MERCHANT BANKING IN AUSTRALIA

Also by Michael T. Skully

Handbook of Australian Corporate Finance (co-editor)
Credit Unions for Australians (co-author)
*Financial Institutions and Markets in the Southwest
    Pacific: a study of Australia, Fiji, New Zealand, and
    Papua New Guinea* (editor)
*ASEAN Financial Co-operation: development in banking,
    finance and insurance*
*Merchant Banking in ASEAN: a regional examination of
    its development and operations*
*Financial Institutions and Markets in the South Pacific: a
    study of the Solomon Islands, Tonga, Vanuatu, Western
    Samoa and New Caledonia*
*Dividend Reinvestment Plans: their development and
    operation in Australia and the United States*
*American Depositary Receipts: internationalising
    Australian fund raising and securities trading*
Merchant Banking in the Far East
A Multinational Look at the Transnational Corporation
    (editor)
*Financial Institutions and Markets in South East Asia:
    a study of Brunei, Indonesia, Malaysia, Philippines,
    Singapore and Thailand* (editor)
*Financial Institutions and Markets in the Far East:
    a study of China, Japan, South Korea and Hong Kong*

MERCHANT BANKING IN AUSTRALIA

Michael T Skully

Melbourne
OXFORD UNIVERSITY PRESS
Oxford   New York

OXFORD UNIVERSITY PRESS

Oxford   New York   Toronto
Delhi   Bombay   Calcutta   Madras   Karachi
Petaling Jaya   Singapore   Hong Kong   Tokyo
Nairobi   Dar es Salaam   Cape Town
Melbourne   Auckland
and associated companies in
Beirut   Berlin   Ibadan   Nicosia

National Library of Australia
Cataloguing-in-Publication data:

Skully, Michael T. (Michael Thomas), 1947–
   Merchant banking in Australia.

   Bibliography.
   Includes index.
   ISBN 0 19 554473 0.

   1. Merchant banks—Australia. I. Title.

332.1′2′0994

Edited by Angela Gundert
Jacket designed by Steve Randles
Typeset by Graphicraft Typesetters Limited
Printed by Kings Time Printing
Published by Oxford University Press,
253 Normanby Rd, South Melbourne
OXFORD is a trademark of Oxford University Press

Contents

Tables and Figures

Tables

Figures

Preface

There is never a good time to write about merchant banking. Whenever one conducts research on the topic, there is always evidence of major change on the horizon and thus a temptation to wait until the industry has once again settled down. However, settling down and merchant banking do not go well together.

Since the Campbell Committee of Inquiry in 1979, Australia's financial sector has been one of continuous change and this is a position which will probably continue for the next few years as institutions adjust to the post Campbell–Martin environment. However, even before the Campbell Inquiry, the merchant banking industry could hardly have been called a staid business and presented a substantial danger to those wishing to study it and, worse still, publish their results.

However despite the speed with which merchant banking changes, it does not mean that the industry should not be examined. On the contrary, there is even a greater need for research and I hope this book will encourage more aspects of merchant banking to be considered in greater depth. The study of Australia's merchant banking industry is also important for much of the financial sector's post-war development is reflected in merchant bank operations and in many cases the merchant bankers or former merchant bankers themselves have been responsible for these innovations.

Although this book is the first in Australia solely devoted to merchant banking, it is my own third examination of the industry. In the first two efforts, the Australian chapter in a title covering the Asia–Pacific region accounted for 48 pages in the first edition and 57 pages in the second edition of what were respectively 274 and 474 page publications. It is a credit to the growth of the region's merchant banking industry that there is now just too much detail to include within one title. Instead the industry must be examined not only on a regional basis, but by taking a country by country approach to each of the Northeast and Southeast Asian areas.

Merchant Banking in Australia, however, has a wider scope and will, I hope, prove of value to those within the industry as well as those with a more general interest in financial matters.

The task of constructing such a publication is considerable and could not have been accomplished without the assistance of a multitude of people. Perhaps the first note of thanks should go to Australia's financial press. When first conducting research on merchant banking in the mid-1970s, the few available articles were generally written by merchant bankers. A decade later, merchant bankers are still ardent contributors to the financial press but today there are many excellent journalists devoted primarily to merchant bank related topics. There has also been a massive expansion in the financial news coverage on the general media as well as the introduction of a number of new business magazines and, most recently, a monthly, *Triple A*, devoted largely to the merchant banking area. Without these publications, the study of merchant banking would be very much more difficult.

The merchant banking industry as a whole must also receive special thanks, for virtually all of those executives contacted were more than willing to give their time to discuss matters which, for them, were probably rather mundane. Without their excellent support this book could not have been possible. Special thanks must go to Australian Ratings; Ian Brown, David Clarke and Robin Wood, Macquarie Bank; Les Coventry and Nigel Dews, Reserve Bank of Australia; Stephen Calder, Sydney Futures Exchange; Edna Carew, *Triple A;* Harvey Crapp, Kuring-gai College of Advanced Education; David Danks and John Hall, Australian Merchant Bankers Association; Bill Evans, Schroder Australia; Graham Hand, Commonwealth Bank; H. Lerbscher, SBC Australia; Toby Marshall of Marshall's Reports; David Macintyre, Rothschild Australia; Paul Murnane, Capel Court; J.A.B. Newton, ANZ Capital Markets; Ian Pollard and Ralph Reily, Delfin Corporate Services; Olev Rahn, BT Australia; Bob Taylor, University of New South Wales; Jeffrey West, Trans City Holdings; Michael Wilson, Barclays Australia; and Phillip Weate, Potter Partners, for their assistance in the preparation and/or review of the manuscript. Finally, thanks must also be given to those who have gone before in this research. In particular, Ross Kolts, who pioneered academic research in merchant banking back in 1970, Norman Leggat for his insights as to the industry's founding in the late 1940s, and R.R. Hirst for his early writings on development finance in Australia.

M.T. Skully, Kensington, December 1985

1 Introduction

... petty banking has thrown open a door to frauds and impositions of a most grievous nature to the country at large. The persons principally concerned in this nefarious practice are to be found among the lowest orders of society ... such being the credulity of the people that notes of hand issued by these wretches are taken and passed into free circulation as if guaranteed by the best securities.[1]

But for an old-fashioned use of English, the above quotation might well have appeared in a letter to the editor following the collapse of Minsec in the mid-1970s or come from the Nugan Hand Inquiry or the Costigan Report. It is somewhat older, from 1810 to be exact, and the words are those of the Governor of New South Wales, Lachlan Macquarie, the first person in Australia to attempt to regulate what was then the merchant banking industry. His report to the Colonial Office unfortunately brought little change to local practices, and the so-called 'petty banking' conducted mainly by merchant firms continued much as before until the trading banks firmly established themselves within Australian finance.

Merchant banking then, as the quote from 1810 suggests, is nothing new to Australian finance. Indeed, merchant banks in various forms were active in Sydney for at least a decade or more before the establishment of the first commercial or trading bank in 1817. This position is not unique to Australia. In most countries the merchant finance operations, from which today's merchant banks trace their ancestry, were in operation long before the first commercial bank ever opened for business.

This book has been structured to give the reader some insight into this historical process, and the coverage of the industry's past, both overseas and in Australia, is provided in Chapters 3 and 4 respectively. However, given some confusion over what constitutes a merchant bank, the book considers this question first in Chapter 2. Also within the introductory section, Chapters 5, 6, and 7 address

1

the industry's relative importance in Australia, its market structure, and its regulation. Most of the remaining chapters, 8 to 17, are devoted to such merchant banks' operations as their money market, domestic lending, offshore financing, corporate finance, investment management, futures business, foreign exchange, overseas expansion, and other activities. A special topic, that of the industry's staffing problems, is discussed in Chapter 18, and the impact of the Campbell and Martin reports is covered in Chapter 19. The last chapter, Chapter 20, considers the industry's future in Australia.

In addition to the text itself, a list of merchant banks together with their shareholders is provided in Appendix II. Though such matters are often quickly dated, it may nevertheless provide some assistance to those researching the industry, as will the select bibliography on Australian merchant banking and the index.

2 What are Merchant Banks?

When the merchant banking industry first developed in Europe in the late fourteenth century, a merchant bank was exactly what the name implies: a merchant trader who helped finance the transactions of other merchants in addition to his own trade. However, as these financing activities became increasingly profitable, some merchants gradually became less merchants and more bankers. In the process they also expanded into other aspects of finance, and today merchant financing comprises only a minimal portion of overall merchant banking revenue.

This change in role and expansion of activities continues to this day and means that what constitutes a merchant bank or merchant banking will vary with market conditions and that the merchant banking business may cover a wide range of financial activities and potentially include a number of different financial institutions.

Within Australia, of many different types of financial institutions, none is more difficult to define than the merchant bank, due mainly to the fact that there is no such thing as a merchant bank licence. Trading banks are licensed, insurance companies are licensed, even credit unions and friendly societies have specific legislation and regulatory bodies, but merchant banks do not. Under the Financial Corporations Act, merchant banks are not classified as merchant banks but as money market corporations. Indeed, it is only recently that the Reserve Bank has used the term merchant bank. Similarly, under the Banking Act, the very institutions calling themselves merchant banks cannot use that title without the Treasurer's approval; such approval has never yet been granted.[1] So, at least one problem with defining a merchant bank, in the Australian context, is that legally the term itself does not exist.

Merchant banks of course do exist, but it seems that the only government body actively using the word is Telecom and then only in its *Yellow Pages* directory. Interestingly, Australia is not unique in this position; within the Asia-Pacific region few countries use the term merchant bank in a legal sense, and, as shown in Table 2.1, only Malaysia has given the term true legal status.

This position is not confined to the 'Mysterious East' for even in England there is some question as to what constitutes a merchant bank. As the then Chairman of Baring Brothers, Sir Edward Reid, explained the problem in that country, merchant bank is a term which 'is sometimes applied to banks which are not merchants, to merchants who are not banks and sometimes to houses who are neither merchants or banks'.[2]

Sir Edward is not alone with this problem. As another very respected title on the subject complained, even 'the so called merchant banks in London are now seldom merchants and by no means always bankers; the title is often misused as a generic description of businesses that operate in the financial sector, whether they perform pure banking services, or merchant banking services, or not'.[3] Some even suggest that 'in part, the air of mystery which surrounds merchant banking has been deliberately fostered. In the United Kingdom [for example] ... some of the largest merchant banks do not even show their corporate titles on their doors'.[4]

Fortunately in Australia there have been some attempts at defining the industry more effectively. One of the earliest was contained in the old New South Wales Securities Industry Act. It defined a merchant bank as

Table 2.1 Merchant Banks in the Asia Pacific Region

Country	Official Term
Australia	Money market corporations
Hong Kong	Deposit taking companies
Indonesia	Investment finance corporations
Japan	Securities houses
Malaysia	Merchant banks
New Zealand	Unofficial money market corporations
Philippines	Investment houses
Singapore	Merchant banks[a]
South Korea	Diversified financial institutions[b]
Thailand	Finance and securities companies

[a] Technically there is no term or licensing for merchant banks under Singapore law. In practice, however, the industry is effectively licensed and regulated by the Monetary Authority of Singapore.

[b] Actual translation from Korean; the term 'merchant bank', however, is used in official English language material.

a corporation which has a paid up capital of not less than $1 million, a public company status, and whose principal functions include one or more of the following: underwriting issues of securities; advising and assisting corporations in relation to the raising of capital, corporate reconstructions and amalgamation, or the acquisition of securities of other corporations primarily for the purpose of exercising control by the first mentioned corporations of such other corporation; and dealing in bills of exchange or otherwise operating in the money market.[5]

For the purposes of the Act, it was not a bad definition as it recognized the functional aspect of merchant banking rather than a licensing provision but in the process covered a much larger group of financial consultants and others who would be considered merchant banks only under this definition. That this wide scope limited the definition's usefulness is apparent. It was dropped from later revisions of the Act and not included in other Australian securities industry legislation.

Another potential definition is found under the Financial Corporations Act, where money market corporations include those firms 'whose short term borrowings are a substantial proportion of their total outstanding provision of finance, which is mainly in the form of loans to authorised dealers in the short term money market and other liquidity placements, business loans and investments in government, commercial and corporate paper'.[6] In the early 1970s, a merchant bank with a set of commercial banking parents was primarily in the borrowing and lending business—much along the lines of the money market corporation definition. Unfortunately, by 1985 this definition was no longer relevant for merchant banks as most firms now provide a much wider range of activities and the money market represents an increasingly smaller portion of their overall business.

Indeed, recent changes in merchant banking have been such that many newer entries have relatively little of the industry's traditional money market involvement. Thus, whereas almost all money market corporations are merchant banks, not all merchant banks are money market corporations. As shown in Table 2.2, one study comparing the 1983 asset figures of the fifty largest merchant banks and the fifty largest money market corporations found that 'whilst 96.1 percent of money market corporations are merchant banks, less than 78 percent of merchant banks are money market corporations'.[7] A similar study in 1985 would find this latter percentage even less for, following the trading banks' new money market freedom in 1984, traditional merchant bank money market activities have become increasingly difficult and many firms scaled down their old deposit-raising and

Table 2.2 Money Market Corporations and Merchant Banks: A Comparison of the Fifty Largest Firms

Category	$ m	% of MMCs	% of MBs	No. of Cos
MMC	13 934	100.0	81.0	50[a]
MBs	17 193	123.4	100.0	50[b]
MMC & MBs	13 384	96.1	77.8	32[c]

Source: Peat Marwick Mitchell, Government Gazette & company annual reports as cited in Nigel Dews, 'Money Market Corporations', B. Comm. (Hons) thesis, James Cook University, 1985, p. 15.

[a] From gazette, not corporate groups.
[b] From Peat Marwick Mitchell's 1984 listings.
[c] Common to both MMC and MBs categories.

on-lending activities in favour of fee-earning areas. In fact, an emerging trend within the industry is to emphasize the investment banking side of the business.

This problem with the term 'money market corporation' was clearly recognized by the Campbell Committee even in 1979 for, despite its official classification, the Campbell Committee often used 'merchant bank' instead. The Campbell Committee nevertheless provided a more recent definition and suggested that merchant banks

operate principally in the area of wholesale, particularly short-term, finance, servicing the financial needs of the larger corporations and public authorities. In addition to their on-balance sheet borrowing and lending operations they trade in government and public authority securities and bank and other corporate debt instruments; they also provide financial advice and services such as underwriting and placements for semi-government securities.[8]

This proved more valuable for, unlike other definitions, it stresses that merchant banks traditionally raise and lend their monies in the corporate and institutional market (wholesale finance) and not in the household sector (retail finance). It also mentions underwriting and financial advisory work, both now important to the industry. As with the earlier definitions, though, some updating is still required as foreign exchange, international capital raisings, and investment management are now important in merchant banking.

It is tempting to amend this definition accordingly and end the chapter here, but there is still a problem when considering merchant banking in Australia compared with merchant banking in Korea or the Philippines. The industry in each country also performs a range of activities which are unique to that country. As one researcher concluded, 'each financial sector in the world has its own concept of merchant banking',[9] suggesting that there are problems associated with relying on a solely functional definition.

A further difficulty is that few, if any, merchant banking services are not performed in some manner by other financial institutions. Accepting deposits and making loans, for example, are hardly unique activities among Australian financial institutions. Australia's trading banks, another example, can perform the same range of activities as any merchant bank. The missing link is perhaps the way in which these various functions are performed.

On first glance one major difference between a merchant bank and a trading bank is size. Where the trading bank employs thousands, the merchant bank at most has a couple of hundred staff. Interestingly, this position is not unique to Australia, and there is a similar size constraint throughout the industry. This is true in the United Kingdom as well. As one author commented, British merchant banks are 'a group of institutions characterised by their relatively modest size against the big commercial banks, their concentration on certain specialised types of activity and their flexibility and speed of decision-making'.[10] Indeed, these British institutions are very small even when compared with Australian banks. As shown in Table 2.3, even the largest British merchant bank has less than 4000 employees and most have less than one thousand. In contrast, the Westpac Banking Corporation has some 3187 staff in New Zealand alone.

Table 2.3 Major British Merchant Banks: Employees and Net Worth as at end 1983

Firm	UK Employees	Shareholder Equity
		$m
Kleinwort Benson	1 090	310
Hill Samuel Group	3 802	230
S.G. Warburg*	1 285	230
Hambros Group*	1 328	200
Schroders	1 162	190
Morgan Grenfell	881	170
Samuel Montagu	774	150
N.M. Rothschild*	596	120
Lazard Brothers	528	100
Baring Brothers	752	70

Source: 'International Banking Survey', *The Economist*, 16 March 1985, p. 6.
* For the year ended March 1984.

It is this relationship between size and speed of decision making that seems an important characteristic of the industry and a major reason for its success against much larger financial institutions. As one writer explained the British position:

merchant bankers lived on their wits, were quick on their feet, and were able to reach snap decisions. Clearing bankers were slow and lumbering, bowed under the weight of their huge bureaucracies. Merchant bankers were nifty at putting together complicated financial packages; clearing bankers came in handy for putting up the money. Brain versus brawn.[11]

Somehow this sort of spirit should be reflected in any merchant banking definition. As another writer explained, 'the essence of merchant banking lies in the people which the banks employ and the environment in which they work'. Merchant bank employees 'can expect a high degree of responsibility at relatively early ages, and are encouraged to adopt an innovative, experimental, flexible and adaptable approach to providing the services that clients require'.[12] This flexibility and speed of decision making, the very psychology of merchant banking, cannot be over-emphasized. As one writer described them, merchant banks are 'the cavalry of banking, cleverer, quicker and more mobile than' the large commercial banks.[13]

Thus, merchant banks, regardless of country, are typically characterized by a high proportion of professionals to total staff; a short chain of command; a substantial delegation of decision making; rapid decision making; a flexible organizational structure; innovative approaches to problem solving; and a high level of financial sophistication.[14] Something of these findings must also be incorporated in any definition.

A final definitional qualification must be size from another viewpoint. Just as a merchant bank may prove unsuccessful if it becomes too large, it is unlikely to offer an adequate range of merchant banking services if it is too small. There is something of a critical mass required. To fulfil the functional qualifications adapted from the Campbell Report requires a substantial investment in at least human capital if not financial capital—something that a one- or two-person office cannot provide. Thus to avoid including all of those listed as 'merchant banks' in the *Yellow Pages*, one must require that all the businesses actually provide, not just advertise, an adequate range of merchant banking services.

An Australian merchant bank could best be defined as a financial institution primarily active in the wholesale money market, lending, corporate finance, foreign exchange, and investment management business whose organization is characterized by a high proportion of professional staff able to approach problems in an innovative manner and to make and implement decisions rapidly. This definition of course may well apply to some of Australia's new foreign bank entries. This is quite intentional, for it appears from discussions with many within the industry that there will be little difference in the services and, more importantly, in the orientation of those organizations operating as merchant banks before and after their operations are reorganized as a trading bank.[15] In the United Kingdom, for example, each of the major merchant banks is also a licensed bank. It is the style and orientation of their operations, not their licensing, that sets merchant banks apart from other institutions.

3 Merchant Banking Overseas: A Brief History

If faced with a trivial pursuit game question on where merchant banks developed, the logical answer might be London, or at least the United Kingdom. After all, it is the old established names such as Barings, Rothschild and Hambros that are associated most with merchant banking overseas and London is where these firms are headquartered. Unfortunately, this answer would mean a lost turn as merchant banking did not originate in the United Kingdom. Furthermore, few of today's great merchant banking houses were established by the British. Instead, merchant banking traces its origins to Italy and the founders of today's top firms, as shown in Table 3.1, the non-financial trading houses in Northern Europe.

For practical purposes, merchant banking dates from the late Middle Ages when, with the emergence of international trade, European merchants found money lending and foreign exchange dealing could be lucratively combined with their normal trading activities. For reasons of location, Italian traders gained the full advantage of this business and, within Italy, those in Florence, due to wool trade, were the most active. Britain, however, was not totally uninvolved in these Italian developments. As early as 1290, the British wool trade and the monarch, King Edward I's need to finance his army, caused the Florentine firm of Bardi and Peruzzi to send agents to London

Table 3.1 Selected British Merchant Banks' Historical Background

Firm	Established	Initial Location	Initial Business
Baring	1717	Bremen, Germany	Clothing & wool
Kleinwort	1792	Cuba	Rum, cigars, etc.
Hambros	1838	Copenhagen, Denmark	Silk & foodstuffs
Rothschild	mid-1700s	Frankfurt, Germany	Textiles & coins
Schroder	1804	Hamburg, Germany	Wheat & coffee
Warburg	1798	Hamburg, Germany	Silver

and arrange for a loan paid by a tax on wool exports.[1] Other Florentine and Genoese merchant firms similarly established London offices and even today, one of the city's main streets, Lombard Street, reflects this early Italian influence on British finance.[2] Unfortunately for the Italians, following King Edward III's ascent to the throne in 1327, England soon defaulted on the loan and ironically so brought to an end much of the then British-based industry.

Italian merchants, however, continued to dominate Europe's international trade for a few more centuries and thus many other merchant-style banks as well as the first modern commercial banks were founded in Italy. Probably the most famous of the former, again based in Florence, was that of Cosimo de Medici, grandfather of Lorenzo the Magnificent, who by the mid-fifteenth century had an international merchant banking operation with offices in London, Bruges, and Avignon as well as throughout Italy.[3] Over time, however, Italy lost its importance and England and Northern Europe began to dominate international commerce. By the 1700s, the German merchant houses had grown particularly significant through good commercial ventures and financing their German principalities' territorial ambitions. These merchants had territorial ambitions too and most were well represented throughout Europe. These overseas offices not only ensured good overseas connections but also diversified the family's exposure over a range of countries rather than just Germany. The most diversified was the Frankfurt-based clothing and coin business established by Mayer Amschel Rothschild. As Rothschild's finance business grew, he sent his sons to establish their own merchant firms in Europe's major capital cities. Thus Rothschild was soon represented in Frankfurt, London, Naples, Paris, and Vienna.[4] These five offices eventually formed the basis for the Rothschild symbol, the Five Arrows, a corporate emblem still used today and the name of Rothschild Australia's local unit trust operations, the Five Arrows Unit Trust.

Through its international network, Rothschild developed an extensive intelligence network and through fast horses, ships, and carrier pigeons, the firm was reportedly the first in London to learn of Wellington's victory over Napoleon at Waterloo. On receiving the news, Nathan Rothschild began openly selling British government paper on the market, causing prices to crash as everyone followed his lead. He then secretly started buying through another broker and profited accordingly when prices soared again on news of the British victory.

Merchant banking has many such tales of intrigue and adventure but not all end with merchant bankers as winners. The worst of the industry tales is that of Baring Brothers, the oldest of London's merchant banks. Baring for most of the nineteenth century was Europe's premier merchant bank with strong representation in North and South America, as opposed to Rothschild's European outlook. Its ties with the United States were particularly close, and when in 1803 President Thomas Jefferson sought funding for the Louisiana Purchase,[5] it was Barings that raised the $15 million Napoleon required. The fact that Britain was then at war with France was seemingly no reason to forgo good business. Baring's American connections, however, were not always so fortunate and by the 1880s Baring was overcommitted in loans and investment in Argentina. Political and economic problems in that country soon followed and in November 1890 Baring was saved only through a rescue effort organized by the Bank of England, Rothschild, and the Banque de France. A special Argentina Committee was established and Baring reorganized as a limited company in early 1891. Unfortunately, while saving Baring Brothers, the Committee could not stop the international repercussions and within a short time a world recession was in progress.[6] It is no exaggeration to say that Baring's financial problems were catalysts even for Australia's 1890s financial crisis.

Britain dominated the world financial sector at least up to the First World War and merchant banking was the key to its foreign capital raisings.[7] London-based merchant banks, for example, financed much of the American railway system as well as providing industrial finance for South America. Over time, however, New York and other financial centres also grew in importance, and by the First World War, London had lost its dominance in international finance. This was partly a result of the country's decline as a world trading power and imperialist, but its merchant banking industry certainly shared some blame. As one writer concluded, during the inter-war period many 'older concerns continued the sedate and amiable pace of the partners' room in a way that reflected past glories and the gentleman's club rather than future challenges. [Indeed] it is difficult to resist the conclusion that the revered City establishment dawdled into the twentieth century'.[8]

Thus London for some time lost its dominant position and it was not until the late 1950s that it began to resume an unquestionable first place financial centre ranking as the home of the Euro-dollar market. Its merchant bankers, too, resumed a role of the premier international financiers, with Euro-market loan and bond raisings their specialty.

Today the United Kingdom continues as world financial centre with its first-place status contested only by New York and Tokyo. It is, however, still the undisputed centre for merchant banking and even many US financial institutions still headquarter their merchant banking operations in London, not New York. A list of today's key merchant banks, those that are members of the Accepting Houses Committee, is shown in Table 3.2.

Merchant banking, however, is hardly a phenomenon that Australia shares solely with London. Quite to the contrary, there is an equivalent of Australia's merchant banking industry in most market economies. Its development in the Asia-Pacific region, not unlike that of the United Kingdom, was mainly foreign initiated. There was certainly the potential for Asian, particularly Chinese, merchants to develop a finance role, just like those

Table 3.2 British Merchant Bankers: Accepting Houses Committee Members

Firm	Date Established*	Early Trade Connections
Baring Brothers & Co.	1890	Wool & general merchants
Brown, Shipley & Co.	1810	Linen merchants
Charterhouse Japhet	1880	n.a.
Robert Fleming & Co.	1909	n.a.
Guinnes Mahon & Co.	1836	n.a.
Hambros Bank	1912	Silk & foodstuffs
Hill Samuel & Co.	1831	Oil, shells & general merchants
Kleinwort, Benson	1792	Rum, cigars & sugar
Lazard Brothers & Co.	1870	General merchants
Samuel Montagu & Co.	1853	Foreign exchange & gold
Morgan Grenfell & Co.	1838	n.a.
Rea Brothers	1919	n.a.
N.M. Rothschild & Sons	1804	Textiles & cloths
J. Henry Schroder Wagg	1804	General merchant
Singer & Friedlander	1907	n.a.
S.G. Warburg & Co.	1934	n.a.

Note: Accepting Houses Committee members should be recognized banks (Banking Act 1979) established under English law and headquartered in the City of London, conducting both British and international banking (including acceptance credits), corporate finance, and investment management. Each firm should be a full member of the British Bankers Association, which means it must be over 50 per cent owned by British residents and with no non-residents likely to act in concert holding more than 33 per cent (including not more than 15 per cent of non European Economic Community residents). Its day-to-day merchant banking business must be managed independently of any non-member parent company.

* Some merchant banking families indirectly entered the business earlier than these establishment dates suggest (see Table 3.1).

in Europe (no doubt some did), but these firms were initially ill-equipped for investment required for Western trade and consequently Western merchant houses soon established local offices to finance this business. By the early nineteenth century, for example, these merchant firms included Jardine Matheson in Hong Kong and Shanghai, Kerr Rawson & Co. in Singapore, Russel & Sturgess in Manila, and MacLane, Watson & Co. and Fraser, Easton & Co. in what is now Indonesia. By providing much the same financial services as the early European merchant banks, these foreign merchants soon dominated their host country's growing trade with the West. Asian trading houses, in contrast, chose to serve as wholesalers to, and to deal through the Western merchants, rather than trade with the West directly. When Western commercial banks later opened in the region, the merchant houses soon relinquished their financial business to concentrate on trade alone and the Asian trading houses either followed suit or established similar relations with the newly-arrived banks. Thus, although there was the potential for an Asian domestic industry to develop, and which it certainly did in Japan, the rest of Asia was not so fortunate and in most cases it was not until the late 1960s and early 1970s that domestic merchant banking, in a modern sense, was established.[9]

A surprising aspect of these later developments, and the reason why this chapter is in a sense a brief history of British merchant banking, is that whereas the British did not invent the industry, they proved its strongest missionaries. Thus, rather than the European houses, British firms were responsible, at least in part, for the industry's development over much of the rest of the world. The US investment banking industry, too, had a close relationship with the United Kingdom, and some trans-Atlantic ownership still remains today. In the Asia-Pacific region, the British influence was also strong and British firms actually established the first merchant bank in a variety of Asian countries. In Singapore and Malaysia, for example, the British merchant bankers Arbuthnot Latham provided the expertise and staffing for the first local merchant bank in each country in March and October 1970 respectively.[10] Similarly, in Hong Kong, British merchant bankers Robert Fleming provided the personnel for Jardine Fleming, the first of many merchant banks established in the Colony. To a lesser extent, this was true also in South Korea. While the British influence is perhaps not so direct in Japan or the Philippines, these countries' securities companies and investment houses were nevertheless very much influenced by the London market.

More could be said of these developments, but the point that should be stressed is that the British industry's importance in the nineteenth century is probably no less than today. London-based firms are still involved with most of the world's major capital raisings. This business often may be in the City of London itself, but it can just as easily happen in Luxembourg, Singapore or Hong Kong—cities where all of the major merchant banks have established operations. Just as from its beginnings, merchant banking remains an international business and one in which industry in Australia thus far plays a minor role. It is a role, however, that is becoming more important and its development and its effect on the industry's future are discussed in more detail in Chapters 11, 15, 16, and 20.

4 Merchant Banking in Australia

For most purposes, Australia's merchant banking industry is a post-war phenomenon. However, even within this relatively short time period it has had a major impact on the Australian financial sector. Indeed the merchant banking industry itself was directly responsible for a large number of Australian financial instruments, markets, and institutions which most financiers today take largely for granted. These accomplishments, however, are not confined simply to the list of 'financial firsts' shown in Table 4.1. The impact of merchant banking has been much more significant. Indeed it is hardly an overstatement to suggest that its local history is really the history of financial innovation in Australian corporate finance.

It is wrong, however, to consider Australian merchant banking as simply a product of the late 1960s or early 1970s even though many merchant banks were established in that period. A closer examination reveals that Australian merchant banking, as an industry, can trace its origins back even to the colonial period. It would be nice to break up this history into specific periods (the era of the money market and so forth) but unfortunately merchant banks have tended to add to their existing services rather than replace one set of products with another. Similarly, due to rapid innovation, particularly in more recent years, it is difficult to classify one period of time as, say, the 'age of the hedge market' in that there were other

Table 4.1 Major Australian Merchant Bank Innovations

Cash management trusts
Commercial bills market
Currency hedge market
Promissory note market
Rebatable preference shares
Unofficial deposit market

equally important developments during the same time frame. Finally, in the money market, for example, merchant bank innovation has continually been at the forefront of the sector's development so that while the commercial bill market in the mid-1960s is probably the industry's most important achievement, one could argue that one-name paper in the late 1970s should deserve an equal ranking. With these disclaimers, the following divisions have been adopted: in the colonial period, the age of merchant trade financing; 1948–57, underwriting Australian industry; 1958–66, developing the money market; 1967–71, tapping the world's capital market; 1972–78, restrictions on growth; 1979–83, responding to deregulation; and 1984 to the present, licensing the leaders.

THE AGE OF MERCHANT TRADE FINANCING

As suggested elsewhere within this book, some trading bank executives may consider merchant banks as 'upstarts' and that the banks could simply wipe them from the market place. An examination of Australia's financial history suggests they are wrong on the first point and possibly right on the second.

It took time for the private sector to establish itself in the Colony of New South Wales, but soon there was a considerable trade between it and points overseas—primarily England. Given the transit time, this trade required finance and it was probably not long before the better-placed merchant houses provided trade financing. Indeed some firms might eventually have grown in stature and in time specialized in trade finance and other financial services. In other words, they would have followed along much the same lines as their English counterparts.

By the early 1800s merchant paper was de facto currency in Australia and merchant finance houses were active in money market, lending, and international operations including foreign exchange. But unfortunately, as reflected in Governor Macquarie's report (see page 1), the industry's reputation was not high. When commercial banks were established, the merchant finance houses found them overly effective competitors. Thus, although the first commercial bank was established only in 1817, by 1835 Butlin could report that one of the last merchant finance houses, Cooper & Levy of Waterloo (a Sydney merchant firm which 'dabbled in banking'), ceased its banking activities.[1]

From then until today, the trading banks have dominated trade finance and it is only in the last few years that Australia's merchant banking industry has attempted to re-enter the business.[2] The only area where banks did not totally replace the merchants was in rural areas. There the wool-broking houses continued to provide customer finance as part of their trading activities and, in a very limited way, continued at least part of this merchant finance tradition.[3]

UNDERWRITING AUSTRALIAN INDUSTRY

The merchant banking industry then commenced operations in international trade financing and foreign exchange, only to be replaced by the trading banks. By the 1930s, though, it was apparent that the trading banks could not meet all of Australia's funding requirements and even the 1936 Royal Commission into Australia's Monetary and Banking System recommended the formation of a mortgage bank and other long-term finance institutions.

The problem was that trading banks then generally offered short-term funds. Public share and debenture' offerings were the major source of long-term corporate capital. Smaller or unlisted companies without access to the stock market had to rely on internally-generated funds. This position grew worse in the post-war period as Australia's secondary industry developed. As the country's economic structure continued to change, it became apparent that the banks could not fulfil these new requirements for medium- to long-term funds.[4] It was just this gap in the capital market that attracted both the finance companies and the modern merchant banks.

The first of Australia's modern merchant banks, the Anglo-Australian Corporation Pty Limited, was established in Melbourne in December 1948[5] (initially as Australian Finance & Development Corporation Limited) as a joint venture of Lazard Brothers, Morgan Grenfell, and the Consolidated Zinc Corporation.[6] All three London-based companies saw substantial potential in Australian underwriting. Investors were extremely optimistic in the post-war period and this was shown in the success of new securities offerings. As one study commented, 'from the end of the war until early in 1948, almost any public share issue or placement of shares in any company new to the stock exchange was certain to be subscribed in full'.[7] Furthermore, there was a pent-up demand for new capital as the National Security (Capital Issues) Regulations, after 13 October 1939, had severely restricted new offerings.[8]

British investors thus were also very interested in the Australian market, and Anglo-Australian's founders offered some important advantages. First, as two of London's leading merchant banks, Lazards and Morgan Grenfell used the latest in financial techniques and had access to the world's largest capital market. Second, although Anglo-Australian had an initial capital of £A125 000 (£A500 000 authorized),[9] then a sizable sum, it could also rely on its parents' considerable financial strength. Third, through parent-company connections, it often had an inside track on British-controlled, Australian capital raisings. Fourth, Anglo-Australian had the advantage of its parents' reputation. Finally, with the company's status, it had little difficulty attracting quality local staff: its first Chairman, Mr H.T. Armitage, for example, was formerly Governor of the Commonwealth Bank of Australia.[10] It also had no major difficulty in attracting business, for in 1964 one study reported 'that the merchant banking services of Anglo-Australian have been used by Caltex, Dalgety, Rootes, General Motors Acceptance Corporation, Shell, Standard and Vacuum Oil'.[11] Other clients included MacRobertsons, Slazengers and Patons and Baldwin.

The other merchant banks that followed—Mainguard (Australia) Ltd (1950),[12] Australian United Corporation (1953), Development Finance Corporation (1953) and Capel Court Corporation (1958)—were initially attracted to the underwriting and venture-capital business and only later added money market, commercial lending and foreign loan raising to their activities. This orientation was also reflected among their initial shareholders and besides British merchant banks included a number of well-known US investment banks. Some examples of the latter included Carl M. Loeb Rhodes in Australian United, Lehman Brothers in Development Finance and, from 1961, Lazard Freres in Anglo-Australian.

Another interesting aspect of these early merchant banks was their organization. As one study concluded:

all these enterprises had a common corporate structure. The parent organization is incorporated as a public company which raises its funds by a public issue of shares...the merchant banking and other functions of the development corporations are performed by a number of affiliated private companies whose shareholders are the parent development corporation...[13]

Australian United, Capel Court and the Development Finance Corporation were all good examples of this position and that of AUCs is shown in Table 4.2. As another study described the rationale, they

set up a complex series of interlocking subsidiaries for reasons of both tax advantage and protection against losses in say one area, as well as operational efficiency in taking into account conditions in the capital market and the state of company law relating both to the corporate entry per se and the securities industry in particular.[14]

DEVELOPING THE MONEY MARKET

By the late 1950s, the merchant banks' initial orientation changed towards that of the money market. The intercompany market had

Table 4.2 The Australian United Corporation Group, 1963

Corporate Name	Specialized Activities
Australian United Acceptance Ltd	Authorized money market dealer
Australian United Development Pty Ltd	Financial assistance to small companies
Australian United Enterprises Pty Ltd	Investment in other companies
Australian United Investment Co Ltd	Managed investment company
Australian United Management Services Pty Ltd	Investment management company
Australian United Projects Pty Ltd	n.a.
Australian United Underwriting Co. Pty Ltd	Share and debenture underwriting
NZ United Corporation	Money market dealer
United Discount Co. of Australia Pty Ltd	Authorized dealer in the official market

developed after the war and by the mid-1950s this and the repurchase agreement or 'buy back' market was sufficient for government
to consider regulating. By 1957 Treasury gave official support to the
idea and on 17 February 1959 the so-called official market was
established.[15] Thus by 1960, in addition to Capel Court, Development Finance and AUC, other companies which were later affiliated,
All States Capital, AMP-Morgan Grenfell, Chase-NBA, Citinational, Short Term Acceptances and Trans City, were also established.

This' brief expansion of the industry, though, was not totally a
function of the money market. As one study found, many merchant
banks 'were incorporated in the 1959–60 boom when there was great
financial activity which created many profitable opportunities for
development corporations'[16]—in other words, the underwriting and
corporate finance side of merchant banking. This, too, was reflected
in an inflow of overseas 'security analysts, market and commodity
researchers, industry and economic surveyors' and other such
'experts' brought to Australia by thirty-four of the world's largest
finance groups, all with representation in Australia's non-banking
sector—primarily through merchant bank shareholdings.[17]

By the time of the commercial bill market's rebirth in 1963 some
official dealers had already found affiliated unofficial dealers an
advantage in certain money market transactions. With the Reserve
Bank's support of the bill market in 1965, these affiliates soon
became a necessity. The new bill market encouraged others to enter
the industry. Indeed, even some trading banks attempted to do so:
the ANZ Bank, for example, reportedly planned 'to set up a

company to act as an intermediary in the bill market in competition with the authorised dealers and acceptance houses which were being established',[18] but Reserve Bank guidelines prevented it.

The commercial bill market greatly improved the merchant banks' earning prospects and this was reinforced by the government's capital-raising guidelines on foreign-owned companies. The latter caused foreign firms to to seek help from their banks overseas. This helped raise the prospect of foreign financial institutions establishing Australian operations, a position which eventuated during the mining boom.

TAPPING THE WORLD'S CAPITAL MARKETS

With the late 1960s came yet another change in merchant banking as the famed Australian mineral development boom began. Indeed,

there were major domestic booms in mining, in commercial building and in some rural products; and there was a boom in world trade and in world money markets. These booms, while they ran, at times gave participants a pretty wild ride; most of them were followed by a near-bust...[19]

From then until the boom peaked in the early 1970s, substantial foreign capital made its way to Australia, as did a wide range of foreign financial institutions. These firms came for three major reasons: first, to lend to local borrowers; second, to share in the underwriting or investment management business that the boom might produce; and third, to take advantages of those market niches not then served by the trading banks. However, as the government precluded their direct entry, foreign banks entered Australia indirectly through equity interests in a variety of merchant banks, finance companies, and other institutions. As most Australian institutions lacked good access to overseas loan funds, they were pleased to enter joint ventures with the foreign banks and these consortiums, for the most part, were formed as merchant banks.

These foreign institutions' initial intentions were quite varied. Some, for example, 'were good at providing financial advice and services for fees. Some knew best how to run a short money book. There were those whose thoughts ran to channeling in funds borrowed abroad. Some had ambitions to specialise in medium-term financing',[20] which would in turn be supported by a range of other merchant banking services.

This growth in the late 1960s was also furthered by a government policy against local borrowings by foreign-controlled companies and restrictions on local commercial bank lending. As early as 1965 the government had controlled such raisings but in September 1969 companies with more than 25 per cent of foreign ownership also became affected. Basically, foreign-controlled enterprises were precluded from raising local debt capital other than for limited working capital purposes, so forcing them to borrow on the overseas markets. This demand sparked considerable interest among overseas financial institutions. Furthermore, as not all the capital could be used immediately, it was invested—primarily in the short-term money and inter-company markets. This 'growth of large corporate deposits during the mining boom since 1967'[21] helped expand merchant bank money market operations and set the basis for their locally-funded domestic lending. Many trading bank affiliated firms established during this period (as shown in Table 4.3) directed much of their attention to these activities. The industry's growth was such that by the mid-1970s the local financial press could publish a list of some seventy-nine different merchant banking styled corporations[22] and even the Governor of the Reserve Bank agreed there could be from 'a low of thirty up to a figure of eighty or more' merchant banks depending on the definition used.[23]

Table 4.3 Major Australian Trading Bank Interests in Australian Merchant Bank–Money·Market Styled Corporations Acquired Over 1967–72

Australia and New Zealand Banking Group Limited	
25% in Australian International Finance Corporation Ltd[a]	6 May 1970
Bank of New South Wales[b]	
33 1/3% in Partnership Pacific Limited[a]	25 Feb. 1969
Commercial Banking Company of Sydney Limited[c]	
33 1/3% in Commercial Continental Ltd[d]	1 July 1970
Commercial Bank of Australia[b]	
25% in Euro-Pacific Finance Corporation Ltd[d]	8 Dec. 1970
20% in International Pacific Corporation Ltd[d]	12 Sept. 1967
Commonwealth Bank of Australia	
23% in Australian European Finance Corporation Ltd[e]	1 Oct. 1970
National Bank of Australasia[c]	
33 1/3% in Chase-NBA Group Limited[a][f]	20 Nov. 1969

Note: The trading banks in many cases wished for a greater percentage of ownership but were precluded from acquiring more than a one-third shareholding by the Reserve Bank of Australia. This limitation was raised to 60 per cent in 1980 and removed in 1984.

[a] Since raised to a 100 per cent holding.
[b] Since merged to form the Westpac Banking Group.
[c] Since merged to form the National Australia Bank.
[d] Since sold.
[e] Since increased to a 51 per cent holding.
[f] Now known as First National Limited.

A continued demand for funds coupled with a booming stock market rapidly attracted additional foreign-controlled firms and encouraged their diversification. Thus, from nine full-service merchant banks in 1970 the industry quickly expanded to over twenty-four by 1972.[24] At its then peak, over 105 foreign banking institutions had official representation or interests in local non-bank financial institutions. With no specific controls over their establishment, the government had no statistics on the industry and even in 1973 the Treasurer could only guess that there were 'somewhere between 50 and 80 corporations operating in the merchant banking area'[25] and was forced to admit that 'the state of knowledge about just what these merchant banks are doing and who they are, is very poor.'[26]

While the perceived profitability of the Australian market was no doubt the main attraction, at least part of this growth in numbers was what is sometimes referred to as the lemming theory of banking. Once a few institutions take a certain action or introduce a particular service, the rest of the industry soon follows. As one executive explained this phenomenon in Australian merchant banking, 'in the event of a number of British merchant banks or a few American trading banks setting up affiliates in Australia, the remainder of each industry believe that they are being left out of the race if they also do not set up some kind of operation as well'.[27]

Once established, these new institutions had to justify their presence and attract as much new business as possible—reflected in an industry cumulative growth rate, between 1965 and 1973, of nearly 50 per cent per annum.[28] This, of course, adversely affected the older merchant banks and whereas 'during the late 1960s four companies, Australian United Corporation, Development Finance Corporation, Darling Holding [now Schroder Australia] and Capel Court Corporation dominated the merchant banks sector' and comprised 82.1 per cent of industry assets in 1969, by 1972 their share was only 20.9 per cent.[29]

Initially, British-based firms dominated the local industry and, as shown in Table 4.4, most major British merchant banks were somehow represented by the late 1960s. Interestingly, few of these original investments survive today, with J. Henry Schroder Wagg's holding in Darling & Company (now Schroder Australia), Hambros Bank's Australian Finance Investment Co. (now Hambros Australia) and N.M. Rothschild & Son's International Pacific Corporation (now Rothschild Australia) being the major exceptions. Today, the merchant banking industry has a much wider base of foreign ownership, with US and Japanese commercial banks being the most significant.

Table 4.4 British Merchant Bank Equity Interests in Australia, late 1960s

British Firm	Australian Equity Holdings
Alexander Discounts Ltd	Westralian International
Anthony Gibbs & Sons Ltd	Merchant Bills Corporation
Baring Brothers	Martin Corporation
Cater Ryder	Martin Corporation
Chartered Consolidated	International Pacific Corporation
Charterhouse Japhet	Australian United Corporation
Crown Agents	Westralian International
	Commercial Continental
Guinnes Mahon	Trans Australian Investment Trust
Hambros Bank	ANZ Hambros Investments
	Trans Australian Investment Trust
	Australian Finance Investment Co.
Hill Samuel	Development Finance Corporation
	Hill Samuel Australia
	Ralli Australia Limited
J. Henry Schroder Wagg	Darling & Co.
	Trans Australian Investment Trust
Kleinwort Benson	Industrial Growth Finance Ltd
	Merchant Bills Corporation
Lazard Bros & Co.	Australian United Corporation
Lehman Bros.	Development Finance Corporation
Morgan Grenfell	Australian United Corporation
N.M. Rothschild & Son	International Pacific Corporation
	Development Finance Corporation
	Realty Development Mortgage
Ralli International	Ralli Australia Limited
SAGIT London	Australian Finance and Investment Corp.
Samuel Montagu & Co.	Capel Court
F.D. Sassoon & Co.	Westralian International
Slater Walker	Thomas Brown
	Mutual & Underwriting Development Ltd
Wallace Brothers	Dier Computer Corporation Ltd
Williams Brandt & Son	Philips—First City—Brandts

Source: James Freemantle, 'Growth of non-bank financial intermediaries and their impact on trading banks in the Australian money market', M. Admin. thesis, Monash University, 1971.

RESTRICTIONS ON GROWTH

The end of the mining boom, the stock market crash, and the 1974 credit squeeze all reduced foreign optimism over Australia's potential and hence the flow of new merchant banks. The government's Financial Corporations Act, first moved in parliament in 1973, and the introduction on 23 December 1972 of the variable deposit requirement (VDR), which precluded much overseas borrowing, further affected the industry. In the first case there was the danger that part IV of the then bill (see Chapter 7) might be passed and implemented, thus removing one of the merchant banks' greatest advantages—little government control. Secondly, many foreign banks viewed their Australian affiliates primarily as marketing agents. As the VDR removed most of this business, many merchant bank shareholders questioned the value of their investment.

The VDR period (1972–74 and again in 1977),[30] while slowing the industry's numbers and growth rate (see Table 4.5), forced those primarily overseas 'agent' firms to otherwise justify their local existence and in the process greatly expanded the industry's activities. The initial effect was to replace overseas money with local funding. The merchant banks' money market operations grew so that, when the Financial Corporations Act's institution classifications were determined in 1975, many firms were really more money market corporations than merchant banks, and the industry was classified accordingly.[31]

The industry has since grown in both numbers and stature but this

Table 4.5 Restrictions on Foreign Fund Raisings, 1972–78

August 1972	Embargo on new overseas borrowings repayable within 2 years
December 1972	Variable deposit requirement of 25% set on new overseas borrowings
October 1973	Variable deposit requirement increased to $33\frac{1}{3}$% on new overseas borrowings
June 1974	Variable deposit requirement on new overseas borrowings reduced to 25%
August 1974	Variable deposit requirement on new overseas borrowings reduced to 5%
November 1974	Variable deposit requirement suspended Embargo on foreign borrowings reduced to those repayable within 6 months
January 1977	Variable deposit requirement of 25% reimposed on most new borrowings Embargo extended to foreign borrowings repayable within 2 years
July 1977	Variable deposit requirement suspended Embargo on foreign borrowings reduced to those repayable within 6 months
June 1978	Embargo lifted on all foreign borrowings

Source: Correspondence with Treasury and Reserve Bank, 1982.

growth differed not only for the reasons just described, but also, since 1973, due to the government's foreign investment guidelines. The government restricted new foreign-owned non-bank financial institutions basically to joint ventures with Australian interests. Thus, from April 1976 to September 1984, foreign interests could establish new ventures without local ownership *only* if Australian interests were unwilling to invest in the enterprise *and* where the venture would provide substantial net benefits to Australia. As the Treasury explained: 'because of the range and depth of financial services available in Australia, particularly in the merchant banking industry, it is generally difficult for foreign interests to demonstrate substantial benefits'.[32]

In effect this meant that all new merchant banks required at least 50 per cent local ownership or in some cases had to find local equity within a specified number of years. Similarly, government policy precluded foreign interests from increasing their ownership of existing firms, and later even the transfer of foreign shareholding could not take place without first increasing the firm's overall Australian ownership.

RESPONDING TO DEREGULATION

It is interesting that much of merchant banking success has been blamed on its lack of regulation compared with its trading bank competitors. It is certainly true that merchant banks developed both more quickly and probably with less difficulty as a result of the direct controls on trading bank deposit and lending operations. However, direct controls did not preclude the trading banks from responding through their own affiliated merchant banks and finance companies and it is notable that the former have traditionally been among the largest of Australia's merchant banks. The direct controls, too, were not a constant problem for the trading banks but rather a diminishing one due to the Reserve Bank's deregulation policies in the 1970s. As shown in Table 4.6, for example, the interest controls on large trading bank loans (then $50 000) were lifted as early as 1972 and restrictions on trading bank shareholdings in merchant banks to 12.5 per cent were lifted in 1975. The year 1979, though, could well be considered the landmark for Australian financial deregulation for in January 1979 the then Treasurer, John Howard, announced the establishment of a Committee of Inquiry into the Australian Financial System under the chairmanship of John K. Campbell. While the Campbell Committee did not present its final recommendations until November 1981, by then it already had a major impact on the speed of Australian deregulation and mapped the path which

Table 4.6 Government Regulatory Moves and their Impact on Merchant Banks

Date	Regulatory Change	Impact
1942–59	March 1942 regulations under the National Security (Wartime Banking Control) Regulations empower the Commonwealth (Central) Bank to fix maximum interest rates on bank advances and deposits. These and other 1944 regulations are subsequently included in the Banking Act (1945). In July 1952 the regulations are revoked but the private trading banks agree to observe uniform rates. In February 1956 the Liquid and Government Securities (LGS) convention reached with major trading banks, with the ratio initially set at 14 per cent of depositors' balances.	E
Feb. 1959	Official short-term money market established.	E
Dec. 1959	LGS ratio increased to 16 per cent.	E
Jan. 1960	New Banking Act (1959) gives Reserve Bank authority to impose quantitative and qualitative controls on bank lending. The Bank continues to influence bank lending without invoking regulations.	E
Jan. 1960	The Statutory Reserve Deposit (SRD) system established under the Banking Act (1959), replacing the special accounts system. The initial SRD set at 16.5 per cent of depositors' balances.	E
Nov. 1960	The maximum term on fixed deposits reduced from 2 years to 12 months; the minimum term remains at 3 months.	E
Apr. 1962	The LGS ratio increased to 18 per cent.	R
Sept. 1962	Maximum maturity of trading bank term deposits extended from 12 months to 15 months.	R
Aug. 1963	Initial Reserve Bank advice given to banks on the principles important in their non-bank associations.	R
Apr. 1964	Maturities for fixed deposits at trading banks of $100 000 and over set at between 30 days and 15 months. Approval also given for trading banks to accept fixed deposits of $50 000 and over for periods between 30 days to 3 months.	R
Sept. 1964	The maximum term for fixed deposits extended from 15 months to 24 months.	R
Mar. 1965	Banks permitted to proceed with moderation with commercial bills.	E, R
	Authorized dealers also permitted to discount and trade in paper bearing the name of an approved trading bank.	E, R

Table 4.6 (cont.)

Date	Regulatory Change	Impact
May 1965	Voluntary 'guidelines policy' introduced limiting foreign-controlled companies' freedom to borrow in Australia.	E
Oct. 1966	The Reserve Bank discontinues active use of qualitative guidance on bank lending.	E
May 1968	Reserve Bank approves trading bank lease financing on a modest scale outside the maximum overdraft interest rate arrangements.	R
Mar. 1969	Approval given for trading bank to issue certificates of deposit with a 2 year maximum maturity and in minimum parcels of $50 000 subject to interest rate maximum and a minimum maturity of 3 months.	E, R
Sept. 1969	'Guidelines policy' confirmed by the Prime Minister and an incentive introduced for foreign companies to admit some Australian equity in the form of extra borrowing rights on the domestic market.	E
Dec. 1970	Approval to extend the maximum term on fixed deposits from 2 years to 4 years.	R
Feb. 1972	Maximum overdraft rate applied only to loans of less than $50 000, with rates on loans of $50 000 and over a matter for negotiation between banks and their customers.	R
Sept. 1972	Embargo imposed on borrowing from overseas of less than 2 years maturity. Portfolio investment abroad allowed in shares, fixed interest securities, and real estate within quantity limits. The previous 'guidelines policy' abolished.	R
Oct. 1972	The Companies (Foreign Takeovers) Act introduced and controls applied to the purchase of shares in an Australian business with assets of more than $A1 million by any one overseas interest or associated group of 15 per cent or more, or by overseas interests in aggregate of 40 per cent or more.	R
Dec. 1972	Variable Deposit Requirement (VDR) of 25 per cent imposed on overseas borrowings exceeding 2 years.	R
Feb. 1973	Embargo and VDR widened to cover inter-company transactions of a capital nature and non-resident deposits with domestic financial institutions.	R
Sept. 1973	The interest rate ceiling on CDs removed and the maximum term extended from 2 years to 4 years.	R
Oct. 1973	VDR increased from 25 to 33⅓ per cent.	R

Date	Regulatory Change	Impact
Late 1973	Additional foreign bank participants in the non-bank sector subject to control.	R
June 1974	VDR reduced from 33⅓ to 25 per cent.	E
Aug. 1974	Financial Corporations Act becomes operative, but Part IV of the Act, which covers non-bank financial corporation regulation, not proclaimed.	R
Aug. 1974	VDR reduced from 25 to 5 per cent.	E
Sept. 1974	Reserve Bank begins trading in bank accepted commercial bills.	E, R
Nov. 1974	VDR suspended. Embargo on borrowing from overseas modified from 2 years or less to 6 months or less.	E
Sept. 1975	Finance is one of the few sectors in which small-scale foreign investment proposals are not exempted from examination by the Foreign Investment Advisory Committee.	R
Sept. 1975	Reserve Bank permits banks to increase their equity in money market corporations from 12.5 per cent up to a maximum of 33.3 per cent.	E
Feb. 1976	The LGS ratio increased temporarily to 23 per cent.	E
Feb. 1976	The size of overdraft subject to maximum interest rate controls increased from $50 000 to $100 000.	E
Apr. 1976	The establishment of new non-bank financial institutions to be examined by the Foreign Investment Review Board. New foreign investment must yield a large net economic benefit to Australia and be unable to find Australian participation. Otherwise, an effective partnership must exist with Australian interests.	R
June 1976	Businesses in the financial sector excluded from the government's general policy of non-intervention in foreign takeovers of small companies.	R
Nov. 1976	The interest rate payable on SRDs increased to 2.5 per cent.	R
Jan. 1977	Embargo on overseas borrowings extended from 6 months to maturities less than 2 years. VDR imposed at 25 per cent; however, certain borrowings for investment in mining and manufacturing sectors exempt from VDR.	R
Apr. 1977	The LGS ratio restored to 18 per cent.	E

Table 4.6 (cont.)

Date	Regulatory Change	Impact
May 1977	Exemption from VDR increased to borrowing by local financial institutions intended for investment in certain mining and manufacturing categories.	E
July 1977	Embargo on overseas borrowing reduced to less than 6 months. VDR suspended. Restrictions on non-resident investment in fixed interest securities modified.	E
June 1978	Embargo on overseas borrowing suspended.	E
Dec. 1978	Previous export licensing arrangement for foreign exchange abolished and more liberal arrangements for export proceeds introduced.	E
Jan. 1979	Treasurer announces that the Government has no objection to the establishment of currency futures trading facilities, provided such facilities are established on the basis of existing exchange control policy (which remains unaltered).	E
	Campbell Committee established.	E
Mar. 1979	Part of the financing requirements of the Australian Wheat Board in 1978–79 met by commercial bill issue instead of Reserve Bank Rural Credits Department advances.	E
June 1979	The trading banks begin foreign currency hedge market.	R
Dec. 1979	Tender system introduced for Treasury notes.	E
Mar. 1980	Trading in currency futures on the Sydney Futures Exchange begins.	E
Apr. 1980	Tap system introduced for Treasury bonds.	E
May 1980	Banks permitted, on a case-by-case basis, to increase their equity in money market corporations from 33⅓ to 60 per cent.	E
Aug. 1980	Committee of Inquiry into the Australian Financial System Interim Report tabled in Parliament.	E, R
Dec. 1980	Ceilings on trading and savings bank deposit interest rates removed.	R
June 1981	Bank of New South Wales and Commercial Bank of Australia merger approved.	R
	National Bank of Australasia and Commercial Banking Co. of Sydney merger approved.	

Date	Regulatory Change	Impact
Aug. 1981	Australian Bank commences operation.	R
Aug. 1981	The minimum term to maturity of trading banks newly issued CDs and small fixed deposits reduced from 3 months to 30 days.	R
Oct. 1981	Banks informed that the Reserve Bank would not object to them sponsoring and/or managing cash management trusts through their partly owned money market corporation subsidiaries.	E
Nov. 1981	Trading banks allowed to offer lines of credit facilities, comprising a limit approved for drawdown at any time, with a minimum monthly balance to be repaid. Maximum interest rates for limits of less than $100 000 restricted.	E, R E
Nov. 1981	Campbell Final Report tabled in Parliament.	E, R
Mar. 1982	Minimum term on trading bank fixed deposits reduced from 30 days to 14 days for amounts of $50 000 and over, and from 3 months to 30 days for fixed deposits of lesser amounts. The minimum term on CDs reduced from 30 days to 14 days.	R
	Notice required on savings bank investment accounts withdrawals removed and savings banks permitted to offer small fixed deposits (under $50 000) for periods of 30 days to 4 years.	R
May 1982	The interest rate payable on SRDs increased to 5.0 per cent.	R
June 1982	Domestic borrowings by major electricity authorities freed from Loan Council controls (i.e., no longer subject to limits on terms, conditions, amounts or timing).	E
June 1982	The Reserve Bank lifts quantitative guideline on growth in trading banks' advances.	R
June 1982	Tender system for Treasury bonds replaces Tap system.	E
July 1982	Changes in the portfolio requirements of dealers in the short-term money market provides dealers with added flexibility in determining its composition, while still requiring dealers to hold at least 70 per cent of their assets in Commonwealth Government securities within 5 years of maturity.	E

Table 4.6 (cont.)

Date	Regulatory Change	Impact
Aug. 1982	Amendments to the Banking (Savings Bank) Regulations announced. LGS to deposits ratio reduced from 40 to 15 per cent: of this, half must be kept in Reserve Bank deposits or Treasury notes. The 100 per cent requirement specifying investments for savings bank depositors' funds broadened to include a maximum 'free choice tranche' (excluding fixed assets) of 6 per cent.	E
Sept. 1982	In principle approval granted to banks to issue Euro-bond floating rate notes on a subordinated basis.	R
Dec. 1982	Proposals involving a rearrangement of shares between existing foreign shareholders in a money market corporation and no decrease in Australian equity, no longer required to provide adequate opportunities to Australians to buy the shareholdings.	E
Jan. 1983	First invitation for foreign bank licences announced but postponed in May 1983.	R
May 1983	The Treasurer announces a review of the recommendations of the Committee of Inquiry into the Australian Financial System (Martin Inquiry).	E, R
July 1983	The Loan Council discontinues arrangements whereby the terms, conditions and timing of domestic borrowings by larger authorities are subject to Loan Council control.	E
Oct. 1983	Greater freedom for trading banks in foreign exchange markets.	R
	Reserve Bank withdrawal from official forward exchange market.	E
Dec. 1983	The Treasurer and the Reserve Bank announce that the spot exchange rate is to be determined by the market and that a major part of the existing exchange controls are to be abolished, effective 12 December. The main changes to exchange controls to be: • removal of restrictions on the timing of trade and other current payments; • removal of the requirement for Reserve Bank approval before residents may enter into any contract with a non-resident;	E

Date	Regulatory Change	Impact
	• removal of all restrictions on overseas portfolio and direct investment by Australian residents; • permission for loans by residents to non-residents; and • permission to financial institutions in Australia to offer foreign currency denominated accounts.	
Dec. 1983	Martin Inquiry Report presented to the Treasurer.	R, E
June 1984	Foreign exchange dealer authorization to forty non-bank financial institutions.	E
July 1984	Trading banks allowed to purchase their own certificates of deposits.	E
Aug. 1984	Fourteen-day rule on bank overnight deposits and prohibition on interest bearing cheque accounts removed, as are maximum maturity restrictions.	R
	Reserve Bank withdraws 60 per cent limit on bank shareholdings in merchant banks.	
	Reserve Bank to enter the money market through repurchase agreements with authorized money market dealers.	
Sept. 1984	Intentions announced for Bank of China banking authorization.	R
	Treasurer announces 12-month moratorium of foreign investment controls on merchant banks and invites applications for banking licences.	E
Feb. 1985	Sixteen foreign banks invited to establish trading bank subsidiaries in Australia.	R
Mar. 1985	Macquarie Bank commences operations.	R
Apr. 1985	Interest rate ceilings removed on trading bank loans under $100 000 for other than housing purposes.	R
May 1985	LGS ratio abolished and prime assets ratio for trading banks introduced.	R
Oct. 1985	Federal government relaxation on foreign investment policies on non-bank financial institutions.	E

Source: Revised and up-dated from Nigel Dews, 'Australian Money Market Corporation Growth, 1959–1983', B.Econ. (Hons) thesis, James Cook University, 1985, pp. 79–82.

E Encouraged the growth of merchant banks.
R Restricted the growth of merchant banks.

has largely been followed since. The appointment of a Labor government review committee and its report (the Martin Report) over 1983–84 generally only reaffirmed this trend.

The trading banks over a fairly short period had the bulk of their remaining controls on deposit rates (December 1980) and lending levels (June 1982) removed. The last major changes came in 1984 when the fourteen-day rule prohibiting their acceptance of overnight deposits or paying interest on cheque accounts was removed on 1 August, and the ceiling on small personal loans in April 1985. Indeed, the only real restriction now remaining on the banking system, other than the statutory reserves deposits (SRD) and prime assets ratio (PAR), is the ceiling on housing loan interest rates.

For the merchant banks then, business has become increasingly difficult as the industry's major competitor has competed on a more and more even footing. Merchant banks have had to respond to these changes and the industry worked hard over the first half of the 1980s to maintain its growth. Significantly, many areas where merchant banks experienced the most success were traditionally areas more associated with the trading banks. The currency hedge market, for example, developed rapidly and provided considerable competition for the trading banks' traditional foreign exchange business as well as servicing markets which banking regulation precluded. The introduction of the cash management trust likewise attracted the larger individual savers who previously may have used bank certificates of deposit (CDs) or other bank deposits for these investments. In each case, there was just that slightly different area of coverage that the trading banks could not or did not serve that made these merchant bank innovations a success.

LICENSING THE LEADERS

The announcement of the new foreign-affiliated banks authorization in 1984 marked yet another major changing point for Australian merchant banking and it is here that one must be careful that what is basically a historical chapter does not overlap too much with the chapter on the industry's future. The most interesting thing is that among those successful in obtaining banking authorizations were what were probably the then most innovative of the Australian merchant banks: most notably, BA Australia, BT Australia, and Hill Samuel Australia. Other equally innovative firms to have obtained approval included Barclays, Citicorp, Lloyds, and Wardley. As of October 1985 only Hill Samuel Australia, as the Macquarie Bank (whose authority was granted separately from the foreign banks),

Chase AMP Bank Limited, and Lloyds Bank NZA Limited had commenced operations. It is therefore too soon for these new entrants to have affected the other merchant banks. Even so, the impact should prove the most important on the industry's operations to date and further blur the distinction presently made between a wholesale oriented trading bank and a merchant bank styled non-bank financial institution.

5 Merchant Banks and Australian Finance

As suggested in Chapter 4, merchant banks are responsible for many innovations in Australian finance. Their accomplishment is even more impressive if one considers the industry's relative size compared to other institutions. As shown in Table 5.1, merchant banks as of 30 June 1984 had total assets of $16 620 million. These holdings, as shown in Table 5.2, accounted for approximately 6.1 per cent of the financial sector's total assets and thus ranked seventh among the sixteen institutional categories used by the Reserve Bank.[1]

This asset ranking position, however, greatly understates the industry's importance. First, a large, indeed a growing portion of merchant bank activities is not directly related to its balance sheet other than eventually through the profit and loss account. A merchant bank, for example, could play a crucial role as an adviser or independent valuer in a multi-million dollar takeover bid but this would not be reflected directly in its assets. Other advisory services, investment management, arranging offshore finance, and similar fee-based work again have no immediate impact on the firm's asset size. Second, even in merchant bank lending, where the loans are shown among the firm's assets, the reported figures substantially understate the true position. Much merchant bank lending, for example, now entails arranging for clients promissory note and other securities issues which are then sold in the market. These too would not appear in the merchant bank's accounts. Third, even the levels for other significant merchant bank assets, such as those related to the money market, are less meaningful when one considers that most dealers actively trade and so turn over these holdings several times during the year. Finally, as discussed in Chapter 2, the Reserve Bank's money market category does not provide complete coverage of the merchant banking industry.

Another indication of the industry's importance is reflected in Australian Ratings' 1985 Top One Hundred Financial Institutions.

Table 5.1 Australian Financial Institutions by Total Assets, year ending 30 June ($m)

	1974	1975	1976	1977	1978	1979	1980	1981	1982	1983	1984
Reserve Bank	5 685	5 356	6 193	8 057	8 679	10 247	12 007	11 880	12 747	15 523	16 888
Trading banks	15 611	18 465	21 245	23 481	25 008	29 494	34 580	41 172	49 274	55 343	64 040
Savings banks	11 765	13 646	15 568	17 294	19 026	21 040	22 684	24 886	27 267	32 820	37 603
Other banking institutions	737	871	1 041	1 105	1 197	1 354	1 648	1 783	2 082	2 394	2 983
Other banks (consolidated)[a]	26 924	31 634	36 512	40 631	44 002	50 366	57 352	66 132	76 311	87 761	101 375
Life offices and pension funds	13 378	14 735	16 567	18 524	20 956	23 423	26 280	30 296	34 524	43 018	49 286
Non-life insurance offices	3 059	3 433	4 390	5 935	6 195	8 349	8 865	9 681	11 602	13 620	15 990
Finance companies	8 699	9 221	10 927	12 785	14 468	15 854	17 780	21 821	25 460	26 015	28 285
General financiers	665	722	870	1 008	1 384	1 643	1 959	2 358	2 920	2 872	3 510
Money market corporations	2 516	2 732	2 980	3 356	3 897	4 932	6 460	8 669	11 966	13 741	16 620
Permanent building societies	3 571	4 126	5 092	6 386	7 496	9 023	10 860	12 326	13 655	15 381	17 549
Co-operative housing societies	797	923	1 014	1 117	1 242	1 374	1 463	1 516	1 560	1 632	1 707
Authorized money market dealers	485	892	1 053	1 145	1 499	1 579	1 698	1 809	1 405	2 006	2 244
Credit co-operatives	484	633	839	1 066	1 342	1 760	2 192	2 559	2 957	3 658	4 470
Pastoral finance companies	850	837	710	760	811	949	1 255	1 305	1 633	1 924	3 176
Cash management trusts	–	–	–	–	–	–	–	180	1 685	2 214	1 476
Other financial institutions	1 479	1 571	1 767	2 116	2 177	2 622	3 555	4 348	5 975	8 043	8 730
Total	68 592	76 815	88 914	102 886	114 148	132 121	151 726	174 880	204 400	237 408	271 306

Source: Reserve Bank of Australia, *Bulletin Supplement: Flow of Funds*, April 1985, p. 6.

[a] Banks, other than the Reserve Bank, with identifiable inter-bank balances netted out.

Table 5.2 Australian Financial Institutions by Percentage of Total Assets, year ending 30 June

	1974	1975	1976	1977	1978	1979	1980	1981	1982	1983	1984
Reserve Bank	8.3	7.0	7.0	7.8	7.6	7.8	7.9	6.8	6.2	6.5	6.2
Trading banks	22.8	24.0	23.9	22.8	21.9	22.3	22.8	23.5	24.1	23.3	23.6
Savings banks	17.2	17.8	17.5	16.8	16.7	15.9	15.0	14.2	13.3	13.8	13.9
Other banking institutions	1.1	1.1	1.2	1.1	1.0	1.0	1.1	1.0	1.0	1.0	1.1
Other banks (consolidated)[a]	39.3	41.2	41.1	39.5	38.5	38.1	37.8	37.8	37.3	37.0	37.4
Life offices and pension funds	19.5	19.2	18.6	18.0	18.4	17.7	17.3	17.3	16.9	18.1	18.2
Non-life insurance offices	4.5	4.5	4.9	5.8	5.4	6.3	5.8	5.5	5.7	5.7	5.9
Finance companies	12.7	12.0	12.3	12.4	12.7	12.0	11.7	12.5	12.5	11.0	10.4
General financiers	1.0	0.9	1.0	1.0	1.2	1.2	1.3	1.3	1.4	1.2	1.3
Money market corporations	3.7	3.6	3.4	3.3	3.4	3.7	4.3	5.0	5.9	5.8	6.1
Permanent building societies	5.2	5.4	5.7	6.2	6.6	6.8	7.2	7.0	6.7	6.5	6.5
Co-operative housing societies	1.2	1.2	1.1	1.1	1.1	1.0	1.0	0.9	0.8	0.7	0.6
Authorized money market dealers	0.7	1.2	1.2	1.1	1.3	1.2	1.1	1.0	0.7	0.8	0.8
Credit co-operatives	0.7	0.8	0.9	1.0	1.2	1.3	1.4	1.5	1.4	1.5	1.6
Pastoral finance companies	1.2	1.1	0.8	0.7	0.7	0.7	0.8	0.7	0.8	0.8	1.2
Cash management trusts	–	–	–	–	–	–	–	0.1	0.8	0.9	0.5
Other financial institutions	2.2	2.0	2.0	2.1	1.9	2.0	2.3	2.5	2.9	3.4	3.2
Total	100.0	100.0	100.0	100.0	100.0	100.0	100.0	100.0	100.0	100.0	100.0

Source: Reserve Bank of Australia, *Bulletin Supplement: Flow of Funds*, April 1985, p. 6.

[a] Banks, other than the Reserve Bank, with identifiable inter-bank balances netted out.

Of these one hundred, some forty companies were classified as merchant banks, and after removing some double counting, merchant banks would account for around a third of the total number of firms.[2] More importantly, despite the vast increase in merchant bank numbers, individually most are relatively small. It is particularly telling, for example, that only one merchant bank, Elders Finance, ranked within the top twenty financial institutions where banks, finance companies, and building societies predominate.[3] Even then, it only made twentieth place.

Possibly a better indication of importance are the deposit levels raised by financial institutions shown in Table 5.3. Here the money market corporations rank fifth rather than seventh place. Their position would be even higher, though, if the deposit figures were restricted to those funds from the wholesale or corporate sector rather than the retail deposit market. This would see the savings banks' and building societies' levels drop considerably and leave the merchant banks vying with the finance companies for second place. Similarly, the gap between the trading banks and these institutions would be much less as the trading banks raise slightly less than half of their deposits from the business sector.

An examination of financial institutions' advances similarly provides a greater insight into the industry's relative importance. As shown in Table 5.4, the merchant banks rise to fourth place behind only the trading banks, savings banks, and finance companies. Again, these figures could be modified to differentiate between corporate and personal lending. First, savings banks effectively would be

Table 5.3 Australian Financial Institutions by Total Deposits, year ending 30 June ($m)

	1983	1984	1985
Trading banks	36 044	38 424	47 109
Savings banks	30 018	34 342	38 878
Other banks	1 505	1 662	1 947
Building societies	14 296	16 564	17 130
Credit co-operatives	2 952	3 708	4 701
Authorized money market dealers	790	953	553
Money market corporations	11 054	13 430	15 419
Pastoral finance companies	470	1 219	622
Finance companies	16 697	17 373	20 043
General financiers	1 231	1 454	1 885
Intra-group financiers	1 364	1 342	1 488
Other financial institutions	360	327	369

Source: Reserve Bank of Australia, *Bulletin*, November 1985.

Table 5.4 Australian Financial Institutions by Total Loans, Advances, and Bills Discounted, year ending 30 June ($m)

	1983	1984	1985
Trading banks	28 687	31 751	39 301
Savings banks	17 820	20 520	26 232
Other banks	2 152	2 430	2 600
Building societies	12 392	14 412	15 212
Credit co-operatives	2 720	3 496	4 560
Authorized money market dealers	1	–	2
Money market corporations	10 951	13 719	17 746
Pastoral finance companies	284	523	694
Finance companies	20 202	21 463	24 472
General financiers	1 922	2 311	2 790
Intra-group financiers	1 584	1 539	1 340
Other financial institutions	135	170	261

Source: Reserve Bank of Australia, *Bulletin*, November 1985.

eliminated as their lending is mainly for personal housing finance. The finance company businesses also lend to consumers. If these were restated to reflect only business loans the total would be about two-thirds of its present size and hence less than the money market corporations. Thus on adjustment, merchant banks would certainly rank second in the advances to business category. Finally, as with the deposits, the actual gap between the trading banks and money market corporation figures would be less when personal and housing loans were removed from the trading bank totals. As only about 60 per cent of trading bank lending is to businesses, the trading bank figures would be in the mid-twenties, certainly still higher than the money market corporations, but not as dominant as Table 5.4 suggests.

As a result of the industry's success in raising deposits from, and lending to, the corporate sector, merchant banks have grown more rapidly than most other financial institutions. This was particularly true in the 1960s when merchant banking experienced a compounded rate of growth of some 39.3 per cent over the decade. This performance was even more impressive if only 1965 to 1970 is considered. Over those years it grew at a compound rate of 55.0 per cent. In contrast, Australian financial institutions' total assets grew at only 9.5 per cent over the 1960s and at 10.1 over 1965–70. After these impressive showings, it is perhaps not surprising, as shown in Table 5.5, that the industry then grew at a slower rate and only resumed something like its previous growth rates in 1979. The most recent slow-down partly reflects trading bank deregulation. The

Table 5.5 Australian Financial Institutions by Percentage Annual Growth Rates, year ending 30 June

	1975	1976	1977	1978	1979	1980	1981	1982	1983	1984
Reserve Bank	-5.8	15.6	30.1	7.7	18.1	17.2	-1.1	7.3	21.8	8.8
Trading banks	18.3	15.1	10.5	6.5	17.9	17.2	19.1	19.7	12.3	15.7
Savings banks	16.0	14.1	11.1	10.0	10.6	7.8	9.7	9.6	20.4	14.6
Other banking institutions	18.2	19.5	6.1	8.3	13.1	21.7	8.2	16.8	15.0	24.6
Other banks (consolidated)[a]	17.5	15.4	11.3	8.3	14.5	13.9	15.3	15.4	15.0	15.5
Life offices and pension funds	10.1	12.4	11.8	13.1	11.8	12.2	15.3	14.0	13.6	14.6
Non-life insurance offices	12.2	27.9	35.2	4.4	34.8	6.2	9.2	19.8	17.4	17.4
Finance companies	6.0	18.5	17.0	13.2	9.6	12.1	22.7	16.7	2.2	8.7
General financiers	8.6	20.5	15.9	37.3	18.7	19.2	20.4	23.8	-1.6	22.2
Money market corporations	8.6	9.1	12.6	16.1	26.6	31.0	34.2	38.0	14.8	21.0
Permanent building societies	15.5	23.4	25.4	17.4	20.4	20.4	13.5	10.8	12.6	14.1
Co-operative housing societies	15.8	9.9	10.2	11.2	10.6	6.5	3.6	2.9	4.6	4.6
Authorized money market dealers	83.9	18.0	8.7	30.9	5.3	7.5	6.5	-22.3	42.8	11.9
Credit Co-operatives	30.8	32.5	27.1	25.9	31.1	24.5	16.7	15.6	23.7	22.2
Pastoral finance companies	-1.5	-15.2	7.0	6.7	17.0	32.2	4.0	25.1	17.8	65.1
Cash management trusts	—	—	—	—	—	—	n.a.	n.a.	31.4	-33.3
Other financial institutions	6.2	12.5	19.8	2.9	20.4	35.6	22.3	37.4	34.6	8.5
Total	12.0	15.8	15.7	10.9	15.7	14.8	15.3	16.9	14.3	14.3

Source: Reserve Bank of Australia, *Bulletin Supplement: Flow of Funds*, April 1985, p. 7.

[a] Banks, other than the Reserve Bank, with identifiable inter-bank balances netted out.

1985 statistics, although not yet available from the Reserve Bank, will probably show an increase not unlike that of 1983–84, but the 1985–86 figures will be much worse as a number of the larger merchant banks, on receiving trading bank authorizations, will transfer most assets to the trading bank category.

6 Market Structure

The merchant banking industry in Australia is characterized by a relatively high level of foreign ownership and a fair degree of concentration. Its operations are also strongly centred around the state capital cities of Sydney and Melbourne. Finally, there is a marked difference between the style of operations or business strategies followed within the industry.

In terms of foreign ownership, most Australian merchant banks were at least foreign initiated, so that the industry has always had a relatively high level of foreign involvement. This was at times accentuated by the practice of many firms to concentrate their activities in de facto banking business. As this entailed raising deposits and making loans, these firms had a greater importance in industry assets than those following a more investment banking approach. The growth of Australian-owned enterprises was further restricted by the Reserve Bank's limitations placed on the local trading banks' shareholdings within the industry. These restrictions did not totally preclude Australian trading bank participation and in time government policy allowed a consolidation of these holdings so that there are at least some major firms now wholly Australian-owned. Indeed, of some fifty-one companies in 1985, approximately seventeen were either wholly or majority Australian-owned and another four had approximately 50 per cent Australian ownership. In terms of assets, Australian-owned or -controlled firms accounted for some 42.2 per cent of the industry's assets and if Australian–foreign joint ventures were included, this foreign content could be raised to 49.9 per cent or approximately half of total assets. Given the recent mass licensing of wholly foreign-controlled firms and the shareholder rationalization programme conducted by many foreign previously part-owners, this position is unlikely to change in the near future and, if anything, as merchant bank lending operations are transferred to existing and expected trading banks, foreign ownership levels are likely to increase.

Besides foreign ownership, Australian merchant banking (as shown in Table 6.1) also has a fair level of concentration, so that relatively few firms control much of the industry's assets. Still, compared with other institutions, this concentration is not extreme —it requires about the ten largest merchant banks before these companies could control half of the industry assets.

In terms of firms, Partnership Pacific has traditionally headed the list as both Australia's largest and, more recently, largest wholly Australian-owned, merchant bank. First National, now wholly owned by the National Australia Bank, traditionally has also been one of the largest firms. Capel Court's number two position, shown in Table 6.2, is a more recent development as it held only sixth place in 1984. This is due partly to its merger with part of what was once Citinational and a repositioning of assets in line with its parent's participation in a new foreign-affiliated trading bank.

Some caution, however, must be taken in examining all but the indicative ratings when using firm asset figures. First, differences in timing of annual report periods can significantly affect asset levels. Likewise, a marked change in assets can just as easily reflect a change in the firm's money market dealing position from one year to another rather than any major expansion programme. Thus a firm's position in such total asset tables can change significantly from year to year. Finally, these asset figures do not reflect contingent assets or liabilities. As a rule, however, those companies with a local trading bank or authorized dealer affiliation tend to rank relatively higher than other companies.

Table 6.1 Australian Merchant Banking Industry Concentration, 1985

Number of Firms	Cumulative % of Total Assets
The largest five	26.6
The largest ten	46.8
The largest fifteen	62.6
The largest twenty	74.9
The largest twenty-five	84.3

Source: Calculated from fifty-one firms' asset figures reported in *1985 Survey of Financial Institutions: a statistical profile*, Sydney: Peat Marwick Mitchell & Co., 1985.

Table 6.2 Selected Australian Merchant Banks by Total Assets

		$m
1	Partnership Pacific	1 339 996
2	Capel Court Corp.	1 119 368
3	First National Group*	899 285
4	Aust. Europlan Fin.	859 716
5	BT Australia	854 006
6	AMP Securities	830 852
7	Wardley Australia	822 019
8	Tricontinental Holdings	773 117
9	Lloyds International	731 484
10	Elders Fin. & Inv. Co.	688 273
11	Barclays Australia	674 166
12	Euro-Pacific Fin. Corp.	610 975
13	ANZ Capital Markets	601 107
14	Trans City Holdings	561 647
15	Citicorp Capital Markets	560 463
16	Morgan Guaranty Australia	491 043
17	Societe Generale	480 958
18	BA Australia	472 097
19	Standard Chartered	467 423
20	French Aust. Fin. Corp.	441 105
21	Spedley Securities	392 795
22	Bill Acceptance	371 125
23	CIBC Australia	347 154
24	Schroder Darling	340 106
25	All-States Cap. Group	334 829
26	First Chicago Australia	328 587
27	Hambro Australia	301 007
28	Security Pacific Aust.	270 195
29	Indosuez Australia	262 460
30	Commercial Continental	244 374
31	SBC Australia	222 795
32	Kleinwort Benson	220 564
33	European Asian Australia	179 819
34	Delfin-BNY Acceptance	163 576
35	Chemical Aust. Intern'l.	161 794
36	BOT Australia	156 106
37	PNB Internl Fin. Co.	142 554
38	Rothschild Australia	132 430
39	Amro Australia	125 325
40	ABN Australia	120 809
41	RBC Australia	120 513
42	Rothwells	108 542
43	Australis Securities	102 862

* Current Sept. 1984.

Table 6.2 (cont.)

	$m
44 CCF Australia	91 550
45 Dai-Ichi Kangyo Australia	88 618
46 Michell NBD	47 686
47 NCNB Australia	42 206
48 DBSM	26 173
49 Bisley Investment Corp.	25 235
50 Oakminster	15 942
51 Morgan Grenfell Aust.	8 440
Average	406 003

Source: Marshall's Reports, *Merchant Banks*, 1985.

While asset levels indicated where a firm is particularly active in deposit and lending, the relative importance of these to other activities is perhaps better reflected in profitability ratios (see Table 6.3). Those firms with consistently low returns on total assets are fairly certain to have a high involvement in the money market compared with companies with exceptionally high returns: these are more likely to concentrate on fee income-based services, particularly the corporate finance and investment management business. Again it is dangerous to comment on one year's results alone, but over time certain firms, such as BT Australia, Hill Samuel/Macquarie, Lloyds International, have earned considerably higher returns on a total assets basis than other major firms.

With some financial institutions, the number of offices also reflect a firm's relative importance within its industry. This is partly true in merchant banking, with the larger firms having the largest number of offices. Until recently, branch offices were important in raising money market deposits. Thus firms with an authorized dealer affiliation generally have offices in all mainland state capitals and often in other major towns as well. For the most part, as shown in Table 6.4, merchant banks have tended to choose either Sydney or Melbourne for their head office and then, often at the same time, open a branch office in the other city. In time, the firm may expand either to Brisbane or, to a lesser extent, Perth. The need for these offices, at least from a money market standpoint, though, has been reduced in recent years due to technological innovations and, as will be discussed in Chapter 9, because there is now a trend to concentrate money market and foreign exchange dealings either in Sydney and/or Melbourne. This is not to say that offices in other states will close but they will probably operate with a smaller staff.

Table 6.3 Selected Australian Merchant Banks' Profitability Ratios

	Net Profit/Total Assets (%)	Net Profit/Shareholder Funds (%)
All-States Capital	0.5	10.3
AMP Securities	0.9	23.0
AUC Holdings	0.1	1.5
Australian European	0.6	13.4
Australian International	0.6	10.1
Australis Securities	1.2	23.4
BA Australia	0.2	4.9
Bill Acceptance	1.2	15.0
Boston Financial	0.7	10.9
BOT Australia	0.3	4.4
BT Australia	2.4	43.7
Capel Court	0.6	17.6
CCF Australia	0.1	2.7
Chemical All-States	0.7	10.9
CIBC Australia	0.1	4.1
Citicorp Capital	0.2	5.1
Commercial Continental	0.5	10.5
Delfin-BNY	1.0	21.9
Elders Finance	1.25	27.5
Euro-Pacific	0.5	13.5
European Asian	0.1	1.2
First Chicago	0.1	4.3
First National	0.1	2.9
First National Securities	1.0	23.9
French Australian	0.2	7.5
Hambro Australia	0.8	12.0
Hill Samuel	2.2	32.9
Japan Australia	0.4	33.0
Lloyds International	1.4	28.0
Midland International	1.3	9.4
NCNB Spedley	0.5	7.3
Oakminster	4.6	17.3
Partnership Pacific	1.0	22.7
Rothschild Australia	0.9	16.2
Rothwells	2.7	32.0
RBC Australia	0.6	8.3
SBC Australia	0.3	5.8
Schroder Darling	0.7	12.5
Security Deposits	3.4	42.5
Security Pacific	0.3	6.6
Spedley Securities	1.0	11.1
Standard Chartered	0.5	11.4
Trans City	1.0	26.5
Tricontinental	0.9	16.4
Wardley Australia	1.1	21.2
Average position	0.8%	16.1%

Source: *1985 Survey of Financial Institutions.*

Table 6.4 Merchant Bank Office Representation, 1985

Firms	Office Representation							
	S	M	P	B	A	H	C	D
ABN Australia	H	–	–	–	–	–	–	–
All-States Capital	B	H	B	B	B	B	B	B
AMP Securities	H	B	B	B	B	B	B	B
Amro Australia	H	B	–	–	–	–	–	–
AUC Holdings	B	H	B	B	B	–	–	–
Australian European	H	B	B	B	–	–	–	–
Australian International	B	H	B	B	B	–	–	–
Australis Securities	H	B	B	B	–	–	–	–
BA Australia	H	B	B	B	–	–	–	–
Barclays Australia[a]	H	B	B	B	B	–	–	–
Baring Brothers	H	–	–	–	–	–	–	–
Barrack House	–	–	H	–	–	–	–	–
BBL Australia	B	H	–	–	–	–	–	–
Bill Acceptance	H	B	–	B	–	–	–	–
Boston Financial	H	B	B	B	–	–	–	–
BOT Australia	H	B	–	–	–	–	–	–
BT Australia	H	B	B	B	–	–	–	–
Capel Court	B	H	B	B	B	–	–	B
CCF Australia	B	–	–	–	H	–	–	–
Chemical All-States	B	H	–	–	–	–	–	–
CIBC Australia	H	B	B	B	–	–	–	–
Citicorp Capital	H	B	B	B	B	–	–	–
Commercial Continental	H	B	–	B	–	–	–	–
Delfin-BNY	H	B	–	B	B	–	–	–
Dominguez Barry Samuel Montagu	H	B	–	–	–	–	–	–
Elders Finance	B	H	B	B	B	–	–	–
Equiticorp Australia	H	–	–	–	–	–	–	–
Euro-Pacific	B	H	–	B	–	–	–	–
European Asian	H	B	–	–	–	–	–	–
First Chicago	H	–	–	–	–	–	–	–
First National	B	H	B	B	B	–	–	–
First National Securities	B	H	B	B	B	–	–	–
French Australian	H	B	B	B	B	–	B	–
Grindlays Australia	B	H	–	–	–	–	–	–
Hambro Australia	H	B	–	–	–	–	–	–
Hill Samuel	H	B	B	B	B	B	–	–
Indosuez Australia	H	B	–	–	–	–	–	–
Japan Australia	H	B	–	–	–	–	–	–
Kleinwort Benson	H	B	–	–	–	–	–	–
Lloyds International	H	B	B	B	B	B	–	–
Michell NBD	B	B	–	–	H	–	–	–
Midland International	H	–	–	–	–	–	–	–
NCNB Spedley	H	–	–	–	–	–	–	–
NZI Securities	H	B	B	B	–	–	–	–
Oakminster	H	–	–	–	–	–	–	–

Firms	Office Representation							
	S	M	P	B	A	H	C	D
Partnership Pacific	H	B	B	B	B	–	–	–
PNB International	H	–	–	–	–	–	–	–
RBC Australia	H	B	–	–	–	–	–	–
Rothschild Australia	H	B	–	–	–	–	–	–
Rothwells	–	–	B	H	–	–	–	–
SBC Australia	H	B	–	–	–	–	–	–
Scandinavian Pacific	H	B	–	–	–	–	–	–
Schroder Darling	H	B	B	B	–	–	–	–
Security Deposits	B	H	–	B	–	–	–	–
Security Pacific	H	B	–	–	–	–	–	–
Societe Generale	H	B	–	B	–	–	–	–
Spedley Securities	H	B	–	–	–	–	–	–
Standard Chartered[b]	H	B	B	B	B	–	–	B
S-T-H-Graham	–	–	–	B	–	–	–	–
Sumitomo Perpetual	H	–	–	–	–	–	–	–
Trans City	H	B	B	B	B	B	B	B
Tricontinental[ab]	B	H	B	B	–	–	–	–
Wardley Australia	H	B	B	B	–	–	–	–
Western United	–	–	B	–	–	–	–	–

Source: Compiled from *1985 Survey of Australian Financial Institutions*, Sydney: Peat Marwick Mitchell, 1985.

H Location of headquarters; B Location of branch.

S Sydney; M Melbourne; P Perth; B Brisbane; A Adelaide; H Hobart; C Canberra; D Darwin.

[a] Also has a branch in Townsville.
[b] Also has a branch in Newcastle.

7 Regulation and Control

Although many suggest that merchant banks succeeded largely due to lack of regulation, merchant banks are subject to some regulation. As corporations, they are subject to the Companies Act and other forms of business regulation. More specifically, they are also affected by the Banking Act, Financial Corporations Act, Securities Industry Code, foreign investment controls, Income Tax Assessment Act and by their own self-regulatory measures.

THE BANKING ACT

To date the Banking Act's most obvious effect on merchant banking is that no merchant bank has legally traded under that classification. As its section 66 provides:

Except with the consent in writing of the Treasurer, a person or body of persons, not being a bank, shall not assume or use, in relation to the business, or any part of the business, or any part of the business carried on by that person or body, the word 'bank'; 'banker' or 'banking' or any word of a like import.[1]

This law was once rather strictly enforced. A restaurant in Sydney, the Old Bank Restaurant, for example, was required to gain such exemption before it could use 'bank' in its name. The law also once rather restricted the description of merchant bank services and even in the early 1970s, composite terms like 'merchant bank' or 'investment bank' were not considered appropriate to appear in merchant bank produced literature.[2] This policy, as merchant bank advertisements indicate, has since been modified and today section 66 presents few difficulties other than using the term 'bank' in a firm's business name.

The Banking Act also had another, possibly more technical effect on the industry. Before the passing of the Financial Corporations Act in 1974, there was always a question as to whether the Banking Act might apply to what were then the standard merchant bank money and lending procedures. As the Reserve Bank itself advised, 'wherever there is any doubt whether a non-bank financial institution may be carrying on business of the character of banking business ... [a firm] should seek an exemption under section 11 of the Banking Act'.[3] It was thus generally considered prudent for merchant banks to apply to the Treasurer for an exemption under section II of the Banking Act. Such an exemption may be granted to institutions wishing to carry on certain banking type business but not engage in the general business of banking. Of equal importance, the exemption also meant that the institution was not subject to the direct and other controls then applied to Australian banking. As the Reserve Bank commented in its 1966–67 annual report:

At the end of the year, exemptions were held by 115 organisations including pastoral finance companies, permanent building societies, finance companies, life offices, authorised dealers in the short term money market and operators in the commercial bill market.[4]

These exemptions, however, were always granted, at least in view of the Vernon Committee, 'with the condition that, in making any advances in the course of banking business, the exempted body shall follow the policy, if any, determined by the Reserve Bank'.[5] Thus, the Banking Act did, and to some extent still does, have some possibility to be used as a form of non-banking regulation. The legal position, though, was sufficiently questionable for the government to introduce a new piece of legislation, the Financial Corporations Act, to cover non-banking institutions.

More recently the Banking Act and its associated regulations have again become more significant in merchant banking industry regulation. This is because the merchant banks receive their foreign exchange licences under the Banking Act. To obtain such a licence a firm technically requires an 'Authority to Deal in Foreign Currencies', 'a minimum level of shareholders' funds of $10 million', and the 'demonstrated capacity and expertise to carry out foreign exchange dealings'. Once the prospective licensee's proposed staffing, control systems, and correspondent arrangements are assessed, it can commence operations provided it observes certain prudential standards, provides the Reserve Bank with certain statistical and other market information, maintains certain operating standards and monitors certain transactions for taxation and exchange control purposes.[6]

While one can only speculate as to the future, press reports suggest the Banking Act might eventually apply directly to part of the merchant banking industry. The reference here of course is to at least two of the new foreign banks, Morgan and Deutsche Bank. These have indicated that they will, as authorized trading banks, operate almost exclusively in the wholesale banking area and take a strong merchant–investment bank approach to such business. There is little question that others among the new authorized banks would take a similar approach but at present seem forced into some retail banking due to promises in their initial licence applications. Given the competition expected in the retail area, some institutions may eventually reduce their retail exposure to the point where they could easily be included in the authorized trading bank section of the then Australian merchant banking industry.

In the past, Reserve Bank guidelines also affected the local merchant banking industry through restrictions on trading bank shareholdings in merchant banks. Initially the Reserve Bank took a similar stance to that adopted for authorized money market dealers and limited holdings to a maximum of 12.5 per cent. This precluded the local trading banks from having a major impact on the merchant banking industry's early development and effectively ensured they would be more a passive investor than an active shareholder. In September 1975, however, this position changed and up to a $33\frac{1}{3}$ per cent shareholding was allowed. This limit was raised to 60 per cent on 28 May 1980 and finally removed altogether on 1 August 1984. Nevertheless the restrictions, while they lasted, had a major impact on the structure of the local industry and acted as a barrier to the rationalization of merchant bank shareholders. Restrictions on trading bank shareholdings are likely to have some further effects as well in that the Reserve Bank has indicated that the new foreign-affiliated trading banks should hold any of their foreign parents' interests in Australian non-banking financial institutions. Thus those presently wholly foreign-owned merchant banks, whose parents have received an Australian banking licence, are likely to be owned in the future by the new Australian banking entity. The only limitation on such holdings is that these non-banking interests should not be unduly large relative to the trading bank itself.

FINANCIAL CORPORATIONS ACT

As mentioned, concern over the growth of the merchant banking industry had existed since the mid-1960s and eventually in the early 1970s the government had considered bringing all potentially non-bank financial institutions under Reserve Bank control. This finally resulted in the introduction of the Financial Corporations Bill 1973 to the House of Representatives on 11 December 1973 'to provide the basis for the examination and, as necessary, regulation of activities in the non-bank financial sector in the interests of effective management of the economy...'[7]. Its first purpose was therefore to gather information on non-bank financial institutions and second to give the government the same potential regulatory powers afforded under the banking legislation.

The Financial Corporations Act (FCA), which became law on 7 August 1974, applies to all corporations whose principal business in Australia is the borrowing of money and the provision of finance, whose assets in Australia resulting from the provision of finance exceed 50 per cent of the corporation's total assets, and whose total assets, including related companies, exceed $1 million. Such corporations existing prior to the FCA were required, under the Act, to register with the Reserve Bank and any other corporations on being subject to the Act, must also file with the Bank within sixty days.

Over a thousand companies subsequently registered and after much discussion and consideration they were either exempted from the Act or classified into specific industry groups. Finally, when the FCA classifications were announced on 17 October 1975, a total of 690 corporations had been placed in ten separate categories: Category A, building societies; B, credit co-operatives; C, authorized, money market dealers; D, money market corporations; E, pastoral finance companies; F, finance companies; G, general financiers; H, retailers; I, intra-group financiers; and J, other financial corporations. A listing of those firms registered as money market corporations is shown in Table 7.1. As mentioned in Chapter 2, the money market categories included those corporations, not authorized dealers,

whose short term borrowings are a substantial proportion of their total outstanding provision of finance, which is mainly in the form of loans to authorised dealers in the short term money market and other liquidity placements, business loans and investments in Government, commercial and corporate paper.[8]

All FCA registered building societies, authorized money market dealers, money market corporations, pastoral finance companies, and finance companies, as well as those general financiers or credit co-operatives within Australia with over $5 million must, since June 1984, file monthly reports with the Reserve Bank using the forms designated for each specific category: Form 4 is used in the case of money market corporations. As shown in Appendix I, this provides extensive details on each firm's financial operations, assets, selected liabilities, and interest rates.

As with other institutions subject to the Act, the merchant banking industry's greatest concerns are the interest rates and other

Table 7.1 Category D (Money Market Corporations) Registered Firms

AIFC Leasing Limited, Victoria
AIFC Leasing Nominees Pty Limited, ACT
AIFC Securities Limited, Victoria
AMP Acceptances Limited, ACT
ABN Australia Limited, NSW
ABN Leasing (Aust.) Pty Limited, NSW
All-States Capital Group Ltd, Victoria
All-States Corporation Limited, Victoria
AML Finance Corporation Ltd, NSW
Amro Australia Limited, ACT
Amro Leasing Ltd, NSW
AUC Holdings Limited, Victoria
AUC Leasing Limited, NSW
Australian European Finance Corporation Limited, NSW
Australian International Finance Corporation Limited, Victoria
Australian United Corporation Limited, Victoria
Australis Securities Limited, NSW
BA Australia Leasing Limited, Victoria
BA Australia Limited, Victoria
Barclays Australia Limited, NSW
Barclays Australia Securities Limited, NSW
Barrack House Limited, WA
Bill Acceptance Corporation Limited, NSW
Bisley Asset Management Pty Limited, NSW
Bisley Investment Corporation Limited, NSW
Bisley Securities Limited, NSW
Boston Financial Limited, Victoria
BOT Australia Ltd, NSW
Broadlands International Finance Limited, WA
BT Australia Limited, NSW
BT Finance Pty Limited, NSW
Capel Court (ACT) Limited, ACT
Capel Court (SA) Ltd, NSW
Capel Court Corporation Limited, Victoria
CCF Australia Limited, SA
CCF Australia Management Limited, SA
CCF Australia Securities Limited, SA
CIBC Australia Holdings Ltd, NSW
CIBC Australia Limited, NSW
Chemical All-States Limited, Victoria
CitiSecurities Limited, ACT
Commercial Continental Ltd, NSW
Delfin-BNY Acceptances Limited, NSW
Dominguez Barry Samuel Montagu Limited, ACT
Elder's Finance & Investment Co. Limited, SA
Euro-Pacific Finance Corporation Limited, Victoria
Euro-Pacific Leasing Limited, Victoria
European Asian of Australia Limited, NSW
Financial Leasing Corporation (Australia) Limited, Victoria

First National Limited, Victoria
First National Securities Ltd, Victoria
French Australian Financial Corporation Limited, NSW
Grindlays Brandts Australia Limited, NSW
Grindlays Securities Australia Limited, ACT
Hambro Australia Limited, NSW
Hill Samuel Australia Limited, NSW
Indosuez Australia Ltd, NSW
Intermarine Australia Limited, NSW
Invia Limited, Victoria
Japan Australia Acceptances Limited, NSW
Kleinwort Benson Australia Limited, NSW
Lloyds International Limited, NSW
Michell NBD Limited, SA
NCNB Spedley Leasing Limited, NSW
NCNB Spedley Limited, NSW
Oakminster Limited, NSW
Partnership Pacific Leasing Limited, NSW
Partnership Pacific Limited, NSW
Partnership Pacific Securities Limited, NSW
PNB International Finance Co. — Australia Limited, NSW
RBC Australia Finance Limited, NSW
RBC Australia Limited, NSW
Rothschild Australia Limited, ACT
Rothwells Limited, Queensland
SBC Australia Limited, NSW
Schroder, Darling and Company Limited, NSW
Security Deposits Limited, Victoria
Security Pacific Australia Limited, ACT
Security Pacific Finance Limited, ACT
Security Pacific Industrial Limited, ACT
Security Pacific Securities Limited, ACT
Short Term Investments Limited, NSW
Societe Generale Australia Limited, NSW
Spedley Securities Limited, NSW
Standard Chartered Australia Limited, NSW
S-T-H—Graham Ltd, Queensland
Sumitomo Perpetual Australia Limited, NSW
Trans City Corporation Limited, NSW
Trans City Holdings Limited, NSW
Transia Corporation Limited, NSW
Tricontinental Corporation Limited, ACT
Tricontinental Australia Limited, WA
Wardley Australia Leasing Limited, NSW
Wardley Australia Limited, NSW
Western United Finance Limited, SA

Source: Commonwealth of Australia, *Gazette No. S 312,* 19 August 1985, p. 7.

Note: The extensive multiple listing of many companies within the same group makes the FCA listings a relatively unhelpful means of determining the real number of firms operating in Australia.

direct controls contained in the as yet ungazetted Part IV of the Act. This section's Division 2—Asset Ratios, for example, would allow the Reserve Bank to prescribe up to 40 per cent of FCA registered firms' assets as well as a range of other ratio requirements related to liabilities or certain specified assets or liabilities. Its Division 3, Lending Policies, could also give the Reserve Bank the power to direct registered corporations to conduct business only within certain categories or for specific purposes or limit its business to only certain classes of transactions. The final of these direct control powers, Division 4—Interest Rates, would allow the Reserve Bank to prohibit the payment or receipt of interest by registered corporations over a certain rate per annum. While Part IV has not yet been declared and thus its powers are not available to the Reserve Bank, the government could proclaim the section with little difficulty or delay. Significantly, some more left-wing politicians have occasionally suggested that Part IV of the Act should be implemented and that non-banking financial institutions, particularly money market corporations (merchant banks), be required to allocate a certain percentage of their assets to housing loans.

Fortunately, it seems unlikely that these direct controls will ever be utilized under the Hawke Labor government. This, of course, may not be true of future governments and from the industry's viewpoint, concern over interest rate controls and specified asset ratio is much more than a matter of politics or corporate freedom. As the Australian Merchant Bankers Association (AMBA) pointed out in its Campbell Committee submission, 'the specification of interest rates for merchant banks ... could immediately put into jeopardy the whole basis of floating rates charged by them'. Furthermore, given their existing Securities Industry Act liquidity requirements, the prescribed asset holdings under the FCA, 'could be treated as an illiquid asset by the Corporate Affairs Commission' and hence put individual merchant banks in breach of their liquidity requirements. Not surprisingly, the AMBA submission concluded its comments with the recommendation that 'Part IV of the Financial Corporations Act be amended to remove provisions for direct control of lending and of interest rates'.[9] The industry's concern over Part IV is also reflected in that most merchant bank loan agreements contain clauses which will automatically pass on all the costs of compliance with any Part IV implementation to the borrowers.

Besides its statistical requirements and the potential of direct controls, the FCA has at times also had an indirect effect on merchant bank operation through special advisory committee meetings between the Reserve Bank and selected industry officials. Initially, these committee meetings served mainly as a forum for government policy and to improve the government's statistical collection system, but between late 1976 and 1982 they were used in part to set de facto growth ceilings for the industry—often as a percentage of total outstandings or advances. For example, in November 1976 the 'merchant banks were told that their lending was excessive and that the authorities wanted it contained within a growth of the money supply [then 10 to 12 per cent a year]'.[10] Perhaps a more significant attempt at moral suasion occurred on 21 May 1981 when the Reserve Bank actually wrote to the fifty-four FCA registered money market corporations, pointing out that their recent growth of over 30 per cent per annum was not consistent with government monetary policy and that more restraint should be shown in the future.[11] For a brief period such actions seemingly had some effect. BA Australia, for example, commented in 1981 that its 'growth in the banking department was curtailed in accordance with requests from the monetary authorities'.[12] With the Reserve Bank's more recent market oriented forms of monetary policy implementation, though, it is doubtful that such attempts at moral suasion are now utilized and it is significant that no advisory committees have been held since April 1984. This does not mean there has been no contact between the Reserve Bank and the government. Indeed, the Governor is now a traditional speaker at the Australian Merchant Bankers Association's annual functions.

SECURITIES INDUSTRIES CODE

As a function of the industry's money market operations, underwriting and investment management activities, merchant banks by definition fall under the Securities Industry Code of their respective states and must be licensed accordingly. To obtain a securities dealer's licence, a merchant bank must lodge Form 5, a copy of its latest audited accounts, and hold and maintain surplus funds greater than $50 000, or an amount equal to 5 per cent of the company's liabilities or 3.3 per cent when satisfactory loan standby facilities have been arranged.[13] Under the Act, surplus funds are defined as current assets less total liabilities with following assets excluded from the current asset calculation: fixed assets; unsecured loans and advances to associates; securities with no ready market; assets not to be realized within twelve months; and any amounts owed of which the recovery is doubtful. In terms of total liabilities, fully subordinated loans to the licensee from its shareholders generally can be excluded from the total liabilities calculations. If the company has capital and reserves of less than $2 million it must also lodge approved security of $20 000.

Once licensed, dealers or advisers are required to submit annual returns on their operations. These include an independent auditor's report of not only the accounts but also whether the firm has complied with the conditions of the licence, maintained adequate accounting and control procedures, and conducted its securities business in an appropriate manner.[14]

Besides the additional reporting requirements, the Securities Industry Code places all merchant banks so registered under a liabilities to capital ratio limitation of 20 to 1, or approximately 30 to 1 if the standby facilities provisions are considered adequate. Thus, as the AMBA complained to the Campbell Committee, 'unless their business is restructured, a small part of their business will bring the whole company under the administration of the Corporate Affairs Commissions, which apply capital and other requirements in their own terms as conditions for issuing licenses'.[15]

The possibility that conditions might vary from state to state also concerned the industry. Given that the Code already exempts banks and insurance companies from its provisions, the industry recommended that 'merchant banks be exempted for licensing under the Securities Industry Act'.[16]

Though the industry would no doubt like itself removed from any potential state government controls under the Securities Industry Act, in practice the liquidity ratio provisions have not presented a significant problem in that most firms restructure their own operations in line with the Act. Indeed, almost every merchant bank has at least one wholly-owned subsidiary with usually the word 'securities' in the corporate title. It is generally this 'securities' subsidiary rather than the merchant bank that is licensed as a securities dealer under the Act. Thus only the subsidiary, and not the entire firm, is subject to the liquidity ratio and other provisions.

Unfortunately, while a subsidiary exempts the parent from the various Securities Industry Code requirements, it also means that the parent is not licensed under the Code and if it provides any investment advice or conducts any underwritings, the parent itself would again either need to register or possibly be in violation of the Act. It could, of course, always use its licensed 'securities' subsidiary and staff for these purposes as a registered securities dealer or dealer's representative can provide investment advice without registered option as an investment adviser. This dual use of staff, however, is generally unpractical and so most firms establish a separate investment management subsidiary for this purpose. A licensed investment adviser is subject to similar provisions as a securities dealer but is subject to corporate net tangible assets of only $20 000 plus, where required, a deposit in the form of approved securities of $20 000. Thus it is not uncommon for a merchant bank's money market operations to have one securities dealer licensed subsidiary to handle certain money market operations, its corporate finance division to have another securities dealer licensed subsidiary to handle its underwriting and advisory work relating to shares, and finally its investment management division to have an investment adviser licensed subsidiary for its activities. Given the registration costs and administrative burden this Act-related restructuring involves, it is little wonder that merchant banks would like an exemption similar to the banks and insurance companies. As a number of major operators in the investment management area, such as BT Australia, become licensed banks it will be interesting to see if their current operations are not restructured. The recent Green Paper on securities industry regulation of course would, if adopted, completely change the current position as it would extend securities industry licensing requirements to cover the banks and life offices.

FOREIGN INVESTMENT CONTROLS

While the Reserve Bank's limitations on trading bank shareholding in merchant banks up to 1984 affected the structure of Australian merchant banking, Australian government limitations on foreign investment in merchant banks and other financial institutions have had a more important impact.

Foreign ownership restrictions in Australia were first introduced in October 1972 under the Companies (Foreign Takeovers) Code which required government approval before the acquisition of a 15 per cent holding by one overseas interest, or an aggregate of 40 per cent by a number of foreign interests of an Australian company, could be allowed to proceed. These restrictions were later expanded to cover foreign investment in certain newly-established enterprises and, as of 31 August 1973, foreign investments in non-bank financial institutions were subject to Australian government control. The specific implementation of these policies towards financial institutions was later stated in more detail in the then Prime Minister, Gough Whitlam's, 'Foreign Investment Policy' speech on 24 September 1975. The government policy was basically that:

Australia is already adequately supplied with non-bank financial institutions and insurance companies. Accordingly, it is the Government's general objective to require foreign interests wishing either to establish, or to participate in the establishment of, a new non-bank financial institution or insurance company, or to significantly increase their participation in an existing institution; to demonstrate that the Australian economy would be advantaged by their doing so.[17]

As a result,

all foreign investment proposals relating to new non-bank financial institutions or insurance companies will be screened, irrespective of the level of funds involved [and] all proposals to increase the overall proportionate foreign ownership of companies by more than 5 per cent will be screened.[18]

These general policies continued until late 1984. Thus, to establish a new foreign-owned merchant bank, the applicant had to show that there was either substantial net economic benefit for Australia or apply in conjunction with an Australian partner. In the latter case, the partnership had to involve Australian interests in the control of the enterprise and generally a beneficial Australian ownership of at least 50 per cent. In the case of foreigners acquiring or increasing their ownership in an existing merchant bank, the applicant had to prove that Australian interests were first given the opportunity to purchase the holding on commercial terms. However, even where no Australian buyer was available, the applicant had still to show that substantial net benefits to Australia would result from the ownership change before approval would be given.

The effects of these investment guidelines have been two-fold. First, all merchant banks established between late 1975 and late 1984 generally had an Australian partner with a 50 per cent interest. As the most desirable partners were usually already merchant bank shareholders, new foreign entries had to be increasingly inventive to find local shareholders. Second, any attempts at rationalizing the shareholders in the early multi-foreign institution-owned merchant bank consortiums were exceedingly difficult unless an Australian entity was buying the shareholdings.

Westpac, for example, took from 1980 to 1982 to rationalize its six shareholdings in different merchant banks down to two. The rationalization problem for foreign enterprises, however, was just as difficult and it took Bank of America some years before it could buy out its previous foreign partners.[19] In the meantime these partners were forced to be long-term passive investors in what was by then a competitor with their own Australian interests.

Probably the most publicized aspect of the foreign investment rationalization process was that of Citibank and its 49.9 per cent owned Citinational. Citibank wanted to obtain a wholly-owned merchant bank and proposed to sell its 49.9 per cent interest in Citinational to its Australian partner. Initially it would sell only if it was allowed to purchase 100 per cent ownership of another wholly foreign-owned merchant bank, Grindlays Australia. When the government, however, indicated that this would be considered a new entity and thus require an Australian partner, Citibank changed its mind and some months of proposals and counter proposals took place between Citibank and the government. Finally, in late 1983, a compromise was reached whereby Citicorp sold its 49.9 per cent holding in Citinational to its partner National Mutual, but retained certain Citinational staff to use as the basis of a new, wholly-owned merchant banking subsidiary, Citicorp Capital Markets Australia, with the proviso that this body became 50 per cent Australian-owned within five years.[20]

The point of these few examples (there are many more), is that the foreign control limitations hampered what otherwise might have been a fairly rapid rationalization of the merchant banking industry, with only the serious players remaining as shareholders, usually with a 50 per cent or more shareholding. As competition increased with trading bank deregulation it became apparent that more rationalization would be forthcoming, and with the announcement of new foreign bank licensing, serious concerns were expressed over the industry's future.

Fortunately, when the foreign bank question was again addressed, this time by the Hawke Labor government, the problem of merchant bank rationalization was realized and a one-year moratorium was granted on the previous merchant bank foreign-ownership limitations. Thus between 10 September 1984 and 9 September 1985, foreign companies could either establish or acquire full ownership of an Australian merchant bank. As the Treasurer, Paul Keating, explained the policy:

the decision was made in view of the fact that merchant banks have been coming under increasing competitive and structural pressure as controls over trading and savings banks have been removed. The establishment of new banks can be expected to add to these pressures ... the setting aside of the foreign investment policy applying to merchant banks will allow the industry to rationalise and adjust to these new circumstances.[21]

Over 1985, this moratorium resulted in a host of shareholder changes, usually to 100 per cent foreign ownership by one company, and new wholly foreign-owned merchant banks being established. Indeed over the year some twenty-four merchant banks were so restructured and around sixty new firms were established or approved.[22] These changes placed the industry in a much better position to meet the new trading bank competition but at the same time encouraged even more savage inter-firm competition than before. Ironically, too, the rush to establish a local office, or at least gain an approval, prior to the 9 September 1985 deadline, proved unnecessary as the moratorium was subsequently extended indefinitely due to a change in foreign investment controls.

As part of the Hawke government's deregulatory efforts, the thresholds at which government foreign investment approval is required were raised considerably, and foreign interests establishing a new non-banking financial institution of less than $10 million will be exempt from foreign investment screening. Those involving new ventures of $10 million or more will be subject to a screening mechanism but even these proposals will be approved unless they are considered against the national interest for reasons such as a 'tax minimization arrangement, a serious reduction in competition in a sub-sector of the market, or adverse effects on shareholders and/or creditors'.[23] Finally, any foreign acquisition proposals of financial institutions involving $5 million or more—other than offshore takeovers between foreign interests which are subject to a $20 million threshold—will also be subject to screening controls.

TAXATION OFFICE

In line with the government's concern over foreign ownership and control, the Australian Taxation Office administers a set of guidelines specifically designed to preclude the transfer of funds from Australia to overseas interests by overseas borrowings or transfer pricing. Basically they preclude an overseas parent company from lending its Australian subsidiary more than six times its subsidiary's equity. In addition, any overseas borrowings by the Australian subsidiary conducted with the overseas parent's guarantee are considered as part of this overseas parent company debt to equity ratio.[24]

SELF-REGULATION

In addition to various federal and state government legislation, the merchant banking industry has long been active in self-regulation both within its own industry and in conjunction with other specialist bodies. Within the industry, a desire for self-regulation was initially at least one reason for the founding of the Issuing Houses Association and the Accepting Houses Association of Australia, now merged as the Australian Merchant Bankers Association. Other bodies where industry members have been active in encouraging higher professional standards include the Australian Investment Planners Association, Sydney Futures Exchange, and the Unit Trust Association of Australia.

The Issuing Houses Association, established on 20 October 1972 by five merchant banks active in securities underwriting,[25] was the industry's first formal attempt at self-regulation. It was based on a similarly named body in the United Kingdom and intended to promote a high standard of conduct among its members. As the late Sir John Marks described, its objectives were

to promote high standards of conduct and practice in corporate finance and to provide a forum for discussion to establish the views of the association in all matters of mutual interest to members. [It] ... will also represent interests of members and put forward their views on matters affecting their activities as issuing houses to all others interested in the operation of the Australian capital market.[26]

In line with its high standards objective, membership was restricted; only those companies which were active in 'the sponsoring of capital issues; the representation of persons making, or the subject of, offers for all or part of a company's capital; the giving of general financial advice; and the sale of securities to the public generally'[27] were subsequently invited by the Committee to become members.

This Association was followed on 8 November 1982 by a similar organization covering merchant bank money market activities. Again following the London model, it was known as the Accepting Houses Association of Australia; the term 'accepting' related to the members' common role as the acceptor on commercial bills of exchange. Given the industry's greater involvement in money market activities, this body had some sixteen merchant banks as founding members.[28] Its objectives, as shown in Table 7.2, also stressed the need for high professional standards. As with the Issuing Houses,

Table 7.2 Accepting Houses Association of Australia's List of Objectives

a to promote the consideration and discussion of all questions affecting the business of Accepting Houses in Australia and to establish a forum for the interchange of views among members;
b to encourage members
　i　to maintain a high standard of ethical performance and integrity,
　ii　to develop a high degree of technical skills,
　iii to maintain appropriate financial strength.
c to represent the interests and views of the members in relation to their activities as Accepting Houses and in particular to provide a medium for placing before Government, Treasury, Reserve Bank, stock exchanges and other public and private organisations, authorities and bodies, the views of the Association on matters relating to or affecting such activities.

Source: Accepting Houses Association of Australia, *Rules No. 4*, p. 2.

members had first to meet certain requirements and then be invited by the Committee to join. These requirements included that the company be incorporated in Australia, have an issued capital of $1 million or more, have shareholders' funds of $1 million or more, carry on the 'acceptance, drawing, endorsing or marketing of bills of exchange in Australia' as one of its main activities, and show a 'willingness to abide by the Rules of the Association'.[29]

Both Associations encouraged greater technical knowledge within the industry as well as generally improving its standing within the business community. In particular, the Issuing Houses were very active in submissions regarding takeovers and other securities industry legislation, while the Accepting Houses produced an excellent booklet on bills of exchange and sponsored a number of forums on money market related matters. Indeed in June 1975 the Accepting Houses' activities eventually required the establishment of a permanent secretariat, and by 1976 it had established the AHAA Prime Rate as the benchmark rate for a large percentage of merchant bank loans.

Though both bodies, as in the United Kingdom, might have continued as separate but mutually supportive organizations, the Campbell Committee of Inquiry into the Australian Financial System provided an incentive for only one industry submission. Thus in 1979 the twenty-three-member Accepting Houses Association of Australia and the ten-member Issuing Houses Association of Australia joined together as the Australian Merchant Bankers Association. As the AHAA commented, 'although the two Associations represent different aspects of merchant banking the combining of resources in a joint submission seemed the most practical approach ... [and] ... steps are now being taken which will lead to the full merging of the two Associations under the name A.M.B.A.'.[30]

As with its two predecessors, the AMBA is also a self-regulatory body, but it is interesting that this objective, as shown in Table 7.3, has dropped from first to fourth place when compared to the Issuing Houses' initial purpose and from second to fourth place in terms of the Accepting Houses. It is not that self-regulation is less important but rather that, as the industry and its members have become well-established fixtures in Australian finance, the organization's emphasis has been more towards encouraging market deregulation and improvement.

The present conditions for continued membership with the AMBA include a minimum capital and a number of ratio requirements, as shown in Table 7.4, as well as the submission of annual accounts and a certificate each year signed by the company secretary

Table 7.3 Australian Merchant Bankers Association's List of Objectives

- Facilitate the structural and operational efficiency of the Australian financial markets and promote the recognition of members of the Association as a fundamental part of those markets.
- Enhance the status of members of the Association as deposit-taking organisations and acceptors/endorsers of bills with the objective of improving the competitive position of the members for borrowing and maintaining those instruments as prime paper in the market place.
- Expand the role of members in the provision and mobilization of wholesale finance to governments, corporations and other institutions.
- Promote the reputation of members for the maintenance of high standards of professional conduct and practice.
- Expand the role of members as intermediaries in the capital markets and promote their activities in underwriting, placement of securities, provision of financial and investment advice and their role and expertise in respect of takeovers, mergers and acquisitions.

Source: Australian Merchant Bankers Association, *Annual Report*, 1984, p. 7.

stating that the company currently meets the two tests and that it has continually complied with these tests throughout the year. If for some reason it is unable to meet these requirements it must advise the AMBA within thirty days of the breach and the actions taken to resolve it.

The importance of industry self-regulation, however, may soon change within the AMBA's list of priorities given the comments of the National Companies and Securities Commission (NCSC). This body's new Chairman, Henry Bosch, has indicated that greater self-regulation is needed in mergers and acquisitions and that if self-regulation is unable to resolve matters he will legislate his own code of conduct.

The NCSC attitude is important in other areas of the securities–investment industry where merchant banks are active. The recent problem with unlisted unit trusts, for example, seems likely to be handled successfully through a more active Unit Trust Association of Australia. Similarly, the difficulties with investment advisers may be resolved through the efforts of the Australian Investment Planners Association. The problem, as with commodities and futures dealing regulation, is these bodies' inability to regulate the activities of non-member firms. What appears, as of 1985, is a trend for governments to force financial market participants, particularly new entries, to become members of their respective industry body as a condition of licensing. While this is not yet formally the case, such membership qualifications may already play an important role in considering new licence applications.

Table 7.4 Australian Merchant Bankers Association's Continuing Prudential Tests for Membership

---

Test 1 Capital Base

A member company must have a capital base of at least $10 million. The capital base includes total shareholder funds plus fully subordinate loans and any provisions certified by the Board of Directors to be in excess of the prudently assessed requirements, less: fixed assets, future tax benefits, and other intangible assets.

Test 2 Ratios

A member company must comply with at least two of the following four requirements:

a Total liabilities defined as:
  Balance sheet total less
  • Shareholders' funds as defined in Test 1
  • Clients' liabilities for the members' acceptánces
  not to exceed twenty-five times shareholders' funds as defined in Test 1 above.

b Members having shareholders, being banks or merchant banks of international standing or other institutions acceptable to the Committee, comprising not less than
  • 33 per cent of ordinary shares in the case of one such shareholder; or
  • 66 per cent of ordinary shares in the case of more than one such shareholder.

c Unconditional undrawn standby facilities (net of any VDR or other similar availability restrictions) providing:
  i an amount not less than 20 per cent of total liabilities as defined in (a) above; and
  ii being in the form of cash drawings or discount facilities.

d The aggregate of the following items (at not above market value) being in excess of 90 per cent of the member's total liabilities as defined in (a) above maturing within six months:
  i   Loans or other non-marketable assets maturing within three months
  ii Marketable securities maturing within *six* months or cash advances convertible into such securities at the option of the Member
  iii Commonwealth and semi-government securities maturing within two years
  iv Stock Exchange listed shares
  v   Other assets subject to firm contract of sale for settlement within *six* months
  vi Unused unconditional standby acceptance facilities from banks in Australia
  vii Standby facilities described by item (c)
  viii *Less* the total of any items included elsewhere under (d) which are required to be available for drawings under such facilities.

Source: Australian Merchant Bankers Association, 1985.

The AMBA is also taking action to broaden its representation within the merchant banking industry where, with only thirty member firms of an estimated 100 merchant banks in October 1985, it represents less than a third of the industry's numbers. Even the present membership could substantially decline as many become licensed trading banks and leave the Association. Under the existing rules, it is unlikely that either these new banks or their restructured merchant bank subsidiaries could continue as members. In response, the AMBA is considering a change in its membership conditions to allow at least these new basically fee-based-income trading-bank-affiliated merchant banks to continue within the Association.

8 Overall Operations

Merchant banks in Australia come in all different shapes and sizes but are generally active in the money market, domestic lending, off-shore finance, underwriting and financial advisory work, investment management, the futures business, and foreign exchange. In addition, some firms have expanded into other financial and non-financial areas both locally and overseas. Each of these aspects of merchant bank operations is discussed in Chapters 9 to 17, but it is also helpful to look at the industry in broader terms both from an organizational and financial standpoint.

ORGANIZATIONAL ASPECTS

Merchant banks are generally structured along operational lines. Just as the merchant banking business can be divided into a few major sub-sets, so can the merchant bank's organizational structure. It is traditional, therefore, to have separate divisions for the money market, lending, corporate finance, international, and investment management businesses. Each division has a manager, general manager, or executive director at its head depending on its relative importance and, generally, the executive titles adopted by its parent or major shareholder. 'General Manager' seems the most common among major division heads.

While the structure depicted in Figure 8.1 is fairly straight-forward, any organizational chart becomes difficult if branch office operations are included. This is because while each state has its own state manager, his or her subordinates are also responsible for their respective specialties at the national level. This approach can also differ between capital cities. With a Sydney headquartered firm, for example, its structure is commonly mirrored in Melbourne under the Deputy Managing Director and each division similarly headed by the firm's number two person for that specialty. Since the floating of the

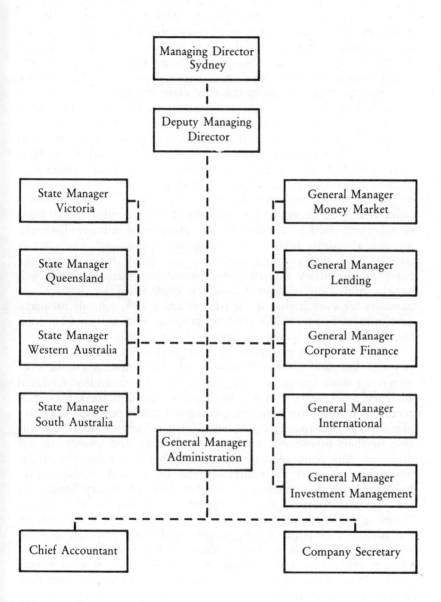

Figure 8.1 Example of a Traditional Merchant Bank Organizational Chart

Australian dollar in 1983 and the granting of foreign exchange licences in 1984, there has been a further problem as the traditional divisional structure is now in transition, with many firms, seeing the close relationship between their money market and foreign exchange work, merging these into a new treasury division. Similarly, the money market division's initial operations have now evolved so that its major functions, that of securities trading and funding the firm's loan portfolio, are now often represented at manager level together with foreign exchange under the new division head.

Further structural changes can be expected as merchant banks continue to adapt to Australia's ever-changing financial sector.

The industry's corporate structure also deserves specific mention. As discussed in Chapter 7 and to a lesser extent in other chapters, there are often legal requirements whereby subsidiary companies become advantageous for specific functions. The money market, where a licensed securities dealer is subject to a specific liquidity ratio, is a good example. Likewise, most firms conduct investment management which usually entails investment adviser licensing through a separate investment management subsidiary. The same is true for the underwriting business, and many have a nominee company subsidiary as well. Thus almost any merchant bank will have a minimum of four subsidiary companies. In practice the numbers are even higher if the firm is active in leasing or property development finance. Most offshore business, too, will entail at least one, if not many, foreign-incorporated subsidiaries.

A final point on merchant bank organizational structure is the physical location of the divisions and the potential conflicts of interest of some businesses. The most obvious problem is in financial advisory work where, as a consultant, a merchant bank may gain access to inside information regarding a client's potential takeover plans or serious financial problems. Such details would be invaluable to their investment management, lending and money market divisions. Any temptation to profit from this knowledge, though, is more than offset by the realization that once client confidentiality has been broken the likelihood of future business is very limited. In the past this conflict has been minimized by the use of so-called 'Chinese Walls' whereby there is at least a mental separation between the advisory, investment management, and other divisions and the staff are directed not to discuss their work across divisional lines. More recently those mental walls have become physical walls as well in that these sections are often located on different floors rather than in the same office area.

FINANCIAL ASPECTS

Merchant banks raise most funds through the acceptance of short deposits and the issue or discounting of money market securities. These deposits are usually on an overnight basis whereas the industry's assets, mainly money market securities (maturities of up to 90 days or more) and advances (short-term up to three years), are for a much longer term. This maturity mismatch between the firms' primarily overnight liabilities and their somewhat longer-termed assets is not a major risk because the securities portfolio can always be resold on the market and most advances can be converted into bills if required. Standby credit facilities can provide further protection against liquidity problems. Another risk in maturity differences between the funding and asset liabilities is the interest rate differential between the two. As will be discussed in Chapters 9 and 10, the traditional term structure of interest rates—where the lowest interest rates are in the overnight market and then rise as the maturity becomes longer—has allowed merchant banks to profit on the difference between their short-term funding rates and their somewhat longer maturity lending rates. This gap is in addition to any credit risk differentials. More recently, though, an inverse yield curve, whereby the short-term overnight rates move higher than the longer-term rates, has become more common and, despite lending at variable interest rates, merchant bank profitability has been affected.

While merchant banks use the bulk of their assets for advances to the private sector, this has not always been the case. Initially, the first merchant banks concentrated on investment banking and as such were frequent participants in corporate share underwritings and, to a lesser extent, direct equity investments. This is reflected in Table 8.1 where in 1960 share investments accounted for 54.2 per cent of the industry's total assets. Similarly, given the nature of share investments, the industry relied heavily on its own funds supplemented by trading bank facilities and other borrowings. With the growth of the unofficial market and the commercial bill market in the 1960s, though, merchant banks concentrated more on the quasi-banking styled business of raising funds and making advances via the money market.

These quasi-banking operations saw merchant bank assets grow rapidly, with the industry (also due to new arrivals) jumping from assets of $60 million in 1965 to $798 million by 1970. This overall growth trend has continued, with the $2732 million level reached in 1975, $6460 million in 1980, and $22014 million in 1985. This growth, however, was not matched by a similar increase in paid-up

Table 8.1 Money Market Corporation Assets and Liabilities by Per Cent of
Total

	1960	1965	1970	1975	1980	1984
Assets						
Cash and bank	4.2	1.7	2.9	8.5	5.4	5.5
Advances	16.7	38.3	26.7	37.5	46.2	41.1
Commercial bills	–	5.0	32.0	28.6	25.2	28.2
Govt & semi-govt secs	–	15.0	8.3	5.9	3.2	2.1
Shares	54.2	31.7	7.8	3.0	3.3	1.7
Debentures, notes & deposits	8.3	3.3	20.7	14.9	14.5	19.1
Stocks & fixed assets	4.2	3.4	0.6	0.3	1.2	1.3
Sundry debtors	12.5	1.7	1.1	1.4	1.1	1.0
	100.0	100.0	100.0	100.0	100.0	100.0
Liabilities						
Shareholders' funds	41.7	35.0	8.7	7.1	5.3	5.8
Advances from:						
Trading banks	12.5	1.7	0.5	0.3	3.6	3.9
Subsidiaries	–	6.7	1.4	0.4)		
Mortgages	–	3.3	22.4	4.1)	13.6	9.5
Others	–	6.7	9.1	8.4)		
Debs, notes & deposits*	29.2	45.0	55.6	78.3	72.2	75.0
Sundry Creditors & Others	16.7	1.7	2.3	1.7	5.7	5.8
	100.0	100.0	100.0	100.0	100.0	100.0
Total $m	24	60	798	2 732	6 460	16 620

Source: Reserve Bank of Australia, *Bulletin Supplement: Flow of Funds*, April
1985.

* Primary deposits.

capital or retained earnings and as a result shareholders' funds have
dropped quickly in relative importance from 41.7 per cent in 1960 to
35 per cent in 1965, and only 8.7 per cent in 1970. The slight rise
shown in Table 8.1 between the 5.3 and the 5.8 per cent in 1980 and
1984 respectively reflects an increase in paid-up capital among some
firms (to the $10 million level) for foreign exchange licensing. This
general trend towards higher gearing levels, however, has been
partially offset by the use of standby letters of credit, parent bank
guarantees, and subordinated loans from shareholders.

The growth of the money market business also saw a similar
decline in the importance of merchant banks' share investments, with
the percentage dropping from 54.2 per cent of assets in 1960 to 31.7
per cent in 1965, and to 7.8 and then 3.0 per cent in 1970 and 1975
respectively. At the same time advances grew from only 16.7 per

cent of total assets in 1960 to 46.2 per cent by 1980. As this growth of assets could not be sufficiently financed through either additional shareholder funds or trading bank borrowings, this rapid growth was funded by an even greater increase in deposit-taking activities. Indeed, from only 29.2 per cent of total funding in 1960 the deposits category rose to 78.3 per cent by 1975. With this funding position and the bulk of its assets related to money market activities, the Reserve Bank's choice of the term 'money market corporation' rather than 'merchant bank' for the industry's Financial Corporations Act category in 1975 is quite understandable. The speed with which the industry could fund its loan portfolio is also important, for as the deposits are for a very short term, merchant banks can quickly adjust their liquidity positions in line with market conditions and their lending requirements.

In conjunction with the growth of strictly deposit and lending styled money market operations also came an increase in the industry's holdings of bills of exchange. These initially grew more quickly than the industry's normal advances, rising from 5.0 per cent of assets in 1965 to some 28.2 per cent by 1984. Accompanying this increase has been a corresponding decrease in Commonwealth and other government securities holdings, which fell from 15 per cent of assets in 1965 to only 2.1 per cent in 1984. This reflects in part both the improved financial status of merchant banks, in that unsecured deposits became dominant, and the availability of substantial stand-by credit facilities which reduced the need for direct liquid asset holdings. The more specific merchant bank assets reflected in Table 8.2 also provide some further insight into merchant bank operations. First, as mentioned earlier, is the very small amount of cash and bank deposits held in a non-interest-bearing form. As one study concluded, the firms 'are cash economisers par excellence. Surplus daily bank balances are placed with other corporations or with the authorised dealers'.[1]

Also of significance are the industry's actual money market placements. The high level of funds with other money market and FCA registered financial institutions relate to the inter-merchant bank market discussed in Chapter 9, while the latter and those placed with other bodies show the industry's overall exposure to the inter-company market. Besides investing any short-term surplus, these monies also constitute part of the industry's liquidity base.

As with the placements, the level of bill holdings in Table 8.2 also reflects a high proportion of funds invested in the securities of other institutions. These bills replace the government securities both as a primary source of potential liquidity for some companies and serve

Table 8.2 Money Market Corporation Assets, April 1985 ($m)

Cash and Bank Deposits	
Negotiable certificates of deposit	1 174.5
Cash and other bank deposits	38.9
Placements	
Placements with authorized dealers	0.5
Placements with related FCA corporations	98.9
Placements with other related corporations	180.5
Placements with other money market corporations	1 510.9
Placements with other FCA registered corporations	1 158.6
Placements with other businesses	2 368.3
Bills of Exchange	
Bank bills of public authorities	5.4
Bank bills of FCA corporations	1 275.0
Other bank bills	1 315.4
Other FCA registered corporation bills	437.8
Other bills	550.9
Promissory Notes	
Promissory notes of public authorities	177.4
Promissory notes of FCA registered corporations	396.3
Other promissory notes	490.2
Government securities	
Treasury notes	161.0
Other Commonwealth securities	267.2
Other government or public securities	60.3
Other Securities	
Shares in related corporations	185.2
Other securities of related corporations	9.4
Shares in other business	386.1
Other securities of other businesses	69.0
Lease Receivables	
Leverage lease receivables	150.5
Other lease receivables	459.5
Loans and Advances	
Loans to related FCA registered corporations	138.2
Loans to other related corporations	459.7
Loans to other FCA registered corporations	810.6
Loans to individuals	138.6
Other loans and advances	5 390.2
Client acceptance commitments	862.0
Other Assets in Australia	660.5
Overseas Assets	627.2
Total Assets	22 014.7

Source: Australian Bureau of Statistics, *Authorised Dealers and Money Market Corporations, Australia, April 1985*, 25 June 1985, pp. 9–11.

* Discrepancy in total due to rounding.

as collateral for secured deposit offerings. As non-bank bills and, so far, most promissory notes serve neither function well, the industry has minimized its holdings of these securities, preferring to re-discount its customer paper to other investors.

Loans comprise the largest group of the industry's assets and, as shown in Table 8.2, most are advances to non-financial institutions. As will be discussed in Chapter 10, the industry has very little lending to individuals other than its own staff.

While the statistics in the two tables, collected under the Financial Corporations Act, are certainly useful in examining merchant banking, some major qualifications should be placed on their use. First, as indicated in the table headings, these figures are collected from money market corporations rather than the merchant banking industry as a whole. As discussed in Chapter 2, while there is much overlap between the two groups, not all money market corporations are merchant banks and, more importantly, a number of merchant banks are not money market corporations. Indeed, given the recent restructuring of merchant bank operations, the non-money market corporation segment of the industry is likely to increase significantly over 1986–87. Second, given seasonal changes in money market liquidity and in the economy in general, there can be major dif-ferences in a merchant bank's assets and liabilities position over the year. As there are no consistent year-end dates within the industry (30 June, 30 September, and 31 December are the most common), an aggregate balance sheet of the overall industry would not be parti-cularly valuable as a standard for ratio analysis. Finally, aggregation of asset categories and their subsequent use also suffer from the major differences in accounting procedures followed by the in-dividual firms. In some cases it is possible to reconstruct the figures but generally, as the *Australian Financial Review* complained, merchant bank financial reporting 'has been nothing other than basic, providing details required by law but excluding backup information to allow full assessment of their operations and per-formance'.[2] In addition, merchant banks also have a significant level of contingent liabilities and assets associated with the firm's and its customers' endorsement of bills of exchange, outstanding under-writing commitments, and guarantees and standbys which are not necessarily shown within normal balance sheet figures.

9 Money Market Activities

Traditionally, merchant bank money market activities provided the bulk of the industry's revenue. Indeed their relative importance was such in the late 1960s and early 1970s that the firms were classified as 'money market' corporations by the Reserve Bank. While the money market continues to be significant in the industry's overall operations, its relative importance is declining. This decline reflects Australia's deregulatory process in which the trading banks were first permitted to pay interest, initially on deposits of 14 days or more (30 days was previously the minimum) and then, as of 1 August 1984, on all deposits. Before then, merchant banks had successfully raised funds in the short-term deposit market, primarily on an overnight basis, with which they could then compete with the trading banks in corporate lending.

As trading banks can now tap this same overnight market, the industry has been forced to pay higher deposit rates, which means less competitive lending rates. While more than a year has passed since the trading banks received this power, the impact on the industry's funding and lending operations is still being felt. Unfortunately this readjustment process is being extended by a number of additional factors. The most obvious is the entry of sixteen new foreign-affiliated trading banks. The increased numbers in themselves would be a matter of concern but so is the background of these new entrants. With the exception of the Oversea-Chinese Banking Corporation, each new entrant already has had a significant operational presence in Australia via its shareholdings in a local merchant bank. Furthermore, most of these existing operations will be restructured to form the basis of their parent's local trading bank operations. Thus what were previously merchant bankers will one day suddenly start wearing a trading bank hat but continue on with their money market funding operations and on-lending much as before. With their new 'bank' status, however, they should be able to raise deposits at a lower cost than their former merchant banking colleagues. They must of course, as banks, place some of these funds into the low-yielding statutory reserve deposits and prime assets in accordance with Reserve Bank directives, but it remains uncertain whether this cost will be sufficient to give the rest of the industry a competitive edge.

At present there is also seemingly another competitive problem yet to be resolved, that of the local trading bank wholly-owned merchant bank subsidiaries. As part of the Campbell concept of deregulation, banking regulations, particularly in the sense of ratios, were eventually to apply to the total banking group rather than simply the trading bank arm of what are really financial conglomerates. Such policies had been stated for the new entities. As yet, however, those additional controls have not been implemented. It would appear that today trading banks can compete first with merchant banks, using their trading bank status to bid for the cheaper or less risky funds, and then bid for the remaining more return-oriented money through their merchant bank subsidiary. It is little wonder then that some merchant bankers view their domestic money market activities as a dying industry and instead now raise medium-term funds from overseas.

In the future, those merchant banks without a trading bank licence will be forced into specialized areas of the money market and will probably concentrate more on securities dealing and other forms of non-deposit based activities.

THE OFFICIAL MARKET

Although technically no merchant bank is an authorized dealer in the official money market, in practice there was a very close relationship between the official money market and the merchant banking industry. In some cases merchant bank money market activities preceded the official market and eventually were restructured to become among the first of the authorized dealers. In other cases it was the official dealers' operations that set the basis for what was eventually a much wider scale merchant banking business. In the first case, for example, the local press in early 1959 commented that Australian United and Development Finance 'are two companies which have been concerning themselves with the establishment of an Australian money market for some time'.[1] Both Development Finance's Delfin Discount Company and AUC's United Discount were among the first four authorized dealers. In contrast, other authorized dealer operations gradually formed the basis from which a number of today's merchant banks developed. From Capel Court

Securities, for example, later developed the Capel Court Corporation, and from City Discount eventually came Trans City Holdings.

Indirectly, though, the official market's role was even more significant, for its support of the bank-accepted or -endorsed bills of exchange from 1965 onwards caused the industry's real growth in the late 1960s and early 1970s. They were also helpful in the early 1980s in attracting an increasing portion of semi-government commercial bills and promissory note issues.

Today this relationship is undergoing a major change as those merchant banks whose parents have obtained a trading bank licence or who have been acquired by a trading bank must sell their shareholdings or reduce them to 12.5 per cent—the maximum trading bank shareholding the Reserve Bank allows in an authorized dealer. This ended a number of long-standing merchant bank–authorized dealer affiliations. Development Finance Corporation, now wholly owned by the ANZ Bank, was forced to sell its authorized dealer subsidiary, Delfin Discount; AMP Acceptances, given its new Chase AMP Bank parentage, AMP Discount; AUC, now Morgan Australia Bank, AUC Discount; and Capel Court, now owned by National Mutual Royal Bank, Capel Court Securities. As Table 9.1 shows, the long-standing tradition of a high level of merchant bank ownership of the official market has been markedly reduced.

THE UNOFFICIAL MARKET

As customers began to understand the official market and the benefits of short-term deposits, they also began seeking the best returns possible on their funds. The inter-company market was the first beneficiary of this trend and recommenced its growth at the expense of the larger deposit end of the official market. The restrictions on authorized dealers to accept deposits of at least $50 000 or more, however, opened another potential market at the lower end and it is from this and the inter-company market that the unofficial market developed.

Unlike the official market, where the authorized dealers are subject to extensive Reserve Bank controls, unofficial dealers are subject only to the securities dealers' licensing requirements of the Securities Industry Code. As mentioned in Chapter 7, besides various reporting requirements, the Code's major impact is on the firm's liabilities position: it must maintain surplus funds equal to the greater of either $50 000 or 5 per cent of the dealer's liabilities (3.3 per cent where satisfactory standby facilities have been arranged). Due to their size, most merchant banks are also classified as money market corporations under the Financial Corporations Act but as yet this regulation only involves statistical reporting and consultation.

Table 9.1 Authorized Money Market Dealers and their Major Shareholders, 1985

All-States Discount Limited (Head Office: Melbourne)
100% A.C. Goode family interests

Colonial Mutual Discount Company Limited (Head Office: Sydney)
(formerly Delfin Discount)
43.5% Colonial Mutual Life
33.0% Kleinwort Benson Australia
12.5% ANZ Banking Group
10.0% State Superannuation Board of NSW

Holst Discount Limited (Head Office: Melbourne)
(formerly AUC Discount)
100% Partners of F.W. Holst and Company

GIO Securities Limited (Head Office: Sydney)
(formerly Capel Court Securities)
100% Government Insurance Office of NSW

First Federation Discount Co. Limited (Head Office: Sydney)
100% Spedley Holdings

NDC Securities Ltd (Head Office: Sydney)
(formerly National Discounts Corp.)
75.0% McIntosh Hamson Home Govett
12.5% Security Pacific Australia
12.5% RESI Permanent Building Society

P.P. Discount Limited
(formerly AMP Discount Corp.)
100% Partners of Potter Partners

Short Term Acceptances Limited (Head Office: Sydney)
25.0% Royal Insurance Australia
25.0% S.C. Healy
12.5% National Australia Bank
12.5% Hindmarsh and Adelaide Building Society
12.5% Hospital Benefits Association
12.5% Former partners of A.C. Goode & Co.

Trans City Discount Limited (Head Office: Sydney)
51% City Mutual Life Assurance
49% Trans City Holdings owned by:
    50% City Mutual Life
    50% Irving Trust

As unofficial dealers, merchant banks are active in accepting deposits of at least $10 000 or more;[2] trading, endorsing, and rediscounting commercial bills of exchange, bank-accepted or endorsed bills of exchange, interest rate futures contracts, certificates of deposits, treasury notes and bonds, semi-government securities, and other related negotiable money market securities and financial instruments; the underwriting and trading of corporate promissory notes; acting as a principal in the inter-company market; and making short advances to customers. In addition to such trading profits, many merchant banks also seek fee income from their money market operations through intra-company market broking, providing clients with money market advisory services, and arranging letters of credit to support corporate money market securities issues.

Recently, the unofficial market has improved its competitive position against the official market in other ways as well. Of these, the introduction of Austraclear in 1984 is perhaps the most interesting. Austraclear is a consortium venture (primarily merchant banks) designed to speed and reduce trading costs by eliminating the need for the physical delivery of money market securities. Instead of arranging for the physical delivery of the securities to the buyer, the seller can now electronically request Austraclear to transfer the ownership of those securities held on behalf of the seller to the name of the purchaser. Thus the securities themselves remain with Austraclear; only the ownership records are changed. As of late 1985 Austraclear planned to handle bank bills, Treasury notes, Treasury bonds, and will eventually expand into certain promissory notes, non-bank bills and secondary mortgage market securities. It also now deals with a potentially larger market, having gained eligibility under the Trustee Act in New South Wales and other states, and soon it is to expand its current Sydney and Melbourne operations to Adelaide, Brisbane, and Perth. This expansion, coupled with other technological advances, should allow firms to concentrate their money market operations in one location rather than running a separate dealership in each state. In practice, however, most firms, while concentrating their dealership business in either Sydney or Melbourne, will probably still maintain some dealing capability in the other cities for marketing reasons.

In conjunction with Austraclear, computer-linked electronic trading systems have become even more viable and the arrangements have now been formalized through the Australian Financial Markets Screen Dealing Association. Through this body Reuter screen transactions now use a $5 million minimum trading parcel in Sydney and Melbourne and $2 million in other capital cities. Unless the quotation is marked with an asterisk, these transactions must generally be settled through Austraclear.

General Deposit Business
The general deposit business of the unofficial market has traditionally been the bread and butter business of Australian merchant banking for it was here that the industry competed so successfully

against the trading banks. These deposits serve two functions. First, and most importantly, they fund their firm's lending activities. Second, they also provide a good source of revenue in their own right as long as dealers raise deposits at rates less than the firm's lending rates or returns on its money market securities portfolio, or adapt the portfolio's maturity to profit from interest rate changes. Once there was a distinct difference in approach between institutions, with some firms concentrating on deposit raisings to fund their loan portfolio, others operating their money market more as a trading and marketing vehicle for their customers' securities, and yet others attempting to do both. Traditionally, those merchant banks with local trading bank affiliations chose the first approach, the smaller consortium ventures the third alternative, and those with a major foreign bank parent either the first or second options.

While most firms will accept either secured or unsecured deposits, there is a preference for the latter. These monies can then fund the firm's lending activities. A secured deposit does not offer the same flexibility. This is because when placing a secured deposit, the customer effectively receives title to a money market security from the merchant bank of equal or greater value in return. To the extent that these securities derive from the merchant bank's loan portfolio, secured deposits can fund the firm's loan portfolio. In practice, however, customers generally require government or semi-government paper or, at the very least, bank-backed paper. As none of these securities is usually a direct product of merchant bank lending, secured deposits provide only indirect assistance, and hence the preference for unsecured deposits.

This loan funding business is often referred to as the 'lending' book. The dealer would be instructed to raise so much money and where possible try to match the maturity of these deposits with that of the firm's loan portfolio. Generally this is seldom possible, for while merchant banks often lend on six month terms or longer, the bulk of merchant bank deposits (over 95 per cent) are comprised of 11.00 a.m. or 24-hour call deposits. Table 9.2 shows some of the other common shorter-term deposit types and their respective conditions. The rates for the longer term deposits, both secured and unsecured, are shown in Table 9.3.

While initially this mismatch between the merchant banks' deposits (short) and loan (medium) maturities might appear risky, most merchant banks traditionally have run a mismatched book by choice. This is because they have generally profited on this position due to the term structure of interest rates. As mentioned earlier, there is usually a direct relationship between the deposit's maturity

Table 9.2 Types of 'At Call' Deposits

11 a.m. call deposit	Same day withdrawal if advised by 11 a.m.
24-hour call deposit	The funds remain for at least 24 hours before giving the required notice.
7-day call deposit	The funds remain for at least 7 days before giving the required notice.
14-day call deposit	The funds remain for at least 14 days before giving the required notice.

Source: Partnership Pacific Limited, 1981.

Table 9.3 Merchant Bank Deposit Rates (%)

	Secured	Unsecured
Call	16.00	16.25
30 days	16.25	16.50
90 days	16.20	16.45
180 days	16.00	16.25

Source: *Australian Business*, 30 October 1985, p. 162.

and the rate of interest expected. The longer the period, the larger the interest rate paid. By accepting deposits on much shorter terms than their loans, merchant banks could often profit from the difference. The other option is to raise funds of a similar maturity to one's advances or hedge the position through futures contracts. Given the general lack of six-month deposit funds, these monies must come either from overseas raisings or from selling similar date securities in the market.

As discussed in Chapter 10, virtually all merchant bank loans carry an option to convert the facility into bills and, when funding becomes a problem, the conversion of one's loan portfolio into bills and their subsequent rediscounting on the market is a common response. Provided the firm can retail the paper successfully, a merchant bank can effectively finance new lending by simultaneously selling the bills provided under the facility for the funds required. The problem is that the merchant bank will normally incur a contingent liability for the discounted paper even if it is not already liable for the bill as its acceptor. At times these liabilities, too, can present a potential funding problem and hence the attraction of a promissory note facility where the money required is (it is hoped) raised in the market directly. Besides customer paper, a number of merchant banks also raise long-term funds in the market by the sale of their own paper. Initially this was usually through negotiable certificates of deposits but in recent years merchant bank promissory note issues have also become common.

At first, merchant bank funding by money market securities issues was a fairly minor arrangement with the instruments marketed on a low key basis to private clients. Capel Court, for example, offered its own negotiable certificate of deposits as early as 1977. Gradually these raisings have become more formal and more important. In the case of certificates of deposits, for example, Partnership Pacific for some time has had a series of weekly issues, generally with a 90 day maturity and with a promise to repurchase up to $500 000 of these securities from private clients on one day notice. It is in promissory notes, however, that the greatest developments have occurred. In 1983, for example, Wardley Australia's $50 million issue was the first Australian merchant bank issue to use the tender system, be supported by a letter of credit, and be underwritten by a major trading bank.

Another aspect of the tightening money market is that merchant banks are making increasing use of standby credit facilities from their parent companies and other institutions. These help reduce the level, from an operational and legal viewpoint, of liquid assets required in one's portfolio, and also add to the merchant bank's credit standing among potential depositors. The magnitude of these arrangements is commonly highlighted in merchant bank annual reports.

In addition to Australian dollar deposits, merchant banks have long accepted what are called simulated or synthetic foreign currency deposits. This is because, while the interest rate paid reflects the offshore rates paid on the foreign currency and the end settlement is adjusted for any exchange rate movements, the deposit, interest payments, and redemption are all made in Australian dollars. As no money is actually converted into foreign exchange, merchant banks offered such facilities even before they received foreign exchange licences or foreign exchange controls were removed. A more recent foreign currency denominated deposit is Partnership Pacific's POSSUM facility. The POSSUM, short for 'Placement Over Seas of Savings Under Management', allows Australian customers to establish fixed deposit accounts denominated in foreign currencies for periods of three to six months and amounts of as little as $10 000 to be split between up to three currencies.

As the trading banks have become more competitive for domestic deposits, merchant banks have been forced to obtain an increasing portion of their funding from overseas. Indeed, as shown in Table 9.4, the industry's borrowing from non-residents has more than tripled in little more than a year.

Table 9.4 Money Market Corporation Borrowings from Non-residents, 1984–85 ($m)

1984	
February	899.0
March	991.6
April	1 084.6
May	1 230.4
June	1 471.4
July	1 537.5
August	1 793.5
September	2 531.3
October	3 051.6
November	2 603.4
December	2 699.4
1985	
January	3 077.2
February	2 803.7
March	3 069.2
April	3 139.1

Source: Australian Bureau of Statistics, *Authorised Dealers and Money Market Corporations, Australia*, April 1985, 25 June 1985, p. 9.

As merchant banks have gained a larger proportion of their funds through medium-term overseas sources, this also has affected their asset structure, in that the previous liquidity balances held in bank or other commercial bills against changes in short-term deposit levels need no longer be as high.

Government Securities
At one time there was little trading in government and semi-government securities in Australia as investors purchased them to hold until maturity. Over time, however, better interest rates on these securities and less regulatory forced purchases caused a trading market to develop. While there is little question that stockbrokers have been the traditional source of most non-financial institutional trading, merchant banks have also had a significant influence. In particular, as the frequency and size of semi-government raisings grew in the late 1970s, their involvement in what were previously primarily share-broker-underwritten semi-government raisings became increasingly influential. Indeed, following the first stockbroker–merchant bank led raising in September 1976, the merchant bank participation grew so consequential that in July 1980 the government's Loan Council finally revised its underwriting fees and procedures to allow for solely merchant bank underwritten raisings.

In the government securities field, too, the once stockbroker, trading bank, and authorized dealer dominated market also began to change as Treasury notes and Treasury bonds offered increasingly market-related rates of interest, so that a marked increase in trading levels resulted. Since the introduction of the Treasury bond tender system, for example, the total secondary trading in register transactions of $100 000 or more has risen from $15.4 billion in 1981–82, to $24.5 billion in 1982–83, and $57.8 billion in 1983–84. There has been a similar growth in turnover as a percentage of Treasury bonds outstanding—from 15.4 per cent of the securities on issue in 1981–82, to 24.5 per cent in 1982–83, and 57.8 per cent in 1983–84.[3] Merchant banks have played a major role in the tender system and become among the most active groups in the secondary market for these securities, a position well reflected in Table 9.5.

As part of its efforts to improve government securities trading, the Reserve Bank on 8 November 1984 gave twenty-one dealers in government securities the status of 'reporting dealers'. Under these arrangements, reporting dealers have exclusive trading access to the Reserve Bank for government securities with a maturity of one year or more. In return, these reporting bond dealers, as the name implies, must make daily reports to the Bank on their overall bond transactions. Unlike the authorized dealer, this reporting status only reflects the various dealers' importance in the government securities market and is in no way a special form of licensing or entitlement to Reserve Bank services or support.

The selection, based on an independent transaction volume comprising greater than 1 per cent of the government securities market, is a mix of stockbrokers, authorized dealers, merchant banks, trading

Table 9.5 Treasury Bond Turnover by Type of Institution

Year to June	1975	1976	1977	1978	1979	1980	1981	1982	1983	1984
Reserve Bank	26	19	19	19	14	12	13	12	5	3
Banks	15	20	26	18	21	20	21	24	31	18
Authorized dealers	31	30	26	26	25	20	19	18	19	16
Money market corps	9	9	9	11	18	14	12	12	12	20
Stockbrokers	7	9	7	11	12	12	17	17	14	21
Life offices	4	3	4	3	3	7	9	9	10	7
Other	8	10	9	12	7	15	9	8	9	15
Total (%)	100	100	100	100	100	100	100	100	100	100

Source: Reserve Bank of Australia, *Bulletin*, February 1985, p. 499.

banks, and life companies. As shown in Table 9.6, stockbrokers and authorized dealers comprise the largest grouping, but not all trading banks or authorized dealers had sufficient volumes to justify a listing.

In addition to more traditional government securities dealings, merchant banks have been fairly innovative in marketing these securities to the general public. One notable method is the use of proprietary acronyms for a range of tax advantaged investments. The DINGO (a discounted investment in negotiable government obligation), for example, was the first of a series of specialized zero or low coupon securities marketed by the merchant banking industry over 1984. Basically these securities are sold on a discount basis with the bulk of or the total return provided from the difference between the initial purchase price and the security's redemption value on maturity. The DINGO thus allows investors a zero coupon government bond by stripping the interest income stream from the bond's redemption value—in effect creating two securities and allowing greater profits for its creator, BA Australia. Other similar products

Table 9.6 Reporting Bond Dealers, December 1985

Firm	Type of Business
Australian Bank Ltd	Trading bank
Australian Gilt Company	Broker
Australian Mutual Provident Society	Life office
Bain & Company	Stockbroker
BT Australia Ltd	Merchant bank
Capel Court Corporation	Merchant bank
Commonwealth Bank of Australia	Trading bank
Dominguez Barry Samuel Montagu Ltd	Merchant bank
GIO Securities	Authorized dealer
Holst Discount	Authorized dealer
Macquarie Bank	Trading bank
McCaughan, Dyson & Co. Ltd	Stockbroker
National Mutual Life Assoc. of Australia	Life office
NDC Securities Ltd	Authorized dealer
Ord Minnett Ltd	Stockbroker
PP Discount Ltd	Authorized dealer
Schroder Australia	Merchant bank
Spedley	Merchant bank
Trans City Discount Ltd	Authorized dealer
Peter Wallman & Co.	Stockbroker
J.B. Were & Son	Stockbroker
Westpac Banking Corporation	Trading bank

Source: *Australian Financial Review*, 19 December 1985, p. 27.

include Trans City's DRAGONS (discounted receipts of Australian government obligatory negotiable securities) and the SGIO Building Society's QUIDS (Queensland Investment Deposit Series). Unfortunately the tax postponement advantage that these zero coupon securities provided were removed on new issue by the Federal Treasurer, Paul Keating, on 16 December 1984 with the requirement that tax be paid annually on the effective interest compounded over the year.

Bills of Exchange

Historically the bills of exchange market has been the most important of merchant bank trading activities and, to many firms, dealing in bills of exchange constitutes the largest single source of money market transactions. There is good reason for this, as the merchant banking industry developed the domestic bills of exchange as a source of short-term finance. The direct responsibility for this innovation must be credited to Philip Miskin, then of Bill Acceptances Corp., who initiated non-bank financing for commercial trade bills of exchange in 1963 and subsequently expanded this to non-trade bills, in other words, strictly financing or accommodation paper. These efforts, quickly copied by other early merchant banks, caused the Reserve Bank to study the bills' potential and subsequently to promote their use in the official market. However, while setting the regulatory framework and support for the bills of exchange market, neither the Reserve Bank nor the trading banks were responsible for developing the bill market to what it is today. Again, this was largely the responsibility of Australia's merchant banking industry. As discussed in Chapter 4, the industry's rapid development in the late 1960s and early 1970s, and its subsequent growth, are directly due to the industry's success with commercial bills.

The bill market originally provided two major functions for merchant banks: first, a source of fee income and second, a means of financing their loan portfolio. The industry's real limitation was the lack of loan funding. Had the industry relied solely on cash deposits, merchant banking would have grown much more slowly and its impact on Australian finance would have been far less than at present. In the early years merchant bank work consisted of arranging bank acceptance or endorsement lines for customers with the trading banks and then discounting the resulting paper. This produced both fee income and at the same time, through rediscounting the trading bank paper to other investors, freed the merchant banks' own funds for other purposes. Indeed, by arranging the bill facilities and then discounting as many bank bills as possible, merchant banks could turn their own funds over and over, producing additional fee income each time. It was the combination of the financial status that bank-accepted or endorsed paper had (and still has) in the market, coupled with the marketing efforts of the merchant banks in placing the paper, that caused the bill market to grow as it did. Later, when the trading banks actively arranged bill facilities themselves and handled their own discounting as well (forcing the merchant banks largely from the bank bill business), the second phase of the bill market—that of the non-bank bill of exchange—was already well advanced. Investors once used to bank bills could see the even higher short-term returns available on bills without a bank acceptance or endorsement. Of course these securities were more risky but as merchant banks grew in stature, and prime non-financial companies began to use this paper, many investors easily accepted this higher risk and return alternative. As a result, merchant banks were soon arranging their own accep-tance–endorsement facilities as well as discounting and rediscounting the resulting paper. Since mid-1984 there has also been some bill trading conducted on a forward basis.

Technically there is no difference between a bank or non-bank bill. Both have three parties: a drawer, an acceptor, and the payee. The drawer (generally the party for whom the financing has been arranged) in theory creates the bill stating that a specific amount will be paid by the acceptor on presentation on a certain date. The acceptor (normally the financial institution) agrees to pay the bill on maturity and thus accepts first responsibility for its payment. If the acceptor for some reason fails to pay the named payee or bearer on maturity, the holder can then seek payment from the drawer. As at least two parties are liable for the bill's payment, bills of exchange are sometimes referred to as two-name paper. In addition to the acceptor and drawer, if the payee has sold the bill by way of endorsement, the payee and any subsequent endorser of the security can also be required to pay the bill if the acceptor or drawer cannot. Very often, as shown in Figure 9.1, the borrower as drawer will also act as the initial payee and first endorser, further registering the liability.

The contingent liabilities created when a merchant bank endorses bills of exchange on selling the bill is typically reported either off the balance sheet as a footnote or as an additional item below the total liabilities. In contrast, while the merchant bank incurs a direct liability when acting as the acceptor of a customer's bill of exchange,

(Face side)

Place of Payment · Date of Drawing · Amount in Figures · Date Payable

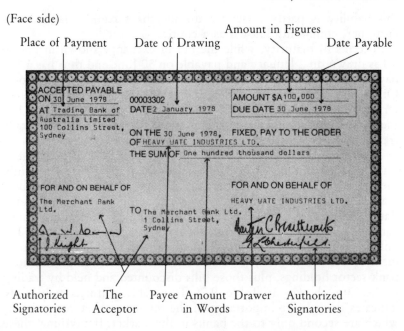

Authorized Signatories · The Acceptor · Payee Amount in Words · Drawer · Authorized Signatories

(Reverse side—part)

Payee's Indorsement

Second Indorser (Who purchased the bill for value)

Third Indorser (Who purchased the bill for value)

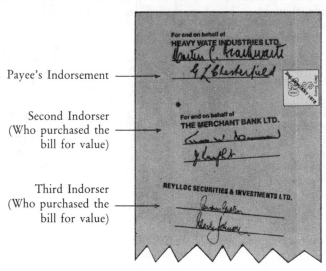

Figure 9.1 Example of a Commercial Bill of Exchange
Source: Australian Merchant Bankers Association, 1985.

this liability is partly offset by the merchant bank's claim on its customer, commonly known as a contra.

In terms of maturity, while the bill of exchange shown in Figure 9.1 is drawn on 2 January and payable on 30 June and thus has a 180 day life, bills are also commonly drawn for 90 and 120 day periods. Other maturities may be arranged but are much less common. In terms of denomination, the $100 000 figure shown in Figure 9.1 is the most common, but again, other amounts, particularly with trade transactions, are possible.

Thus there are today two major providers of bills of exchange—trading banks and merchant banks—with the trading banks certainly the more important. While there are no official figures on the bills market, a rough idea of market share can be obtained from Reserve Bank statistics. As of June 1985, for example, the trading banks had bill acceptance or endorsement commitments of some $17 133 million, with $10 495 million outstanding, and discounting commitment of $13 942 million, with $8475 million outstanding. The non-bank sector holdings, plus those bills discounted and held by trading banks, are shown in Table 9.7. This table unfortunately only indicates the relative importance of the money market corporations which are second only to the banks in the market. If anything, these figures greatly understate their importance, for they do not include bills drawn or accepted by the reporting corporations themselves or those bills that have been marketed to non-financial institution investors.

Table 9.7 Bills of Exchange and Promissory Notes Discounted and Held

	June 1985 $m
Money market corporations	5 023
Authorized dealers	349
Building societies	1 476
Finance companies	498
Credit co-operatives	70
General financiers	107
Intra-group financiers	10
Other non-bank financial corporations	165
	7 707
Plus Bills of Exchange discounted and held by banks	706
Total	8 413

Source: Reserve Bank of Australia, *Bulletin*, August 1985.
Note: Excludes bills drawn or accepted by the reporting corporations.

Besides reporting the total bills outstanding it would be helpful for the Reserve Bank to divide the present total holdings of bills and promissory notes into bank bills, non-bank bills, and promissory notes. The figures would then show changes in the use of these securities. Since the removal of quantitative lending controls, trading banks have been less pressured to rely on bills as a de facto means of lending. More importantly, when the prime asset (PA) ratio is fully implemented by the existing trading banks, there will be a further switch away from the traditional bank bill facility. This is because, unlike the SRD–LGS ratios which covered only bank deposits, the PA ratio covers all domestic liabilities. Thus the other traditional advantage of the banks' bill facility, the avoidance of the SRD–LGS requirements had the loan been funded by deposits, will be greatly reduced.

The other interesting change over time may be the level of merchant bank investment in bank bills. As was shown elsewhere in Table 8.2, reporting money market corporations in April 1985 held $2595.8 million in bank accepted or endorsed paper. For the most part, this paper is held for liquidity purposes and, to a lesser extent, as collateral for secured deposits. While merchant banks would no doubt prefer not to fund bank lending by holding these securities, bank acceptances are easily traded and provide the unofficial market's basic liquidity.

Promissory Notes

As mentioned, promissory notes are an important source of merchant bank Australian and foreign currency denominated funding. These notes, however, are even more important in de facto lending and securities trading. Due to their de facto lending function, 'pro note' facilities combine both lending and money market services. The merchant bank's lending staff assess the issuer's credit risk and handle the facility's documentation and administration, but the merchant bank's money market division is responsible for its sale; if held, the promissory note becomes a money market rather than lending division asset.

The Australian promissory note market can be traced directly to January 1977 when the then Citinational merchant bank had a number of prime corporations conduct note issues for $2 to $5 million which it then marketed to others in the money market. Over time the size of the issues and number of issuers grew and came to include semi-government bodies as well, with Telecom Australia being the first in June 1978. The turning point, though, came in September 1979 when BT Australia led a $636 million semi-government issue together with the Commonwealth Bank, the CBC (now National Australia) Bank, and AML Finance (now Elders) for another semi-government body, the Australian Wheat Board. Other semi-government authorities have since followed suit but the Australian Wheat Board continues to be the largest single issuer. In late 1985, for example, it announced plans to raise some $1.5 billion of its $4 billion 1985–86 borrowing requirements through this means.

The significance of semi-government issuers in the promissory note market cannot be over-emphasized, for a market which had been limited to perhaps one hundred prime corporate note issuers suddenly easily doubled in size. Given their government status in the market, many semi-government bodies could now raise short-term debt—often at rates cheaper than from the banking system. Thus, not only did promissory notes suddenly become respectable but they also created some feeling of urgency in that rates might rise if too many semi-government bodies began using the market.

The significance of semi-government promissory notes was not restricted to the issuer side, for their entry was important to potential investors too. First, many investors were uncertain whether to purchase securities with only one company's backing. However, as the semi-government issues usually had federal or state government backing, investors could purchase their promissory notes without this concern. Semi-government status was also important as investors restricted to trustee investments could invest in semi-government issues, but not ordinary promissory notes, unless they had bank backing. Cash management trusts were attracted for similar reasons. Savings banks and life offices, too, found these semi-government notes attractive alternatives in meeting their then respective LGS ratios. Finally, semi-government status was important to the authorized money market dealers whose participation in many major promissory note facilities greatly added to the market. As of May 1985, there were an estimated 124 promissory note issuers in Australia (26 public authorities, 29 financial intermediaries, and 69 non-financial corporations) with promissory note facilities of some $10 550 million available.[4]

Besides the issuers and investors, money market dealers also benefited from semi-government promissory notes, for the issue sizes soon allowed active trading in these securities as the many firms involved in the underwritings helped ensure a secondary market. A recent Australian Wheat Board notes raising of $1.5 billion, for example, included the four major trading banks as well as BA Australia, BT Australia, Citicorp Capital Markets, First Chicago Australia, and Trans City Holdings among the eleven-firm syndicate. More importantly in secondary trading, the promissory note's major advantage is its bearer nature. While technically a bill of exchange is also a bearer instrument, sellers have always been required to endorse these securities on delivery, thus creating a contingent liability equal to the bill's face value. Logically, a similar endorsement requirement should have been extracted on the sale of any promissory notes, but Citinational successfully argued that this should not be required and the market has treated them strictly as bearer instruments ever since. Thus, when a promissory note is resold, no contingent liability is created.

The avoidance of contingent liabilities has been a major attraction of promissory note trading and over time many merchant banks have actively sought to replace bank bills with promissory notes for an increasing proportion of their liquidity holdings. Besides the contingency problems, another attraction was, of course, that by holding bank bills in their money market portfolios, merchant banks were simply funding the lending activities of their trading bank competitors. With promissory notes the banks were less likely to gain a direct advantage.

As mentioned, the key difference between a bill of exchange and a promissory note is that whereas the bill is dependent on at least two parties (the drawer and acceptor), a promissory note relies on the good faith and credit of one party—the issuer—hence it is sometimes called one-name paper. It is simply a promise by the issuer to pay the bearer of the security so much on presentation on a certain date. The example shown in Figure 9.2, for example, Heavy Wate Industry, has promised to pay the bearer of the note $100 000 on presentation on 30 June at the offices of the Trading Bank of Australia. Since it was issued on 1 June, the note could have been bought and sold by a number of investors. The only signature required, however, is that of the end holder who presents the security to the bank for payment. This signature acknowledges the receipt of payment by the then holder rather than creating any contingent liabilities.

In terms of maturity, although the Heavy Wate rate is for 30 days, 90 and 180 days are the most common issuing maturities. There is no requirement, however, that issuers confine themselves to any particular alternatives. The 1985–86 Wheat Board facility, for example, will allow maturities ranging from 7 to 185 days. Longer promissory note maturities are also possible, but less common within the Australian market.

In terms of denominations, $100 000 is the most common but this too can be adjusted according to market conditions. Again, to use

(Face side)

Amount in Words   Issuer (Maker)   Amount in Figures   Date Payable

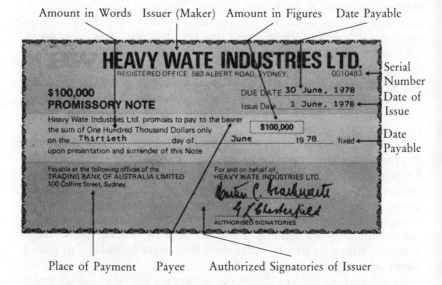

Serial
Number
Date of
Issue

Date
Payable

Place of Payment   Payee   Authorized Signatories of Issuer

(Reverse side)

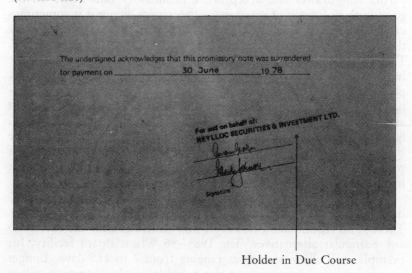

Holder in Due Course

Figure 9.2 Example of a Promissory Note
Source: Australian Merchant Bankers Association, 1985.

the recent Australian Wheat Board as an example, the paper under that facility can be issued in multiples ranging from $20 000 to $1 million.

Initially, promissory notes issues were arranged much like a discount facility for commercial bills: the issuer would present the notes (in multiples of $100 000) to the merchant bank concerned in return for a lesser amount in cash. The merchant bank in turn would either rediscount the notes or hold them for investment. As promissory notes gained popularity, the size of the issues themselves grew from $2 to $5 million and up to $25 million or more and eventually became too large for one merchant bank to handle comfortably. Instead, larger issues used a tender panel system. Basically, one firm arranged the issue and formed a panel of other merchant banks for the bidding. On the appropriate day, the tender panel members bid for the notes, with the discount rate expressed as a yield; the one with the highest bid (the lowest yield) then purchased the securities. However, the panel had no obligation to acquire them. This was corrected in September 1979 when Citinational introduced an underwritten tender concept whereby the underwriters acquire any unsold notes at an agreed rate.

Larger promissory note issues today involve a manager or joint managers who arrange the tender panel and the administration of the issue, the tender panel members who place bids for the issue, and an underwriting group to acquire any securities not purchased. Generally one or two firms serve as managers, three to five as underwriters, and around five to ten as panel members. As a rule the managers also serve as underwriters and underwriters in turn serve as panel members. An indication of the tender panel participation in mid-1985 is shown in Table 9.8. Not all issuers, however, utilize either an underwritten facility or the panel system.

As more institutions entered the market it has been increasingly costly for investors to monitor the financial position of each participant, so the service offered by Australian Ratings, an independent body which assesses and monitors the financial health of the major participants, has become essential. This monitoring role is particularly important because financial positions can change. In mid-1985, for example, CIBC Australia's rating was increased from a BBB+ to an AA− as a result of a guarantee issued on its liabilities by its parent bank, the Canadian Imperial Bank of Commerce. A selected listing of these merchant bank credit ratings is shown in Table 9.9.

A further extension of the promissory note market happened in November 1983 when what was then AUC introduced a promissory note styled preference share called a rebatable note or, more recently,

Table 9.8 Major Promissory Note Tender Participation, May 1985

	Frequency of Representation on Tender Panels
AMP Acceptances	16
ANZ Bank Group	9
Australian Bank/Australis Securities	11
Australian European Finance	7
BA Australia	13
BT Australia	17
Barclays Australia	13
Capel Court Corporation	7
Citicorp Capital Markets Aust.	15
Commonwealth Bank of Australia	14
Elders Finance & Investment	11
French Australian Fin./BNP	12
Grindlays Australia	8
Kleinwort Benson Australia	8
Lloyds International	22
Macquarie Hill Samuel	12
Morgan Guaranty Australia	15
Partnership Pacific	6
Schroder Darling & Co.	14
Trans City Holdings	9
Tricontinental Corp.	7
Wardley Australia	11
Westpac Banking Corporation	9
Average of the 23 major promissory note dealers	11.6
Average of all 57 institutions surveyed	6.0

Source: Investment & Econometrics Research, *Promissory Note Survey*, 27 September 1985.

a floating rate short-term preference share. These 60- to 180-day securities had an advantage over normal promissory notes in that the return could be in the form of preference share dividends rather than interest and hence be subject to a Section 46 rebate, effectively making the returns tax-free to most corporate investors. While these securities as equity were much less secure than normal promissory notes, this position was more than offset in AUC's case in that the issuer's preference shares were also supported by a letter of credit from the Chemical Bank of New York and reconfirmed by the Commonwealth Bank. Since then there have been many similar issues by other major corporations, generally with some form of letter of credit or other guarantee as security.

Table 9.9 Australian Merchant Bank Financial Ratings

Company	Rating 2 yr/unsec.
ABN Australia Limited	(A.1)
All-States Capital Group Limited	B
Amro Australia Limited	BBB
ANZ Capital Markets Corp. Ltd	AA−
Australian European Finance Corp. Ltd	A+
Australis Securities Limited	BBB+
BA Australia Limited	A−
Barclays Australia Limited	A
BBL Australia Limited	(A.1)
Bill Acceptance Corporation Limited	A
BNY Australia Limited	BBB
Boston Australia Ltd	BBB+
BOT Australia Limited	BBB
BT Australia Limited	A
Capel Court Corporation Limited	A−
CIBC Australia Limited	AA−
Citisecurities Limited	A−
Dominguez Barry Samuel Montagu Ltd	BBB
Elders Finance & Investment Co. Ltd	(B.1)
European Asian of Australia Limited	BBB
First Chicago Australia Limited	BBB
First National Limited	AA−
French Australian Financial Corp. Ltd	A
Hambro Australia Limited	BBB
Indosuez Australia Limited	BBB
Kleinwort Benson Australia Limited	BBB
Lloyds International Limited	A+
Michell NBD Limited	BBB−
Midland International Aust. Ltd	A
Partnership Pacific Limited	AA−
Rothschild Australia Limited	BBB−
Sanwa Australia Limited	BBB
SBC Australia Limited	A−
Schroder, Darling & Company Limited	BBB−
Security Pacific Australia Limited	BBB
Societe Generale Aust. Limited	AA+
Spedley Securities Limited	BB
Standard Chartered Australia Limited	A−
Tans City Holdings Limited	BBB+
Tricontinental Holdings Limited	A+
Wardley Australia Limited	A+

Source: *Australian Ratings*, September 1985, pp. 10–13.

Note: Rating in brackets represents the firm's commercial paper rating when a two-year unsecured rating was unavailable.

Inter-Company Market

Though it is difficult to distinguish the general deposit section of the unofficial market from the inter-company market, the main differences are those of orientation, transaction size, and the firms involved. First and foremost, the inter-company market is the informal wholesale side of the unofficial market. Virtually all deposits are on a short-term unsecured basis, with a minimum of at least $250 000 and most in multiples of millions of dollars. Secured deposits can also be arranged, with the security normally of overseas bank guarantees over the borrowers' debentures.

In addition to normal inter-company market transactions there is also a sort of inter-merchant bank market or inter-financial institution market operating as a major sub-market towards the end of the day's closing whereby dealers, after taking most of their positions in the morning, try and balance out their positions in the afternoon.

Secondary Mortgage Market

Another specific sub-sector of merchant bank money market operations is the secondary mortgage market. The trading of money market securities, backed by a pool of first mortgages, has been particularly successful in the United States and many merchant banks have long seen the potential of these securities to refinance traditional home lending institutions such as savings banks and building societies.

The earliest merchant bank involvement in this area came in November 1978 when the Bill Acceptance Corporation established a mortgage portfolio (insured by the government-owned Housing Loan Insurance Corporation) against which it then drew bills of exchange. These bills were rediscounted on the market and the proceeds used to acquire another portfolio of HLIC backed mortgages and the process was then repeated.

While a number of other similar schemes have also been tried, the stamp duty charges on mortgage transfers greatly limited the market potential. Both the Australian Merchant Bankers Association and the Mortgage Bankers' Association of Australia had long pushed for the removals of these and other regulatory inhibitions and in 1984 their recommendations were finally heeded.

Unfortunately, early hopes for a national mortgage market body were dashed when traditional rivalries between the major financial capitals caused New South Wales, Victoria and Queensland to go their own way in an attempt to gain the new market for themselves.

In the end the Victorian government was probably the most successful, for its National Mortgage Market Corporation obtained the equity support of both the Victorian and South Australian governments (sharing a total of 26 per cent) and some twenty-six other financial institutions as shareholders. Its first 'Aussie Mac' promissory note, issued against the security of a pool of insured mortgages, was held on 10 April 1985. The New South Wales body, the First Australian National Mortgage Market Acceptance Corp., will also operate as a consortium venture between the New South Wales government with 26 per cent and a group of financial institutions. Given the initial short term (30 to 185 days' maturity) orientation of the Aussie Mac certificates, the New South Wales body plans to concentrate on longer maturity instruments, with a period of five years expected for its first 'FANMAC' certificate issue. In addition to the maturity difference, the NSW body plans to market these securities aggressively overseas as well as within Australia. In practice, both will eventually adopt very similar market strategies. In addition to the two state government sponsored bodies, there are a number of other secondary mortgage securities operators, including the Austnat Mortgage Pool Agency Ltd (Annie Mae) and Forward Mortgages Ltd, Queensland's first registered issuer under the state's Queensland Mortgage (Secondary Market) Act.

For the most part the merchant banking industry has tried to work within the two state bodies rather than establish its own secondary mortgage market. This is due to a realization that the market must be well established before it could succeed and a state body offers the best potential for success. As a result a number of merchant banks are already shareholders in one or both state bodies and Wardley has even seconded one of its executives to assist in the Victorian body's operations.

10 Domestic Lending

In domestic lending, merchant bankers compete directly with trading banks and finance companies. Initially they were particularly successful due to restrictions on bank lending and the finance companies' instalment credit–real estate financing orientation. But as these institutions entered more into merchant bank style lending, loan margins became lower, and often previous advances were refinanced at lower rates. The gradual deregulation of the trading banks has also hurt the funding and lending side of merchant banking, and Reserve Bank pressure on the industry's lending growth—particularly over 1976–77—also hampered its operations. The greatest market pressures are of course yet to come. The sixteen new banks expected over 1985–86 are all familiar with the type of lending in which merchant banks have excelled. With the funding cost advantages afforded by their trading bank status, these institutions will make the industry's traditional lending activities all the more difficult and more expensive. This lending will also become more dangerous for, unlike its funding side, the bulk of merchant bank lending is on a fixed interest basis for at least 90 to 180 days. Admittedly, these rates are adjusted periodically to the market conditions on what would appear very short periods, but even 90 days can prove too long if interest rates move against one's position.

The industry's liquidity holdings in the form of NCDs, promissory notes, and other securities are similarly affected by such rate movements. The problem then, as was shown in Chapter 9, is that the traditional margin between average overnight rates and those for the industry's 90- and 180-day bills had narrowed and on occasion represented a negative return. Thus far the impact on lending portfolios has been minimized by raising funds with maturities more in line with the industry's loan portfolio, but the new banks also bidding for these funds will reduce margins further and in the process force the rest of the industry either into more risky or more specialized lending areas. One alternative, of course, is to do neither and it is interesting that of the newer merchant banks, Dominguez Barry Samuel Montagu chose not to enter the lending side of merchant banking, and one of the oldest firms, Schroder Australia, sold its term loan portfolio to Midland in 1984.

The reason for these firms' decisions is more obvious when one again considers the relationship between the industry's funding and lending rates. The bulk of its domestic money is still obtained through short-term deposits, with the majority placed on a 24-hour call basis. It is exactly the latter funding which until 1 August 1984 had been free of trading bank competition. As the existing and newly-arrived trading banks expand their use of overnight money, there should be greater pressures on market rates; in the process merchant bank funding will become more reliant both on overseas raisings and on marketing an increased percentage of client bills and promissory note holders to other investors. The latter is an attempt to shrink, or at least contain, the growth of merchant banks' own loan portfolio holdings. These present pressures will worsen over 1986–87 and some firms may follow Schroder Australia and quit the term loan portion of the market. This is not to say that merchant banks will stop lending; rather they will have to offer more specialized lending and support services just to maintain a market share. At present, though, domestic lending falls within ten major areas: cash loans; bill acceptance and discounting facilities; letters of credit; term loans; Australian dollar syndications; leasing; guarantees and performance bonds; trade finance; property finance; and other specialist lending. In addition to these direct Australian dollar lending activities, merchant banks are also active in foreign currency loans (see Chapter 11). There are two other areas which, although technically not lending at all, play an increasing part in the industry's commercial lending divisions. These are the management and provision of promissory note facilities and the placement of redeemable preference shares.

CASH LOANS

Most merchant bank cash advances are a function of their money market operations and for practical purposes are short-term inter-company loans with the merchant bank acting as principal. For short-term borrowing the interest is paid on maturity but with longer term advances interest is paid monthly or quarterly in arrears. For short periods the interest rate is generally fixed but longer term loan rates are periodically adjusted—often every 90 days. Merchant bank cash advances for longer than six months, however, are not common as a bill or a term loan facility is normally used instead. These facilities, though, can be rolled over.

Cash loans are normally made on an unsecured basis and are thus limited only to more credit-worthy borrowers; generally a capitalization of $10 million and a good balance sheet are among the minimum requirements.

In addition to normal cash loans, another facility, the so-called simulated US dollar loan, developed during the peak of the hedge market. Though technically no foreign exchange is involved and the loan is denominated in Australian dollars, the interest rate follows an equivalent US dollar borrowing and the repayment in Australian dollars is adjusted for US and Australian currency movements. The advantage to borrowers anticipating future US dollar receipts is that they can use this money now without foreign exchange exposure or Australian withholding tax.

BILL ACCEPTANCE AND DISCOUNT FACILITIES

A bill acceptance and discount facility are two separate services which are often combined. The acceptance part is where the merchant bank simply acts as the acceptor on the client's bill of exchange; in other words, paying the amount due when the bill is presented on maturity. The discounting, on the other hand, involves the actual selling of the security. As bills of exchange pay no specific interest, they are initially sold at less than their face value to achieve the desired yield to maturity, hence the term discounting. As a rule the borrower signs the bill as the drawer, payee, and first endorser and presents it to a merchant bank or other financial institution for acceptance. The same institution will then commonly sell or discount the security in the market and pay the borrower the proceeds less the institution's fees. A similar discounting facility may also be arranged for promissory notes and trade bills; they need no additional acceptor.

Merchant bank bill acceptance and discount facilities can take a variety of forms, with the popularity of each dependent on market conditions. For example, merchant banks once commonly arranged acceptance facilities with trading banks for clients and then discounted the resulting bills. In time, however, banks became more aggressive as acceptors and initiated many of these arrangements themselves; the merchant bank only discounted the bills. As the banks established their own money market departments, they often assumed this function as well, and thus merchant banks now avoid trading bank lines where possible in favour of their own facilities or the arrangement of promissory note sales.

Table 10.1 Buying Rates for Commercial Bills

June	1976	1977	1978	1979	1980	1981	1982	1983	1984	1985
90-day bills										
Bank bills[a]	10.45	11.10	10.80	10.35	13.85	16.00	18.57	13.60	12.80	16.50
AMBA bills[b]	11.35	11.88	11.38	11.01	14.43	16.75	19.47	14.46	13.44	17.05
180-day bills										
Bank bills[a]	10.35	10.60	10.45	10.35	13.10	15.15	18.35	13.50	12.50	15.55
AMBA bills[b]	11.15	11.45	11.16	11.00	13.80	16.02	19.03	14.20	13.19	16.12

Source: Reserve Bank of Australia, *Bulletin*, May 1979, p. 39 and Australian Merchant Bankers Association, *Annual Report*, 1981, p. 15; 1985, p. 17.

[a] Bank accepted or endorsed bills of exchange.

[b] Originally known as the Accepting Houses Association of Australia, then the Australian Merchant Bankers Association (AMBA) prime rate, this became the Australian Merchant Bankers' bill rate on 1 October 1982. It is now calculated as the lowest rate at which AMBA members would buy a 90, 120 and 180 day bill of exchange bearing the acceptance of another AMBA member at 10.00 a.m.

Bill facilities are usually established for at least $250 000 over a period of one to three years and range from fully drawn advances (for bridging finance) to revolving credit facilities (for seasonal working capital). Standby acceptance facilities may also be arranged. Depending on conditions, these facilities may be unsecured or established against a specific mortgage over fixed assets, a floating charge, overseas guarantees, letters of credit, letters of awareness, or other collateral. Once established, customers may borrow up to a prescribed limit by drawing 90-, 120- or 180-day bills as required. The specific period chosen can generally be nominated by the borrower at the end of each period. These are then accepted by a trading or merchant bank and discounted, with the customer receiving the proceeds less the appropriate fees. These include an acceptance fee and a discount line or establishment fee. Historically, as shown in Table 10.1, these rates change markedly in line with market conditions, but in each case the AMBA rates have been at a margin of around 0.7 to 0.5 per cent higher than for bank bills.

LETTERS OF CREDIT

Letters of credit have long been used for Australian trade financing—particularly in the import and export trade. However by the late 1960s, letters of credit issued by overseas banks were also being used within Australia to raise ordinary domestic finance. Basically, an overseas bank's irrevocable letter of credit, generally confirmed by a local trading bank, effectively guarantees the local firm's borrowings and allows it to raise funds more easily and often at less cost.[1] Overseas parent company guarantees and letters of awareness or comfort[2] are now also commonly used to improve the borrowing power of foreign-affiliated Australian borrowers.

In recent years overseas bank letters of credit, particularly on a standby basis, have grown in popularity and, where once confined primarily to foreign-affiliated firms, now many Australian companies also use this facility. Although much business is placed directly by the banks themselves through their representative offices,[3] merchant banks, with their foreign bank shareholders' support, also market these facilities. The fees, especially if supported by a parent company guarantee, involve around 0.4 to 1.0 per cent per annum to the overseas banks, a local trading bank confirmation for perhaps 1.0 to 1.25 per cent, and something less than 0.15 per cent for the merchant bank arranging the facility. A bill acceptance facility (established under the letter of credit) is still attractive as bank acceptances are discounted at lower rates. Overseas irrevocable letters of credit can also be issued in favour of a trustee to secure debentures, promissory notes, leveraged leases and, given many multinationals' desire to fund locally, no doubt other uses will be found. They are also commonly used to support overseas borrowings.

Overseas bank letters of credit have also been attractive due to the cash management trusts (CMTs) (see Chapter 13). Most CMTs restrict their investment to government or bank-backed securities but include most major international banks within this bank-backed category. By arranging an overseas letter of credit, any money market securities issued under the guarantee would become a potential CMT investment. Thus merchant banks with a cash management trust affiliate can easily fund client paper via their CMT without using their own resources. Overseas bank letters of credit to support corporate promissory note issues have also made these securities eligible CMT investments and again allow certain merchant banks to profit on both sides of the arrangement.

TERM LOANS

Aggressive term loan lending by merchant banks is another reason for the industry's past growth. Trading banks and finance companies are now also aggressive lenders in this area, but the merchant banks' past experience and flexibility in structuring term loans and project finance work still provide some competitive advantage in Australian dollar lending. Term loan facilities are normally provided for plant and equipment and working capital purposes and are for $500 000 or more with a maturity of three to five years, and are usually convertible into bills at the merchant bank's option. By converting a term loan to bills, the merchant banks can then sell these securities for cash—effectively converting long-term assets to liquid ones when required. The bills may also be used as security to obtain additional deposits. Those merchant banks with low deposit bases tend to rediscount their bills regularly—not unlike a revolving credit facility—while those with substantial deposits act more as direct lenders. Chase-NBA (now First National), for example, described itself as 'essentially a cash borrower and a cash lender . . . [with] a panel of some 3000 private and corporate depositors who advance funds on an unsecured basis in amounts from $10 000 to $5 million for periods ranging from 24 hours to more than a year'. Its loans are 'typically between $500 000 to 5 million, for periods up to 5 years'.[4]

Unlike trading bank loans, merchant bank term loans are frequently unsecured and rely on a facility letter from the borrowers to protect their position. Besides detailing the specific term and charges, the letter also provides certain representations and warranties on the firm's financial position and indicates the borrower's agreement to certain financial covenants. Typically, these require the maintenance of certain financial ratios, particularly in respect of the borrowers' working capital and liabilities, as well as a negative pledge and security up-grading on other secured borrowings. Where security is required, however, merchant banks are typically more flexible than trading banks and instead of a traditional mortgage may accept overseas guarantees or letters of credit or debentures issued by the borrower.

Merchant bank term loans are traditionally fixed as to the amount and maturity but are variable in terms of interest rates, with the charges adjusted at agreed monthly to six-monthly intervals. As one merchant bank explained, 'the use of variable interest rate loans helps to insulate PPL's profitability against violent upward movements in interest rates'.[5] The rates themselves are usually based on the merchant bank's then cost of funds or some external index plus an agreed margin, which itself may be subject to periodic review. As there was no real Australian equivalent to the London Interbank Offered Rate (LIBOR), the Australian Merchant Bankers Association introduced a published rate for this purpose in 1976. This rate, now known as Australian Merchant Bankers' Bill Rate, is published in the financial press for 90-, 120-, and 180-day securities and represents the average of the lowest buying rate Association members would pay for a bill bearing the name of an Association member. As the AMBA rate is a money market rather than a lending rate, not all institutions find it sufficient and some produce their own, more loan-related quotations similar to the trading banks' prime rate concept. Partnership Pacific's Base Lending Rate, for example, has been published weekly since 1974 and daily since 1978. The prime rate, as another firm explained, 'provides a strong degree of interest rate stability and is designed to overcome the daily and seasonal volatility of the AMBA quotations'.[6] It was not uncommon over 1985 for better borrowers to pay a margin of 0.25 to 0.75 per cent over the AMBA rates shown in Table 10.1. In addition, a line or establishment fee of 0.1 per cent or more and, where appropriate, a commitment or unutilization fee of 0.25 per cent to 0.5 per cent may also be applicable, the former based on the total facility and latter on only the amount unused.

Many clients prefer fixed rate borrowings to the normal variable arrangement, but merchant bank funding is generally too short term to allow this. However, since 1979 customers can fix their interest commitments for up to two years through the interest rates futures market. Generally, the merchant bank will buy the appropriate number of contracts for the months desired on the customer's behalf, but recently some firms have marketed fixed rate borrowings with the cost of the futures contracts built into the interest rate. For example, Partnership Pacific's PPL Ratelock loans offer a fixed rate of interest up to five years in advance.

AUSTRALIAN DOLLAR SYNDICATIONS

If a borrower requires a term loan or bill of exchange accommodation in excess of $5 million, most merchant banks will arrange with other institutions to help finance the amount. This service is commonly referred to as a syndicated credit facility. The borrower has the advantage of dealing directly with one institution, the syndicate manager, rather than negotiating with a number of lenders. It also means, as there is only one set of documents, that the loan terms and conditions are the same for all syndicate participants. Because each institution has a much smaller loan commitment, the lender might also borrow on slightly longer terms through a syndication than would be available with a larger loan from one lender. Otherwise, the terms and conditions are much the same as any other merchant bank term loan.

As with offshore loans, the instigator, or lead manager, of the syndication receives a management fee in addition to his or her normal lending compensation, and thus syndications are generally more profitable for the organizer than straight lending. Understandably, competition is intense for the lead manager's position especially as the merchant banks are competing with, but generally require the support of, the trading banks. Besides good marketing and customer relations, a firm must develop a reputation as a successful loan syndicator, participate strongly in the actual lending, and take part in other firms' syndications for reciprocity reasons. In addition to actual syndicates, merchant banks also will arrange standby credit facilities so that a potential borrower can be assured of raising funds at a later date.

Although all merchant banks would claim both expertise and involvement in syndications, in practice those merchant banks with a major bank as their parent are best placed and in the case of Australian dollar syndication, those with an Australian trading bank parent are at a particular advantage.

LEASING

Leasing is a somewhat newer form of merchant bank advance and even as late as 1979 was not significant for the industry.[7] The problem was that ever since 1960, when lease finance began in Australia,[8] it operated on a fixed contract basis; the payments, and hence the imputed interest rate, were set at the beginning of the period. Unfortunately, as most financial leases were for more than a year, merchant banks could seldom fund these advances on the money market. Thus, while the merchant bank could set the contract based on present interest rate expectations, a change in rates could produce substantial losses. As a result, the industry generally avoided leasing or limited their exposure.

By the late 1970s, most major merchant banks were active in leasing and today offer conventional fixed and variable rate lease finance as well as arranging leveraged lease packages. In addition, many merchant banks have specialist leasing subsidiaries as well. This position is due to many factors, among others the 40 per cent investment allowance over 1978–80, the development of variable interest rate leases, the introduction of leveraged leasing, and the establishment of the interest rate futures market.

The catalyst for merchant bank leasing was the introduction of the 40 per cent investment allowance in 1978. Although the allowance was subsequently reduced and then removed on purchases after 30 June 1985, the first few years at 40 per cent were more than enough to change corporate attitudes towards lease finance. The reason was that due to the quantitative lending constraints and interest rate controls, the trading banks could not finance all the capital equipment investment that the investment allowance encouraged. Finance companies and merchant banks were the only major other alternatives for medium- to long-term funds. Thus, to gain the funding, many borrowers considered variable or flexible rate leases for the first time. To some extent concern over interest rate changes could be offset by fixing the interest rates and by payments for up to two years through bank bill futures contracts. Today, the bulk of merchant bank leases are written on a similar basis as their other financing, with the rate set at a certain margin over an agreed market lending rate, commonly the AMBA bill rate.

The development of leveraged leasing was another major attraction for merchant banks as they could act as an organizer rather than lender and earn substantial fees in the process. The difference between a normal and leveraged lease is first one of size: leveraged leases are only for relatively large transactions. One merchant bank, for example, suggests them as being 'an appropriate financing method for substantial entities operating depreciable fixed assets worth more than $8 000 000, especially when the entity is not expected to pay income taxes in Australia for a number of years'.[9] Second, there is the lease's structure. With a normal lease the lessor acquires the asset and rents it to the lessee who then uses the item. A leveraged lease is much the same except that the lessor acquires the asset with borrowed funds up to 80 per cent of the purchase price. By a leveraged purchase, the lessor gains the full tax advantages of ownership as well as the deductibility of interest payments for a relatively small investment. If the lessee cannot take full advantage of the tax deductions, the lessee can also benefit by transferring them to the lessor in return for lower lease payments. Finally, the lenders are generally more secure in advancing money to the lessor (generally a joint venture established for lease between a few major institutions) than the lessee and receive a slightly higher interest return in that the loan is made on a non-recourse basis. Because of the money required, merchant banks seldom act as lenders, but often participate in the lessor group and, more importantly, in the lease structuring and organizing.

As the investment allowance on purchases ceased after 30 June 1985, one of the strongest tax incentives in leveraged leasing, and normal leasing too, disappeared. Other taxation changes have also restricted the industry's growth. By effectively precluding tax-exempt bodies in December 1981, and overseas plants by non-residents, and existing plants from the allowance in June 1982, the federal government removed the industry's major growth area. Indeed it was the 1981 $1600 million de facto leveraged lease for the Eraring Power Station, under which the New South Wales Electricity Commission effectively financed one of its major power station developments, that brought an end to this area.

The other problem area, from the industry's viewpoint, was

Section 82AQ of the Income Tax Assessment Act, which effectively means that only banks, finance companies, and certain other financial institutions can be lessors for the leverage lease's equity. While merchant banks can usually qualify too, there are an insufficient number of equity participants. The participants, particularly during the investment allowance, gained substantial tax deductions for a relatively small cash outlay, but most financial institutions were concerned that too much leverage leasing would reduce their taxes to politically too low a level. Thus most allocated a quota of lease participation far short of their total taxable income, and leverage lease organizers experienced difficulty in finding willing equity participants. Worse still, most banks and major finance companies established their own leverage leasing sections and restricted their equity involvement almost exclusively to leverage leases in which they or an affiliate was the organizer. Indeed, the lack of trading bank participation in independent leverage lease packages reached the point that in early 1985 the Trade Practices Commission began investigations into the position.

As a result of these market changes, non trading bank affiliated merchant banks increasingly have been forced to become fringe operators in the business. Many, for example, now market leverage lease packages to much smaller companies as well as specially tailoring their structure, term, repayment mode, and frequency to the client's cash flow and taxation requirements. These also include options for adding or removing additional leased items at short notice, or choosing between a number of currencies. The latter is particularly important with leveraged leases for, whereas the equity portion of the lease is in Australian dollars, the debt could be raised in any currency. If so, the lease payments are then adjusted in line with currency movements so that the lessee absorbs the currency risk or arranges appropriate cover.

Merchant banks are also constantly devising lease finance to service new businesses. With the depreciation allowance on buildings at 4 per cent and a five-year write-off on most plant and equipment, leverage leasing is now used frequently in property financing. In early 1985, for example, BT Australia arranged a $44 million leverage lease for fitting out a newly-completed building. This allowed the owners to finance their tenants' office fittings at much cheaper rates than they could have obtained individually. While individually none of the tenants' requirements would justify a leverage lease, together the total more than justified the exercise.

Another new leasing area is operational leasing. Traditionally, merchant banks were interested in financial leases and left the maintenance of the assets to the lessees. The introduction of Australian Accounting Standard AAS17 on 15 April 1985, however, has changed this preference in that lessees must now capitalize all financial leases, reflecting them as on balance sheet—the item leased showing as an asset and the lease as a liability. Thus by 1987 companies will no longer be able to use financial leases as a method of borrowing but seemingly not increasing their financial risk.

Operational leases, being merely rental agreements, are not incorporated into the balance sheet and it is on this point that merchant bank leasing executives are seeking business. To date the most interesting development is that organized by Kleinwort Benson Australia and National Automotive Fleet Administrators to provide fleet package financing for large company car owners. In line with the new accounting standards, these arrangements are made through an operating lease, with National Automotive providing all the maintenance for the vehicles and Kleinwort Benson, through its newly-formed Wheelease Partnership, providing the lease financing. This partnership, comprised of four merchant banks (Kleinwort Benson Australia, Societe Generale, Hambros, and New Zealand Securities) and a finance company (Beneficial Finance Corporation) is undoubtedly the first of many such arrangements. There may also be new leases in which the lessor retains all the residual risk on the assets but covers this exposure through insurance which the lessee effectively pays through higher payments.

These measures should ensure that merchant banks continue as an important, though limited, part of Australia's leasing industry. Of the more than $12 billion in leases outstanding in 1984, merchant banks probably still account for some $1 billion. Within these totals, according to a Marshall's Report study in late 1984, the leaders in merchant bank commercial leasing were AIFC (ANZ Capital Markets), Euro Pacific (Toronto-Dominion), Partnership Pacific, Chase-NBA (First National), and Barclays; all but the latter were trading bank affiliated firms. Within leverage packaging, BT Australia, Chase-NBA (First National), Hill Samuel (Macquarie), Euro Pacific (Toronto-Dominion), and Dominguez Barry were among the industry leaders.[10]

GUARANTEES AND PERFORMANCE BONDS
In addition to arranging overseas bank letters of credit or credit standby facilities, merchant banks may also support client obligations by a merchant bank guarantee. While the potential revenue is probably higher, the problem is that a merchant bank's name does not have the same status as that of a trading bank. Furthermore,

as the guarantee is in effect a contingent liability, some observers consider that this increases the merchant bank's overall gearing levels.

Besides a direct guarantee of a specific client's debt security, merchant banks also provide performance and surety bonds for Australian manufacturers and exporters. This area may become more important in the future, for in April 1985, a change in New South Wales government requirements allowed merchant banks with sizable local or overseas financial institutions support to provide the performance bond guarantees required on contracts for government departments and authorities.

TRADE FINANCE
Another financing area for some merchant banks is that of trade financing. Merchant bank trade financing through domestic bills of exchange represented the first merchant bank involvement in the bills of exchange market. Today the industry still handles some domestic trade bills, particularly trade bills where firms like BHP are one of the participants, but the bulk of this business is done by the finance companies and trading banks.

In practice, most merchant bank trade financing is now for international trade transactions and commonly involves foreign currencies as well as Australian dollars. Traditionally, most merchant banks arranged both pre- and post-shipment finance for Australian import–export transactions. As the AMBA explained, 'merchant banks are able to use their overseas connections to draw trade bills in major overseas money markets, have them first accepted by a commercial or merchant bank in that market and then discounted, with proceeds being used to pay for the goods imported'.[11] These transactions financed in foreign currencies have some exchange rate risks but may be covered through hedging or forward cover arrangements. As with overseas letters of credit, the merchant bank gets a placement fee for providing the business.

While a few merchant banks were active in trade financing, foreign exchange licences have made international trade financing more attractive and many firms have since entered the business. Grindlays Australia, for example, once operated a specific Trade Finance Division which took advantage of its parent's extensive international banking network; following Grindlays' acquisition by the ANZ Bank Group, Grindlays Australia was merged as part of the ANZ Capital Markets Corporation in 1985 and its trade finance work discontinued. Standard Chartered Australia also opened a special trade finance section, again quite separate from its normal commercial lending. The Standard Charter Bank's recent success with a local banking licence again questions the future of this division. Another specialist in this area is Intersuisse. It is active in trade finance to high risk countries on longer than normal terms, as well as barter trade and non-recourse finance. Such trade specialists may also handle the issuance, subsequent negotiation, and confirming of sight or term letters of credit, export collections, and the packaging of multi-currency trade facilities.

PROPERTY FINANCE

Though many merchant banks may effectively finance property in that it is used as loan collateral, some merchant banks have a specialist division to handle first mortgage and bridging finance. As with other merchant bank lending, these loans are generally for a shorter maturity than those from other institutions and take the form of cash advances or bill of exchange facilities of up to five years for amounts of $500 000 or more secured by first mortgages over income-producing properties.

While probably more appropriately discussed under specialist lending, some merchant banks actually provide housing loans to non-employees. Partnership Pacific's Executive Housing Scheme, for example, allows non-financial institution employees effectively to fund their executives' housing loans without lending the money directly.

These property specialists are also involved with the sale and lease-back of commercial, industrial, or other income-producing property and in conducting more real estate agencies services. These latter services, together with mortgage broking, are discussed separately in Chapter 17.

OTHER SPECIALIST LENDING

As the foreign bank entry and more aggressive local trading banks take an increasing portion of traditional merchant bank acceptances and term loan facility business, specialist lending is the industry's logical response. The industry has already introduced a number of new forms of lending to the Australian market and further specialist loan packaging can be anticipated.

One area pioneered by RBC Australia, for example, is franchise financing packaging. Given its parent expertise in this area, it developed a series of packages to assist franchisees of local companies. It already provides financing for such operations as Barbara's House and Garden, Clancy's Foodstores, and Computerland franchises, and no doubt other operators will take advantage of its experience.

Another area, where both RBC and Partnership Pacific have been active, is in financing professional businesses. Partnership Pacific's Partners' Loan Facility, for example, provides individual partners with the capital required in a partnership so that the debt incurred is only an obligation of the partner and not of the partnership as a whole.

In line with the industry's expansion into more retail financial products, Elders Finance also entered specialist lending in 1983 through a new share margin trading facility which allowed investors to finance up to 70 per cent of their purchase of eligible securities.

Another specialist area is lending commodities rather than funds as such. Tricontinental, Rothschild Australia, and Hill Samuel, for example, have each made cash advances which are repayable in so many ounces of gold rather than a stated dollar amount. Rothschild's $1 million advance to Spargos Exploration to finance its Bellevue gold-mine operation required some 2051 ounces of gold in return plus 2.5 per cent interest per annum.

PROMISSORY NOTE FACILITIES

As discussed in Chapter 9, the extensive use of promissory notes in Australian corporate finance today is yet another example of merchant bank financial innovation, for prior to 1977 these securities played little part in corporate financing. As the note's security relies solely on the good faith and credit of the issuer, only major companies have issued promissory notes in their own right and the market would be quite limited had not semi-government authorities and statutory bodies' issuers become involved. The use of bank guaranteed or letter of credit supported promissory notes also allowed lesser companies to tap this market.

As mentioned, a merchant bank promissory note facility is organized much as a bill facility: the issuer can present promissory notes in multiples of $100 000 (up to an agreed limit) to the merchant bank and receive a lesser amount of cash in return. The merchant bank then either rediscounts the paper on the market to other investors or holds the notes as an investment. The terms are also much the same as a twelve-month to three-year facility. For organizing the tender panel, a merchant bank receives a fee as would any underwriters for their services. From the issuer's standpoint, though, the main incentive has been one of cost, with promissory notes being sold at relatively low margins of 0.10 to 0.30 over the bank bill rate.

REDEEMABLE PREFERENCE SHARES

There is some question as to whether redeemable preference shares are more a lending or a corporate finance activity. Technically, it is the latter as merchant banks commonly arrange for the private placement of these securities with institutions just as they would do for a normal share placement. More recently, however, redeemable preference shares have become much more of a tax-affected form of merchant bank lending.

This relates to the Section 46 rebate on corporations receiving dividends from other companies so that preference share dividends are tax free when received by tax-paying resident corporations. Due to the tax position, potential investors could seemingly accept a much lower return on preference shares (compared with an equivalent debt instrument) and still be better off. The difficulty, however, was that a preference shareholder's position as an owner was more risky than as a creditor with a debt security; the tax benefits were thus offset by the added risk premium. Recently, however, bank guarantees or letters of credit have been used to reduce the risk to an acceptable level. There has also been a change of maturity used, the typically five-year period being replaced with money market oriented securities of less than 365 days.

From the borrower's standpoint, these preference dividends lack the tax deductibility of interest payments and are thus paid from after-tax profits. But this point may not be important to firms with little profit or those wishing to preserve tax loss carry forwards for other purposes.

While redeemable preference shares are not suited to every potential borrower, merchant banks have successfully marketed these facilities to the point that there are some $3.5 to $4 billion worth of redeemable preference shares outstanding. The introduction of corporate tax imputation on corporate dividend payments announced on 19 September 1985 should make these preference shares issues less attractive to issuers who for various reasons are not paying corporate tax. While the actual position regarding preference share dividend imputation has not yet been finalized, it is suggested that the government will differentiate between the traditional preference shares and those used as de facto borrowing facilities.

11 Offshore Financing

Merchant bank offshore finance traditionally involves arranging rather than on-lending money directly as merchant banks are too small, and already highly geared, to place major overseas borrowings in their portfolios. Instead they arrange for clients to borrow directly from their foreign commercial bank shareholders or on the overseas capital markets. Alternatively, some companies use an overseas subsidiary, usually in a tax haven, to borrow offshore and re-lend directly to the client. Merchant banks, however, arrange only a small portion of offshore borrowings as the local trading banks and foreign bank representative offices actively market these same services. Usually those merchant banks active in offshore lending work are successful because their shareholder banks use them for this purpose. Nevertheless the situation is changing due to the 1984 granting of foreign exchange licences and the ability of some merchant banks to raise medium-term foreign currency funds themselves for on-lending with the assistance of parent company guarantees. Finally there is the development of the Euro-Australian dollar market where Australian borrowers can raise medium-term funds offshore at generally less than domestic rates but without the foreign exchange rate.

This chapter examines the merchant bank involvement in foreign currency loans, overseas loan syndications, Euro-bonds, Euro-notes, other foreign securities, and Euro-Australian dollar issues.

FOREIGN CURRENCY LOANS

As mentioned in Chapter 10, most merchant banks provide foreign currency loans via arrangements through a parent company or an offshore subsidiary. As one merchant bank explained in the latter case, it 'has a wholly owned subsidiary in Hong Kong, BA (Australia) H.K. Limited, which can provide foreign currency advances to approved Australian companies'.[1] Partnership Pacific offers a similar service through its own Partnership Pacific Bank NV.

Generally these are for at least $500 000, with the interest rate structured at a margin over the London or Singapore Inter-Bank Offered Rate for a maturity of up to five years. The effective interest costs, including hedging the foreign exchange exposure, is normally about the same or slightly higher than a normal domestic loan. These loans can cover a range of purposes and may have the option to switch currencies denomination during the loan's term or even borrow in a basket of currencies. They may also be used as a standby facility, short-term advance, or term loan—the latter being the most common. For its services, the merchant bank normally receives a placement fee as well as some compensation for any local liaison work. Of course, in the case of a subsidiary arranged loan, it also benefits from the loan itself.

To some extent, the decision to retain the loan even indirectly in the merchant bank's portfolio or simply to arrange the advance is dependent on the loan size. If the amount is relatively small, a merchant bank may lend directly through its subsidiaries. With amounts over a few million dollars, a merchant bank will normally act solely as an arranger.

The merchant bank's traditional position of an 'arranger' was also until 1983 a function of the Australian government's withholding tax requirements. The then Section 128 of the Income Tax Assessment Act exempted overseas borrowings by Australian 'entities' (resident companies at least 60 per cent Australian-owned, with not more than 20 per cent held by one foreign owner) but applied a 10 per cent withholding tax on borrowings by others. As few merchant banks met this requirement, they were poorly placed to borrow overseas and then on-lend locally to Australian companies. The removal of this exemption from overseas borrowings made after 20 May 1983, has since improved the industry's competitive position. In practice, the continued exemption available for widely-held bearer debt securities has meant that there is now a preference for these raisings rather than traditional foreign currency loans.

FOREIGN CURRENCY LOAN SYNDICATIONS

As in domestic lending, syndications are reserved for large-scale borrowings (generally $50 million or more) and, depending on the amount and the currency options, may require a syndicate of a dozen or more institutions to provide the funds. Due to their relative size and limited foreign currency holdings, merchant banks normally just initiate and in some cases manage the syndication, while the commercial banks provide most of the financing.

Most loan syndications are similar to share underwritings in that they may be conducted either on a best endeavour or underwritten basis. In the former, the client and the syndication's manager agree to the terms and conditions (most are set at a margin over LIBOR). The manager then raises the money on that basis but there is no legal obligation to do so. With an underwritten offer of finance the client is legally assured of the funds. In more recent years the difference between the two has become less important and in effect all syndications are underwritten; once the merchant bank agrees to the terms, its professional reputation is at stake.

The syndication may be organized by one institution but in practice most large loan syndication 'tombstone' advertisements list a number of institutions from a variety of national backgrounds. First, there are the so-called 'lead banks', the group of commercial and merchant banks responsible for the issue's success. There is then often a second tier of co-managers who are also involved in underwriting the loan. The next group, usually the largest, comprises firms who actually provide the funds. There may be a number of these tiers depending on the amount lent: the larger the print in the 'tombstone' advertisement and the higher the position on the list, the more funds the firm advanced. The final participant, usually listed at the bottom of the advertisement, is the loan's agent, the firm which handles the loan's administration.

The lead banks or management group may consist of a number of institutions but in practice one firm—usually the firm that initially organized the proposal—has the primary responsibility for the loan's success. Some merchant banks in Australia have served in this capacity, generally in conjunction with an experienced overseas syndicate manager, but more often a specialist such as BA Asia, BT Asia, or Chase Manhattan Asia (with Hong Kong based raisings), assumes these duties in full. As the management group is responsible for setting the loan's terms and conditions, preparing all the related documentation, investigating the borrower's financial position, and ensuring all corporate and legal requirements are fulfilled, experience is of prime importance.

In the past most loan syndications were conducted solely for term loans as it was unlikely a firm would require the funds for a shorter period. Recently, with the spate of takeovers in Australia, much of the funding has been obtained through large syndicated standby facilities. Merchant banks may make similar arrangements for overseas lines of credit on behalf of their Australian clients. The US$800 million line of credit arranged for Coles by BA Australia with the Bank of America is one of the more notable examples over 1985. As a rule, these standby facilities, if used, are a somewhat more expensive form of funding than a normal advance.

EURO-BOND ISSUES

For larger companies or government bodies, a Euro-bond issue is an attractive means of raising medium- to long-term debt finance. As a rule such issues have a longer maturity than afforded through a normal loan—generally three to ten years—and a fixed rather than a variable interest rate. Euro-bonds also are generally unsecured, with often less restrictive trust deeds and financial covenants: hence the restriction of such issues to only the most secure borrowers. Besides access to less restricted fixed rate medium-term debt, the Euro-issues also give the issuer's name a greater exposure in the international financial markets and, if quoted, will ensure that the firm's name appears daily in the financial press.

Hammersley Holdings Limited's US$40 million 8.5 per cent and 9.5 per cent bond issue in December 1976 was the first Australian corporate borrower to take advantage of the Euro-bond market and there have since been a number of issues, including a convertible bond issue by Thomas Nationwide Transport. Though the issuers are not restricted to US dollars, this is the most common foreign currency denomination. A listing of such Australian Euro-dollar issues over 1983–85 is shown in Table 11.1.

As with loan syndications, Euro-bond issues are usually arranged by one institution, the bookrunner, who is responsible for the issue's documentation and for organizing the syndicate. Due to their lack of overseas representation, most Australian merchant banks pass the bulk of this business to their overseas parents or affiliates.

EURO-NOTES

In addition to bond issues, quality Australian borrowers can also raise shorter-term funds through the issuance of Euro-notes. Under a note insurance facility (NIF) these notes can be rolled over (the existing notes are redeemed on maturity with the proceeds of a new notes issue) so that these short-term securities, usually with a maturity of one to six months, can provide much longer term funding. A Euro-note facility in 1985 would typically have been for a three- to five-year period during which its underwriter would guarantee the issuer refinancing at no more than a certain margin over the then London Inter-bank Offered Rates. Such an arrangement is called a revolving underwriting facility or more commonly a RUF.

These Euro-note facilities have the advantage that the notes' margins over LIBOR and hence borrowing through a Euro-note facility are somewhat less than with a loan syndication. In 1985, for example, a note facility was commonly 0.25 per cent over LIBOR plus expenses compared with up to 1 per cent for a loan. This rate difference partly ensures that the notes can always be resold on the market, whereas a loan is seldom negotiable and the facility itself is frequently reviewed. As with a Euro-bond, the note facility also has the advantage over an overseas loan in that the effective interest paid by an Australian borrower is normally exempted from interest withholding tax.

Since 1982 Euro-note issues have used an administrative structure first developed on the Australian money market whereby the notes are sold via a tender panel, with any unsold notes purchased by the facility's underwriters. The idea is that a tender panel comprised of interested financial institutions will help ensure that the issuer receives the best possible price for its securities. An additional incentive for tender panel participation is that the facility's underwriters are also members of the panel.

More recently, as in domestic promissory note issues, higher status issuers will sell their notes through non-underwritten or partially underwritten facilities. Some issuers also forgo the tender panel system in favour of a dealer-based distribution.

As with other offshore financing it is not common for Australian merchant banks to be listed in these Euro-note facilities even though the firm itself might have initiated the facility with the issuer and completed at least part of the work required. One of the few exceptions is BT Australia, which, due to its active Hong Kong subsidiary and London office, has handled much of the work itself. Furthermore, by running its own offshore deposit book it has even funded a small part of these facilities.

Where Australian merchant banks do participate in Euro-facilities it is with multi-currency option issues. Under these facilities, the issuer can choose the currency as well as the maturity of the new notes when the old ones are rolled over. In the case of Australian borrowers, the choice generally includes an Australian dollar promissory note issue. This allows the issuer to cover the foreign exchange exposure when desired as well as take advantage of domestic rates when they are low. This enables Australia's merchant banking industry to participate in both the Australian tender panel and underwriting as well as occasionally to take a management role in such issues. The US$60 million multi-option facility arranged for Thomas Nationwide Transport (TNT) in August 1985 is a case in point. As shown in Figure 11.1, Wardley Australia gained top billing as a joint lead manager with itself and four other merchant banks acting as managers and underwriters of the Australian dollar portion of the facility and a host of others among the Australian dollar

Table 11.1 Australian Euro-dollar Bond Issues, 1983–85

Issue Date	Name	Amount $m	Coupon	Issue Price
1983				
29.3	PIBA	20	14.5000	100.0000
30.6	AIDC	30	14.5000	100.0000
2.8	PIBA	30	14.2500	99.6250
14.9	AIDC	30	14.0000	100.0000
7.10	Woolworths	30	14.2500	100.0000
26.10	Newscorp Securities	30	14.0000	100.0000
28.10	PIBA	40	13.6250	100.0000
5.12	G.J. Coles	35	13.6250	100.0000
Total 1983		**245**		
1984				
10.2	PIBA	50	12.3750	100.0000
17.2	AIDC	42	12.1250	100.0000
17.2	State Bank of NSW	40	12.2500	100.0000
2.3	National Australia Bank	40	12.5000	100.0000
13.6	G.J. Coles	25	13.5000	100.0000
16.7	Statewide Australia	24	13.3750	100.0000
26.10	CBA	35	12.6250	100.0000
13.11	Citicorp Australia	35	12.6250	99.7500
29.11	James Hardie Industries	30	13.0000	100.0000
11.12	State Bank of NSW	40	12.7500	100.0000
Total 1984		**36**		
1985				
30.1	Long Term Credit Bank	65	12.7500	101.5000
8.2	Bank of Tokyo	50	12.6250	101.5000
26.2	AIDC	30	13.0000	100.0000
1.3	Statewide	30	13.1250	100.0000
12.3	G.J. Coles	25	13.2500	100.0000
20.3	BT Australia	40	13.8750	100.3750
10.4	P.K. Banken	47.8	13.8750	100.8000
24.4	Woolworths Ltd	30	13.8750	100.0000
29.4	CBA	50	13.1250	100.0000
7.5	AVCO	35	14.0000	100.2500
7.5	Westpac	50	13.5000	100.0000
22.5	Government Insurance Office	40	13.1250	100.0000
30.5	National Australia Bank	40	13.3750	100.2500
15.5	ANZ	60	13.5000	100.2500
30.5	NISHO	30	13.2500	100.2500
30.5	GZB	50	13.2500	100.3750
4.6	Security Pacific	60	13.1250	100.2500
5.6	Chrysler Finance	55	13.6250	100.2500
5.6	AIDC	40	12.8750	100.3750

Term	Fees	Yield Annual	Lead (Books)	Final Maturity
5	2.2500	15.17	Orion	21.4.88
5	2.1250	15.14	Orion	15.7.88
5	2.1250	15.00	Nikko	11.8.88
5	2.1250	14.63	Orion	15.9.88
5	2.2500	14.92	Orion	1.10.88
5	2.1250	14.63	Hambros	15.11.88
5	2.1250	14.25	Orion	11.11.88
5	2.1250	14.25	Orion	15.12.88
5	2.0000	12.94	Orion	22.3.89
6	2.1250	12.65	Orion	15.2.90
5	2.0000	12.82	Morgan Stanley	29.3.89
5	2.0000	13.07	CSFB	4.4.89
5	2.0000	14.08	Hambros	15.7.89
3	1.5000	14.02	Morgan Stanley	17.8.87
5	2.0000	13.20	Orion	29.11.89
3	1.5000	13.37	Citicorp	14.11.87
5	2.0000	13.58	S.G. Warburg	19.12.89
6	2.0000	13.25	Morgan Stanley	31.1.90
7	1.8750	12.83	LTCB Intl	6.3.92
7	1.8750	12.71	Bank of Tokyo	2.4.92
3	1.5000	13.64	Orion	28.2.88
3	1.5000	13.77	Banque Indosuez	19.4.88
5	2.0000	13.83	Hambros	3.4.90
7	2.1250	14.29	Bankers Trust Intl	23.4.92
6	1.8750	14.15	Salomon Bros Intl	15.7.91
5	2.0000	14.46	Orion	16.5.90
5	2.0000	13.70	Orion	30.5.90
5	1.8750	14.48	Salomon Bros Intl	18.6.90
3	1.5000	14.15	Orion	6.6.88
4	1.7500	13.72	Bankers Trust Intl	25.6.89
7	2.0000	13.78	Orion	26.6.92
7	2.0000	13.91	Orion	17.6.92
5	1.8750	13.72	J. Henry Schroder Wagg	27.6.90
7	2.0000	13.62	Orion	27.6.92
5	2.0000	13.63	Orion	27.6.95
7	2.0000	14.03	Paribas	19.8.92
3	1.5000	13.35	Orion	28.6.88

Table 11.1 (cont.)

Issue Date	Name	Amount $m	Coupon	Issue Price
7.6	Finance Corp. of NZ	25	14.0000	100.2500
11.6	CSR Finance Ltd	40	13.2500	100.1250
13.6	Societe Generale (Aust)	⌠30	13.2500	100.3750
		⌡25	13.2500	100.1250
14.6	Elders IXL	45	13.2500	100.2500
14.6	Citicorp	40	13.5000	100.5000
19.6	CBA	125	12.8750	100.2500
21.6	Die Erste Oesterreichische	60	13.1250	100.6750
25.6	Finance Overseas Ltd (DFC)	50	13.0000	100.6750
28.6	Midlands (Aust.)	50	13.3750	100.1250
28.6	NSW Treasury	75	12.8750	100.3750
2.7	Cooperative Bulk Handling Ltd	30	13.5000	100.0000
3.7	CRA	80	13.1250	100.5000
3.7	SBC Australia Ltd	50	12.5000	100.0000
5.7	ANZ	100	12.7500	100.6750
5.7	SA Financing Corp.	50	12.6250	100.7500
10.7	Bayerische Vereinsbank	60	12.5000	100.7500
12.7	G.J. Coles & Coy	100	13.1250	100.5000
13.7	R & I Bank of WA	50	13.2500	102.0000
13.7	Genfinance NV	50	12.6750	100.3750
16.7	Westpac	50	12.7500	100.6250
17.7	State Bank NSW	75	12.7500	100.7500
17.7	General Motors Acceptance	35	12.8750	100.6250
19.7	Ford Motor Credit A/A	50	12.8750	100.5000
23.7	AGL	50	13.0000	100.3750
24.7	Heinz	37.5	12.1250	100.5000
25.7	SBSA Finance Corp.	50	13.0000	100.0000
26.7	West LB	50	12.6250	100.6250
26.7	NZ Forest Products Fin	50	13.2500	100.6250
26.7	Deutsche	65	12.3750	100.5000
26.7	Metropolitan Estates	50	13.3750	100.0000
26.7	Toronto Dominion	50	12.7500	100.7500
29.7	Dresdner	90	12.3750	100.0000
1.8	AIDC	50	12.7500	100.8750
1.8	GIO	50	13.0000	100.5000
1.8	Commerzbank	75	12.6250	100.5000
5.8	Barclays (Aust.)	50	12.6250	100.2500
6.8	Telecom	60	13.0000	100.7500
9.8	Den Norske	70	12.8750	100.6250
14.8	BFG Bank	45	13.0000	100.7500
14.8	DG Bank	60	12.8750	100.6250
16.8	Creditanstalt	50	12.8750	100.7500
21.8	MGN Holdings	30	13.0000	100.5000
22.8	Merrill Lynch & Co. Inc.	60	13.0000	100.6250
23.8	IKB Finance NV	30	12.8750	100.5000

Term	Fees	Yield Annual	Lead (Books)	Final Maturity
5	1.8750	14.48	Banque Gutzwiller	18.7.90
5	2.0000	13.79	Hambros	8.7.90
3	1.5000	13.73	Bankers Trust Intl	18.7.88
5	2.0000	13.79	Bankers Trust Intl	18.7.90
5	2.0000	13.76	Paribas	6.6.90
3	1.5000	13.93	Citicorp	11.7.88
5	2.0000	13.38	SBC Intl	25.7.90
5	2.0000	13.51	Orion	18.7.90
5	2.0000	13.38	Orion	23.7.90
5	2.0000	13.92	Bankers Trust Intl	5.8.90
5	2.0000	13.34	Bankers Trust Intl	2.8.92
7	2.0000	13.97	Orion	1.8.92
6	2.0000	13.51	Orion	6.8.91
5	2.0000	13.07	SBC Intl	1.8.90
5	2.0000	13.13	Orion	8.8.90
6	2.0000	12.94	Hambros	1.8.91
10	2.1250	12.75	Orion	26.6.95
6	2.0000	13.51	Orion	14.8.91
3	1.5000	13.04	Merrill Lynch	8.8.88
5	2.0000	13.14	Morgan Stanley	5.9.90
5	2.0000	13.14	Bankers Trust Intl	29.8.90
5	2.0000	13.11	Morgan Stanley	22.8.90
3	1.5000	13.25	Hambros	2.9.88
5	2.0000	13.30	CFSB	22.8.90
7	2.0000	13.37	Orion	29.8.92
5	2.0000	12.55	Orion	28.8.90
3	1.5000	13.64	Morgan Guaranty	22.8.88
5	2.0000	13.02	Orion	28.8.90
7	2.0000	13.57	Hambros	1.9.92
7	2.0000	12.71	Deutsche	9.8.92
7	2.0000	13.84	Hill Samuel	29.8.92
3	1.5000	13.07	Morgan Stanley	28.8.88
5	2.0000	12.94	Dresdner	13.8.90
5	2.0000	13.07	Orion	3.9.90
5	2.0000	13.43	Bankers Trust Intl	29.8.90
5	2.0000	13.05	Deutsche	22.8.90
5	2.0000	13.12	Barclays	10.9.90
7	2.0000	13.29	Orion	10.9.92
3	1.5000	13.25	Bankers Trust Intl	22.8.88
5	2.0000	13.36	Paribas	7.6.90
5	2.0000	13.27	Orion	19.9.90
5	2.0000	13.23	Orion	30.9.90
5	2.0000	13.43	Manufacturers Hanover	3.10.90
5	2.0000	13.39	Merrill Lynch	7.10.90
5	2.0000	13.30	Deutsche	30.8.90

Table 11.1 (cont.)

Issue Date	Name		Amount $m	Coupon	Issue Price
29.8	Transcanada		40	13.5000	100.5000
30.8	Kellog Co.		30	12.7500	100.5000
30.8	Tokai Aus. Finance		40	13.6250	100.3750
30.8	Pepsico Capital		50	13.0000	100.8750
2.9	SEK		40	13.0000	100.7500
2.9	Morgan Gty Aus.		60	13.5000	100.5000
4.9	Privatbank		45	14.0000	100.7500
4.9	Midland Int. Aus.		50	13.5000	100.3750
23.9	BMW		50	13.0000	100.5000
24.9	NV Amew	A	25	13.6250	100.0000
		B	25	13.6250	100.0000
24.9	Bayerische Vereinsbank		50	13.0000	100.5000
24.9	Nordlb Finance NV		50	13.1250	100.0000
25.9	GM Acceptance Corp.		40	13.0000	100.5000
25.9	Holstein Kejl		30	13.0000	100.5000
1.10	Christiania Bank		30	13.3750	100.5000
2.10	Security Pacific Aust Ltd		50	14.0000	100.6250
8.10	Sanwa		30	14.1250	100.5000
31.10	De Nationale Investingsbank		50	13.6250	100.0000
5.11	NZI Securities Australia		40	15.0000	100.3750
Total 1985			4 120.3		

Source: Commonwealth Bank of Australia, December 1985.

portion of the tender panel; none is included among the multi-currency groupings. Wardley Australia is also the agent for the Australian portion of the facility.

It should be stressed that despite the industry's participation in the Australian portion of these Euro-note facilities and the resulting occasional management position, Euro-note facilities remain dominated by overseas institutions and are commonly conducted through their London offices. Among the major organizers are First Boston and its affiliate, Credit Suisse, First Boston Limited, as well as the Orion Royal Bank.

While Euro-note issues are limited to only prime Australian borrowers, recently more firms have tapped this market through an international parent company or bank guarantee. Indeed, many Australian merchant banks have also raised this type of medium-term funding. Security Pacific Australia's US$200 million certificate of deposit facility in August 1985 (guaranteed by its parent, Security Pacific National Bank) allows for certificates of deposit in multiples of US$1 million with a range of maturities from one to twelve

Term	Fees	Yield Annual	Lead (Books)	Final Maturity
5	2.0000	13.94	Hambros	15.10.90
3	1.5000	13.17	Salomon Bros	1.10.88
5	2.0000	14.10	J. Henry Schroder Wagg	2.10.90
5	2.0000	13.32	Orion	26.9.90
3	1.5000	13.32	Bankers Trust Intl	27.9.88
5	2.0000	13.94	Morgan Guaranty	26.9.90
3	1.5000	14.32	Morgan Stanley	2.10.88
3	1.5000	13.98	Samuel Montagu	4.9.88
5	2.0000	13.43	Orion	29.10.90
4	1.7500	14.23	Pierson, He	24.10.89
5	2.0000	14.21	Pierson, He	24.10.90
5	2.0000	13.43	Bayerische	22.10.90
7	2.0000	13.59	Orion	6.11.92
5	2.0000	13.43	Hambros	4.11.90
5	2.0000	13.43	Deutsche	23.10.90
3	1.5000	13.80	Bayerische	17.10.88
3	1.5000	14.38	Orion	29.10.88
5	2.0000	14.57	J. Henry Schroder	21.11.90
7	2.0000	14.09	Morgan Guaranty	18.12.92
3	1.5000	15.50	Paribas	16.12.88

months to be offered to a tender panel which then bids for the securities based on a margin over the London Inter-bank Offered Rate. Security Pacific Australia has also recently raised a US$100 million line of credit from a group of Japanese banks, a US$235 million subordinate loan from Mitsui Bank, and US$100 million in a five-year Euro-bond at a coupon rate of 9.875 per cent and also guaranteed by its parent, Security Pacific National Bank.

Other examples of Australian merchant bank offshore fund raisings include Midland International Australia's US$100 million Euro-note organized from Hong Kong; BT Australia's US$100 million Euro-note facility in August 1984; and Wardley Australia's US$80 million Euro-note facility in January 1985. A selected listing of other Australian issues is shown in Table 11.2.

OTHER FOREIGN ISSUES

In addition to Euro-currency issuers, some Australian companies also raise debt funds by domestic issues in certain overseas capital markets. Of these the United States is the most important and many

This announcement appears as a matter of record only

THOMAS NATIONWIDE TRANSPORT LIMITED

U.S.$60,000,000 Multi-option Facility

Lead Managers

The Hongkong and Shanghai Banking Corporation
Wardley Australia Limited

Managers and Underwriters

Australian Dollar Facility

Amro Australia Limited
Barclays Australia Limited
BOT Australia Limited
CIBC Australia Limited
Commonwealth Bank of Australia
Wardley Australia Securities Limited

Multicurrency Notes and Advances

Amsterdam-Rotterdam Bank NV
Barclays Bank PLC
BOT International (HK) Limited
Canadian Imperial Bank of Commerce (Asia) Limited
Commonwealth Bank of Australia
The Hongkong and Shanghai Banking Corporation

Tender Panel Members

Australian Dollar Facility

AMP Acceptances Limited
Amro Australia Limited
Australian European Finance Corporation Limited
Barclays Australia Limited
BOT Australia Limited
BT Australia Limited
CIBC Australia Limited
CitiSecurities Limited
Commonwealth Bank of Australia
Elder's Finance & Investment Company Limited
Hambro Australia Limited
Kleinwort Benson Australia Limited
Macquarie Bank Limited
Schroder Darling and Company Limited
Security Pacific Australia Limited
Societe Generale Australia Limited
Wardley Australia Securities Limited

Multicurrency Notes

Amro (Finance and Securities) Limited
BA Asia Limited
Banque de la Societe Financiere Europeene
Barclays Bank PLC
BOT International (HK) Limited
BT Asia Limited
Canadian Imperial Bank of Commerce (Asia) Limited
Citicorp International Limited
Commerzbank (South East Asia) Limited
CTB Australia Limited
Dai-Ichi Kangyo Finance (Hong Kong) Limited
IBJ Asia Limited
Kleinwort, Benson (Hong Kong) Limited
Kyowa Finance (Hong Kong) Limited
Morgan Guaranty Limited
Saitama International (Hong Kong) Ltd
Sanwa International Finance Limited
Schroders Asia Limited
Security Pacific Bank Asia Limited
Wardley Limited
Yokohama Asia Limited

Arrangers and Facility Agents

Wardley Australia Limited   **Wardley Limited**

June 1985   4017

Figure 11.1 Euro-note Multi-currency Option Facility Advertisement
Source: *Australian Financial Review*, 16 August 1985, p. 75.

Table 11.2 Selected Australian Euro-dollar Note Issues

Issuer	US$m	Date	Margin	Arranger
Adelaide Steamship	80	Apr 1985	0.1665	Citicorp
Avco Financial Services	50	July 1985	0.1185	BT Asia
Boston Financial Corp.	70	June 1985	0.0464	BT Asia
BT Australia	150	July 1985	0.0380	BT Asia
Citicorp Capital Markets	100	July 1985	0.0781	Citicorp
James Hardy Finance*	75	July 1985	0.1020	BT Asia
IEL Finance*	155	July 1985	0.1180	BT Asia
Midland Internat. Aust.	100	July 1985	0.0314	BT Asia
SBSA Finance Corp.*	50	July 1985	0.0762	BT Asia
Town & Country Bldg Soc.	50	n.a.	n.a.	Citicorp
Wardley Australia	80	n.a.	n.a.	Wardley

Source: BT Australia as cited in the *Australian Financial Review*, 14 August 1985, p. 49.

* Issue guaranteed by parent.

firms now raise US dollar denominated capital through the private placements of medium- to longer-term debt issues or (with prime borrowers) the sale of US commercial paper. The latter can be arranged specifically or included within a multi-currency option Euro-note facility. The lack of Australian merchant bank representation in the United States has meant that the industry has played little role in these issues other than introducing the potential Australian issuer to a US commercial or investment bank.

In addition to US domestic raisings, some Australian borrowers have also raised sterling in the British domestic market (bulldog bonds), yen in Japan (samuri issues) and Swiss francs in Switzerland. Again the local merchant banks' role in these issues has been quite limited.

EURO-AUSTRALIAN DOLLAR ISSUES

One feature in the 1985 Euro-currency markets has been the popularity of Australian dollar denominated Euro-notes and Euro-bonds. Technically, the Euro-Australian dollar bond dates back to 15 August 1972 when the Rural and Industries Bank of Western Australia made the first Australian dollar denominated raising, a fifteen-year, $30 million issue with a 6.5 per cent coupon. Possibly as a result, the Bank included an option for the holders to be paid in German marks instead of Australian dollars at a fixed exchange rate of 3.7831 marks to each dollar.[2] This issue, however, did not encourage other issuers to follow suit and it was not until September 1976 that the second issue, a $15 million seven-year raising by the

AIDC, took place.[3] Even over 1977–80, there were only four Euro-Australian issues totalling some $97 million.[4]

Indeed it was not until October 1983, with the first Australian corporate issue—a $30 million five-year bond raising by Woolworths—that the market broadened to include non-government related issuers.

The growth from 1983 onward (shown in Table 11.3) was largely due to the devaluation of the Australian dollar following the election of the Hawke Labor Party government in March 1983. Overseas investors began to view the Australian dollar more favourably and became particularly attracted to the currency following Euro-Australian dollar issues, the strength of the US dollar, and lower US interest rates.

As the rates declined and investors became less pleased with holding US dollars, they turned to other higher-yielding currencies, of which the Australian dollar was one of the more attractive. Thus, as of mid-1985 high Australian interest rates relative to European currencies plus investor expectations that the Australian dollar was a cheap, if not an undervalued currency, caused the Australian dollar to 'become the Euro market's preferred currency for shorter [up to seven years] fixed interest securities'.[5] A July 1985 OECD study found that the Australian dollar ranked fourth place after the US dollar, German mark, and European Currency Unit in terms of the

Table 11.3 Euro-Australian Dollar Issues, 1972–85

Calendar Year	No. of issues	$m
1972	1	30
1973	0	0
1974	0	0
1975	0	0
1976	1	15
1977	0	0
1978	0	0
1979	0	0
1980	1	30
1981	1	10
1982	1	10
1983	8	245
1984	10	361
1985[a]	82	4 120.3

Source: Graham Hand, 'The Euro-Australian Dollar Bond Market', *Commonwealth Bank of Australia Economic Newsletter*, July 1985, p. 4 and correspondence.

[a] Until 5 November 1985 only.

denomination of international bond raisings.[6] By late 1985, however, worries about Australia's balance of payments deficit, overseas debt levels, and high inflation coupled with a poor secondary market and too many issues, had made these issues less popular.

Nevertheless there are many attractions for borrowers to seek Australian dollar funding on the Euro-market. As with other Euro-currency securities neither Euro-bonds nor Euro-notes normally require security collateral. Similarly, unlike domestic Australian debt issues, there are no trust deeds to affect a firm's financial operations and any debt covenants that do exist seldom impose many restrictions. The key advantage of borrowing in Australian denominated securities of course is that the issuer avoids a foreign exchange exposure and at the same time raises the funds at less cost than a similar maturity issue within Australia. The demand for these issues in Europe has been such that rates for selected prime corporate Euro-Australian raisings are actually 0.7 per cent less than for the equivalent Australian government security within Australia. In August 1985 some Australian companies could issue Australian dollar bonds in Europe and then invest the proceeds in Australian government securities at a profit.[7]

At least part of the interest rate difference in local and Euro-Australian dollar corporate raisings is due to Australia's traditional withholding tax requirements on overseas interest payments. Interest on Australian-issued fixed interest debt instruments paid to overseas investors is subject to 10 per cent interest withholding tax. In contrast, most companies raising funds in the Euro-market are able to obtain an exemption on such payments as the securities are widely held and issued in a bearer form. The bearer nature of these Euro-Australian dollar issues, a marked contrast to the registered-owner requirements for most Australian domestic debt, is another reason for the different interest rates for, as interest income is more difficult to trace, holders may be able to avoid tax in their home countries as well. Finally, as Euro-market investors compare the interest rates against other currencies and rates, as opposed to the Australian domestic market, Euro-Australian issues are much less affected by the Australian seasonal interest rate changes.

Even when the potential borrower does not require either fixed rate interest or Australian denominated debt, there can still be some advantages at present for a Euro-Australian dollar issue. This is because the Australian obligation can then be converted, by means of a currency and interest rate swap, into floating rate borrowing in another currency but with an effectively lower cost than might otherwise be available in that currency. Alternatively, it could simply convert its fixed rate Australian dollar debt into an Australian dollar floating rate obligation. Indeed, the attraction of fixed rate Australian dollar borrowing has been such that foreign companies have raised some $400 million by this means. These companies include the German car producer, BMW; the Austrian bank, Genossenschaftliche Zentralbank; and the German bank, Commerzbank. It is unlikely that these borrowers needed Australian dollars. They instead probably converted these obligations via a currency–interest rate swap into floating rate US dollar debts.

Interestingly, many foreign issuers have raised funds much more readily than equivalently sound Australian companies. This is partly because any European issuer would probably be better known and hence more readily saleable to European investors than Australian issuers. Of equal importance, though, is the burden placed on Australian firms under Section 128 F of the Income Tax Assessment Act. Under this section a withholding tax exemption requires not only a public foreign issue and that the securities be widely held, but also that the security's payments be made in other than Australian dollars. Thus to obtain the exemption, the actual payments are typically made in the equivalent amount of US dollars rather than Australian currency. As non-Australian-based firms' raisings are not affected by Australian holding tax, they can pay directly in Australian dollars. While this may not appear important, the US dollar equivalent requirement makes the Australian-based securities somewhat more complex and hence more difficult to sell.

In terms of Australian-based issuers, government bodies have been the largest users in the Euro-Australian dollar market and the Australian Industry Development Corporation has been the most active. The Commonwealth Bank has had the largest single issue to date, one in June 1985 for $125 million, while Coles' $100 million of six-year paper is the largest corporate issue. A selection of the other major Australian users of the Euro-Australian market are listed in Table 11.4.

Australian merchant banks, too, have found these Euro-Australian issues particularly helpful as sources of medium-term Australian dollar funding not normally available to the industry within Australia. Thus they can structure their liabilities more in line with their assets' maturity. For example, in June 1985 Security Pacific Australia raised $60 million in five-year 13.125 per cent notes with the guarantee of its parent bank's holding company, Security Pacific Corp. Morgan Guaranty Australia similarly raised $60 million in five-year 13.5 per cent coupon issue guaranteed by its US parent.

One minor exception to these parent-guaranteed issues was BT Australia's $40 million seven-year 13.875 per cent bond issue sold in

Table 11.4 Leading Issuers of Euro-Australian Dollar Bonds, 1983–85

Issuer	Amount $m	Number
Commonwealth Bank	210	3
AIDC	172	5
PIBA	140	4
G.J. Coles & Co.	85	3
National Australia Bank	85	2
State Bank of NSW	80	2
NSW Treasury Corp.	75	1
Long Term Credit Bank	65	1
Woolworths	60	2
ANZ Bank	60	1
First Austrian Savings	60	1
Security Pacific Australia	60	1
Societe Generale Australia	55	1
Chrysler Financial	55	1
Statewide Building Society	54	2

Source: Graham Hand, 'The Euro-Australian dollar bond market', *Commonwealth Bank of Australia Economic Newsletter*, July 1985, p. 5.

March 1985 at 100.325 per cent. Like many of these issues, the securities were denominated in $1000s and listed on the Luxembourg Stock Exchange. Significantly, the issue was not guaranteed, but it did have a proviso that a guarantee must be arranged if Bankers Trust reduced its ownership in BT Australia below 51 per cent during the life of the note.

There is little question that as Euro-Australian dollar raisings continue, borrowers will begin to adopt a wider range of securities than the present straight debt issues. This should further add to the present popularity of Australian dollar issues as well as possibly encouraging similar issues in Australia's domestic capital markets.

Given the obvious Australian connection, Australian merchant banks should have a considerable advantage over their foreign counterparts in handling these Euro-Australian issues, but this has generally not been the case. The true market for these securities is in Europe, not Asia, and few Australian merchant banks have direct representation in that region. They rely instead on their parents' London connections and in the process their involvement is generally overshadowed. Orion Royal Bank, the market leader shown in Table 11.5, has received support from its Australian affiliate, RBC Australia and more recently Capel Court, but neither firm is reflected on the tombstone advertisements for these raisings. Bankers Trust International has gained even more support from BT Australia and as a result of having BT Australia staff in both

Table 11.5 Lead Managers of Euro-Australian Dollar Bond Issues by Number of Issues, 1983–85

Firm	1983 No.	$m	1984 No.	$m	1985 No.	$m	Total No.	$m	%
Orion Royal	6	185	3	127	11	520	20	832	41.6
Bankers Trust Int.	0	0	0	0	5	260	5	260	13.0
Swiss Banking	0	0	0	0	1	125	1	125	6.3
Hambros	1	30	1	25	2	65	4	120	6.0
Paribas	0	0	0	0		100	2	100	5.0
Salomons Bros	0	0	0	0	2	83	2	83	4.1
Morgan Stanley	0	0	2	80	0	0	2	80	4.0
Citicorp	0	0	1	35	1	40	2	75	3.8
Others	1	30	3	94	5	200	9	324	16.2
Total	8	245	10	361	29	1 393	47	1 999	100.0

Source: Graham Hand, 'The Euro-Australian dollar bond market', *Commonwealth Bank of Australia Economic Newsletter*, July 1985, p. 5.

London and Hong Kong, BT Australia has been the most successful merchant bank packager of Euro-Australian currency raisings within the Australian market.

In terms of the issue, the lead manager is responsible for the legal documentation and for structuring the underwriting group as well as its sale, distribution, and eventual trading arrangements. In return for these services the managers receive as a selling concession a fee of 1.375 per cent (paid to the end retailers) of the issue's face value as well as an underwriting fee of 0.375 per cent. The lead manager also receives a 0.25 per cent fee for its efforts.

As with a normal securities issue, the end composition of the management group depends on its past relations with the borrower, geographical coverage, and client base. Australian issues, though, differ from many other Euro-issues in that they have relatively large management syndicates even though the issues themselves are not large by market standards. This is because the Australian issues, particularly the more recent ones, have been marketed more to individual investors rather than to wholesale placements to institutions. For example, initially most Australian denominated securities were sold to institutional investors. However, as Australian dollar issues have become popular with individual European investors, retail oriented European firms have become more common within the management and selling groups. As of mid-1985, for example, Belgian and Swiss investors have been particularly active purchasers of these securities, often in amounts as little as $1000 to $5000. It is now primarily a retail market.

12 Corporate Finance

A merchant bank's corporate finance work closely approximates that of an American investment bank and includes the advising and underwriting of new issues, acting as a sub-underwriter, the private placement of securities with institutional or major private investors, advising clients on raising equity capital, term loans, mortgage finance, debentures, leases, project finance and foreign currency raisings, guidance on mergers and acquisition practices, capital reconstructions, trust deed revisions, dividend policy, employee stock options, dividend reinvestment plans, inward foreign investment and medium- to long-term financial strategies, project analysis and feasibility studies, and help with complying with government regulations. Through overseas affiliates, most foreign-controlled merchant banks can advise their Australian clients on overseas investment matters as well. Though wide-ranging, these basic corporate finance activities can be divided into two very much interrelated areas: underwriting and financial advisory work.

UNDERWRITING

The underwriting business in its most basic form is a type of insurance,[1] that is a guarantee that a company will be able to sell so many shares at a certain price by a set date. In practice, however, underwriting in Australia is a combination of three services: insurance against the risk of not selling all of the securities; the marketing or distribution of the shares; and advice on the terms and conditions.[2] The degree of risk assumed and the services provided vary with each offering. This discussion first examines the background to the merchant banks' involvement in the underwriting business, then discusses the various types of underwriting agreements, the participants involved, the underwriting process itself, and finally some comments on underwriting film investments.

Background

As mentioned in Chapter 4, it was underwriting that attracted the first merchant bank, Anglo-Australian, to Australia. However, once established, the company soon found its potential limited as an outsider in a closely controlled market and as a corporation where the local stock exchange only allowed individual members.

There is good reason for underwriting in Australia being traditionally the stockbrokers' domain. As Australia has no 'over-the-counter' market, a company wishing a public offering must generally seek a listing on the stock exchange,[3] and the stockbrokers control the exchanges.[4] This control, while understandable, ensured their dominance of underwritings: first, as shown in Rule 2.8 of the *Sydney Stock Exchange Memorandum Rules, By-Laws & Regulations*, 1977, by requiring a broker to be appointed to initial public offerings:

Where a company makes an issue of shares or loan securities without availing itself of the services of any member of an Australian Associated Stock Exchange as either an underwriter or broker, members or member firms shall not lodge any application in connection with such flotation or issues unless the company has agreed to pay all members and member firms lodging any such application brokerage calculated at the relevant rate on the value of securities allotted but this rule shall not apply where securities of a similar class are already quoted...

and second, by restricting stockbrokers' activities in conjunction with non-members, as shown in Rule 5.1:

no member or member firm shall, unless with authority of the Committee and subject to compliance with such conditions as the committee may require, act or agree to act as a broker or underwriter in connection with such flotation or issue.

The first, Rule 2.8, was the more important as it forced initial public offerings to have a broker to the issue. Thus, even if a merchant banker gained an underwriting, the brokerage industry benefited all the same—seemingly either the brokerage was paid or the securities were not listed. This of course, affected the merchant bank's ability to compete. Its cost was based totally on the underwriting, while brokers gained both the underwriting and brokerage fees. As one stockbroker admitted, this 'allows them to take profit at a smaller rate from the actual underwriting [thus allowing a lower tender price than many merchant banks can give] which is made up from profits on brokerage'.[5] Furthermore, unlike underwriting commissions, brokerage fees operate on a fixed schedule of charges. This advantage continued even to recent times as brokers could underwrite a rights issue for only a nominal fee in the knowledge that the brokerage from the extra trading and short-fall sales would offset the added risk.

For Anglo-Australian to succeed in underwriting, it needed the co-operation of a local broker and in this it was fortunate to have the support of Ian Potter & Co. (now Potter Partners). Not all brokers, however, viewed this arrangement favourably. Most considered Anglo-Australian a serious potential competitor and would have nothing to do with it.

Eventually, in April 1950, the company held discussions with the Stock Exchange of Melbourne and by June 1950 both the Sydney and Melbourne exchanges were in general agreement on how their members should treat (both as brokers and underwriters) non-member organized underwritings. Further modifications to the specific provisions were subsequently made and in March 1951 the agreement, known as the Anglo-Australian Agreement, was referred to Australia's other stock exchanges. While the agreement was not ratified by the respective exchanges until 1953–54[6] in practice the agreement was basically in effect from March 1951 (Melbourne was then Australia's chief underwriting centre) to 31 January 1975 when it was no longer applicable due to the Trade Practices Act.

As shown in Table 12.1, the Anglo-Australian Agreement placed substantial restrictions on any member non-broker underwriting agreements: all were to the member's advantage. Basically, it ensured that the member firm would always be broker to the issue (the brokerage fees are an important source of new issue revenue) and dominate the underwriting, as the best a non-member could obtain was underwriting fees on only 20 per cent to 30 per cent of the issue and brokerage on only 5 per cent to 10 per cent; the broker got the rest. Furthermore, the non-member had to promise not to build up a private clientele or otherwise act as a broker in the securities business.

Given that the terms were so much in the broker's favour, one might wonder why Anglo-Australian agreed. It was apparently because 20 per cent to 30 per cent of something was better than 100 per cent of nothing. The brokers controlled the stock exchanges, and most companies, if they were to go public, required a listing. They also controlled the then existing sales distribution network through which the issue was retailed. Similarly, the merchant banks were more interested in serving as an issuing house and concentrating on the sub-underwriting and sales to larger institutional investors. The brokers realized this position and many felt that even this agreement represented the thin edge of the wedge and their eventual loss of

Table 12.1 Anglo-Australian Agreement's Terms and Conditions

Where a member wishes to act with a non-member underwriter etc., it is essential to obtain Stock Exchange approval to such joint venture and this is only given where the non-member undertakes to comply with the so-called 'Anglo-Australian Agreement', to the effect that:

1 The non-member underwriter will not be named in the prospectus as a medium for the receipt of applications.

2 The non-member underwriter will make its issue to the public in association with the member as broker for the issue.

3 The non-member underwriter may place firm with institutions not more than:
   20% of ordinary shares,
   25% of preference shares, or
   30% of loans.

4 That in respect of the balance, not less than the prescribed rate of brokerage will be allowed to the official broker or to other members of Stock Exchanges who may be instrumental in procuring applications, subject to the proviso that the non-member underwriter will not be required to allow any brokerage on 'clean skins' up to 5% of the amount of its underwriting.

   N.B. Brokerage need not be allowed in respect of 'short fall' allotments.

   The non-member underwriters may not act as brokers though they may place outside the markets any stock left with them as a result of a short fall.

   In the case of a non-member underwriter with British principals, an additional 5% of the issue may be placed with those principals as desired.

5 It is not the intention of the non-member underwriter to build up a private clientele for the purpose of brokerage transactions.

6 The non-member underwriter has no intention of acting in the capacity of broker, but looks forward to dealing with the Stock Exchange members for the greatest part of any transactions they may do in securities.

Source: Stock Exchange of Melbourne, 1982.

Note: A clean skin is an application to purchase securities whose form does not carry a broker's stamp. The brokerage that would have otherwise been paid is divided, as above, between the underwriters.

control. Nevertheless the agreement did allow Anglo-Australian direct access to Australian underwritings and during the rest of the 1950s it handled a number of major issues including many foreign company subsidiary flotations and the first unsecured note issue in Australia.

In 1962 Anglo-Australian merged with Australian United Corporation (now Morgan Guaranty Australia), but merchant bank underwriting in Australia still suffered as the agreement proved the blueprint for other member–non-member underwritings and ensured the brokers' dominance of the business.

The brokers' traditional partnership structure, however, was unsuited for accumulating the equity backing good underwriting requires and even in the late 1920s and 1930s some brokers had established affiliated investment companies to improve their financing. Through these companies brokers could create their own in-house underwriting group as well as reduce their own direct risk exposure.[7]

As the underwriting sizes grew, however, even these affiliates often proved inadequate. As one study in the late 1960s complained, that brokers 'assume for several weeks risks which are sometimes very large indeed in relation to their own capital resources is one of the major weaknesses of the present market organization' and that, furthermore, 'the exchanges make little effort to see that their members have adequate capital resources in relation to the risks they are bearing in their underwriting activities'.[8] Such conditions should have allowed the better capitalized merchant banks to replace the brokers in all but the selling group, but instead—due largely to the Anglo-Australian Agreement and their exclusion from exchange membership—underwriting remained broker dominated.

More to the point, brokers were no longer needed in an underwriting role. Besides merchant banks and investment companies, a host of corporate investors (primarily life offices) had entered the business. Thus, in contrast to the early 1950s where underwritings centred 'around the support brokers could gather from groups of individuals and private companies', they could now rely on the 'extensive sub-underwriting support given by institutions'.[9]

Because brokers controlled the stock exchanges, successful merchant banks generally had a major stockbroker among their shareholders (see Table 12.2), and even today these firms are often the most active. Nevertheless, other merchant banks eventually entered the business and by 19 October 1972 formed the Issuing Houses Association of Australia to support their efforts. The Association, whose membership required at least a certain percentage and level of new issues and funding, provided an industry view on such matters as securities legislation, mergers, and takeover rules, and reflected the merchant banks' growing significance in underwriting. The Association has since become part of the Australian Merchant Bankers Association, but its former membership, shown in Table 12.3, shows those then active in underwriting. With the addition of First National and BA Australia, this list would probably still reflect those merchant banks active in underwriting, with Hill Samuel (Macquarie), Schroder Australia, BT Australia, and CIBC Australia as the leading firms.

Table 12.2 Selected Merchant Banks and their Initial Sharebroker Affiliation

All-States Capital	A.C. Goode
AMP Acceptances	Horden Utz & Bode
Australian United Corporation	Ian Potter
BT Australia (Ord BT Company)	Ord Minnett
Barclays	Constable Bain
Capel Court	J.B. Were & Son
Citicorp Capital Markets	Philips Kitchen
Citicorp Capital Markets	Wallace H. Smith
First National (Chase-NBA)	A.C. Goode
Intermarine (Australia) Ltd	Patrick Partners
Rothschild Australian (Inter. Pacific Corp.)	Horden Utz & Bode
Schroder Australia (Darling & Company)	Ord Minnett
Trans City	Ord Minnett
Tricontinental Corporation	Sir Ian Potter

Table 12.3 Issuing Houses Association of Australia's Former Membership

Australian United Corporation Ltd[a]
BT Australia Ltd
Capel Court Corporation Ltd
Development Finance Corporation Ltd
Hill Samuel Australia Ltd[b]
International Pacific Corporation Ltd[c]
Martin Corporation Group Ltd[d]
Schroder Darling & Co. Ltd[e]
Tricontinental Corporation Ltd

Source: Issuing Houses Association of Australia, 1979.

[a] Now Morgan Guaranty Australia.
[b] Now Macquarie Bank.
[c] Now Rothschild Australia.
[d] Now CIBC Australia.
[e] Now Schroder Australia.

While today stockbrokers still underwrite the bulk of new equity issues, merchant banks now have more influence and serve not only as co-underwriters but in some cases as joint managing or lead underwriters. What is now CIBC Australia, for example, in April 1981 was the joint underwriter for the $90 million Caltex Australia Limited issue—at the time the largest public flotation in Australia—but in April 1982 Hill Samuel acted as the sole underwriter for the even larger $130.5 million Westfield Trust flotation, a true indication of the industry's success. Until recently these successes were probably more the exception than the rule as the brokers still dominate most underwritten rights issues. This explains at least part of the enthusiasm with which merchant banks have acquired a 50 per cent share in locally incorporated stockbrokers (the maximum presently allowable) and most will purchase the remaining shares when 100 per cent ownership is allowed in 1987.

As stock exchange membership had not had the same significance in underwriting of government, semi-government, and offshore securities issues, or in private placements of corporate debt and equities, merchant banks have concentrated more on these aspects of investment banking. This has been particularly true of fixed interest securities as their money market talents were equally applicable to government, semi-government, and corporate debt issues. Indeed, since the Citinational's first joint semi-government underwriting for Telecom in 1976, merchant banks have become a major force in semi-government underwritings. Similarly, merchant banks have also been significant in current semi-government and corporate offshore capital raisings. One reason for their success has been the integration of the respective fixed interest dealing and financial packaging skills of their money market and corporate finance personnel. Many firms have restructured these personnel into a new, capital market division. There will no doubt be further changes as the industry's new share-broker affiliations (see Chapter 17) are better utilized.

The Participants

Underwriting participants can generally be divided into four basic groups: the issuing company or offeror; the underwriting syndicate; the selling group; and the investing public. While the first and the last groups require little discussion, the underwriting syndicates and selling groups are more complex.

As shown in Figure 12.1, the underwriting syndicate is comprised of a lead or managing underwriter and a number of supporting co- and sub-underwriters. Large issues, such as the ACI rights issue shown in Figure 12.2, might include one or two managing or co-managing underwriters, a few co-underwriters, and a variety of sub-underwriters. While these firms share the underwriting risk, the managing underwriter is responsible for the issue's distribution or wholesaling. A syndicate is almost a necessity as few underwriters could absorb an issue's shortfall on their own. However, in Australia there is a tendency to rely more on sub-underwriters rather than underwriters or co-underwriters; the largest share underwriting in Australia for example, CSR's $376 rights issue to finance its Theiss Holdings acquisition, involved only a ten-member underwriting syndicate. As most sub-underwriters assume only a portion of the risk, a large issue may require as many as 300 sub-underwriters. These would include probably around 100 sub-underwriters each

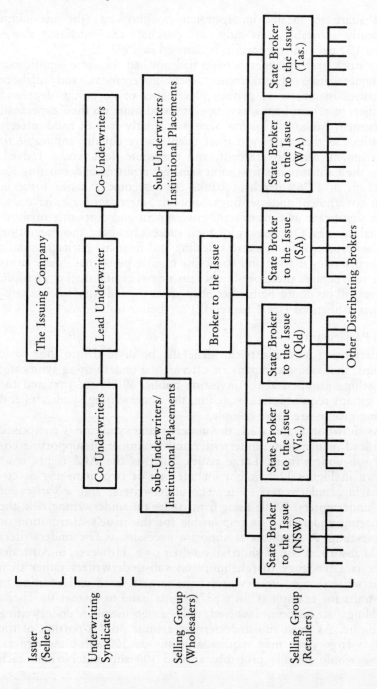

Figure 12.1 Underwritings Structured by Participants

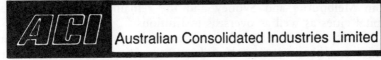

Underwriting of the issue of up to 106,749,618 ordinary shares of $1.00 each at $2.00 per share to finance the cash element of the acquisition of the outstanding ordinary stock units and convertible notes in Acmil Limited with resulted in the allotment of 32,383,550 shares in May 1981.

Managing Underwriters

Potter Partners   J.B. Were & Son

Members of The Stock Exchange of Melbourne Limited

Co-Underwriters

Australian Mutual Provident Society
Australian United Corporation Limited
Bank of New South Wales Group
   Companies
Capel Court Corporation Limited

The Colonial Mutual Life Assurance
   Society Limited
Mutual Life and Citizens' Assurance
   Company Limited
The National Nominees Limited
Schroder, Darling and Company
   Limited

Major Sub-Underwriters

Australian Foundation Investment Co. Ltd.
Banque Nationale de Paris
Barclays Australia Securities Limited
Chase-N.B.A. Underwriters Limited
The City Mutual Life Assurance Society Ltd.
Commercial Union Assurance Co.
   of Australia Ltd.
Euro-Pacific Securities Pty. Ltd.
Robert Fleming & Co. Limited
Government Insurance Office of
   New South Wales
Gwynvill Properties Pty. Ltd.
Hambro Securities Limited
International Pacific Corporation Ltd.

Legal & General Life of Australia
   Limited
Martin Corporation Limited
Mercantile & General Life
   Reassurance Company of
   Australia Ltd.
Nauru Phosphate Royalties Trust
Ord Minnett
Portview Nominees Pty. Ltd.
Provident and Pensions Holdings
   Pty. Ltd.
Royal Insurance Australia Ltd.
S.E.C. Superannuation Fund
State Superannuation Board
   of New South Wales
T & G Mutual Life Society Limited
Tricontinental Securities Ltd.

This announcement appears as a matter of record only.

Figure 12.2 Australian Consolidated Industries Limited

from Melbourne and Sydney and the remainder from the other capital cities as well as overseas institutions.

Besides a better geographic and numeric spread, most life companies and institutional sub-underwriters are probably end buyers of the security. Thus in most cases the underwriter makes the sub-underwriting agreement contingent on the institution taking a firm allocation of (promising to buy) so many shares. For example, the offer might be to sub-underwrite 100 000 shares on condition that one subscribe for 50 000 shares and a general allocation for 50 000 with a maximum commitment for 100 000. Effectively the issue thus can be partially sold in advance and the underwriting risk distributed at the same time. The larger sub-underwriters, particularly major institutional investors, may also help informally support the issue by selective buying both during and for perhaps a week after the offering. This helps stabilize the share price and reduces the risk of a shortfall. Finally, the institutions are more likely to hold any shares acquired through a shortfall. In contrast, most professional underwriters, such as another merchant bank or broker, will usually try to sell their position once the shortfall is known. This of course puts further pressure on the share price and only exacerbates the lead underwriter's difficulties.

The extent of sub-underwriting depends on the issue and the managing underwriter's risk preferences. Most would prefer as little risk as possible and sub-underwrite the entire amount but as a rule the lead underwriter should retain at least some portion. To do otherwise suggests the underwriter lacks confidence in the issue.[10]

Basically, underwriting syndicate members participate on either a fixed or shared basis. As the name implies, with a fixed arrangement one takes a stated proportion of the offering and is responsible only for this amount. Alternatively, under a shared or general commitment, one shares in the success or failure of the overall offering; an individual firm which disposes of its own portion may still suffer. Generally Australian underwriters and co-underwriters participate only on a shared basis while sub-underwriters assume only a fixed commitment.

Whereas the underwriting syndicate often includes many institutional investors, particularly as sub-underwriters, the issue's selling group is comprised of licensed broker dealers—usually stock exchange members—who are sometimes known as 'distributing brokers'. Merchant banks, for example, may have their own investors and pension and superannuation fund clientele, but unless members of the underwriting group, are unlikely to receive any brokerage on these sales. Brokerage is generally restricted to stock exchange members' lodged applications. Sub-underwriters do not participate in the issue's retailing. Most stockbrokers participate in the selling rather than the underwriting due to the risk. Within the selling group they receive a commission or 're-allowance' fee based on their efforts but are not liable for additional shares if their own efforts or the overall offering is unsuccessful.

The Underwriting Process

As lead underwriter, a merchant bank will help plan the issue's terms and conditions, the timing, and the pricing of the eventual sale. Other factors (as shown in Table 12.4) such as meeting Foreign Investment Review Board guidelines and other government regulations should also be considered. Once these are decided, the merchant bank's underwriting arrangements commence. First the terms and conditions of the underwriting are finalized and the price determined. The agreement, however, is seldom formalized at this time and the underwriter has only a moral rather than legal commitment to conduct the offering.

The merchant bank and offeror then enter a rather lengthy administrative process. This generally involves the firm, the firm's solicitors, the underwriter, and the underwriter's solicitors. Often

Table 12.4 The Underwriting Process in Australia: New Equity Flotations

- Consultations between the issuer and its advisers.
- Discussions, if applicable, with Foreign Investment Review Board.
- Planning the strategy and type of issue.
- Negotiation of underwriting terms and conditions.
- Managing underwriter selected.
- Preparation of financial information and investigating accountant's report.
- Preparation of draft prospectus.
- Finalize prospectus.
- Filing application with the State Corporate Affairs Commission and stock exchange.
- Stock exchange approval of listing application and prospectus.
- The issuer and underwriter sign underwriting agreement.
- Registration of prospectus approved by the Corporate Affairs Commission.
- Public announcement of the offering and formal sub-underwriting offers made by the underwriter.
- Sub-underwriting agreements signed.
- Distribution of final prospectus and public offering.
- Collection of proceeds by managing underwriter and payment to issuer.
- Share certificates allotted and any over-subscriptions refunded.
- Certificates posted to shareholders.
- Shares listed for trading on the stock exchange.

the offering company and its solicitors produce the first draft and then the underwriter and its solicitors consider the contents; many revisions are usually required. As time is an essential element in an underwriting (market conditions might change), printers proofs are commonly produced at this stage. Though revisions may increase this cost, the later delay avoided is more than worth while.

The final prospectus is submitted to the Corporate Affairs Commission and the stock exchange for approval. The matter then rests with these bodies, with the delays dependent on their work load and the quality of the prospectus. Once the stock exchange has approved the prospectus and listing application, a formal registration is made with the Corporate Affairs Commission. However, as the Commission has already examined the prospectus, the final submission is largely a formality and approval is immediately forthcoming.

Prior to registration, the underwriter formalizes the position with the offeror by signing the underwriting agreement. This makes the underwriter responsible for providing the issuer its funds and, as sub-underwritings are normally signed only after final approval is obtained, the managing underwriter may be exposed on its own for several days. As one (now dated) study complained, in extreme cases 'the primary underwriter carries the whole risk for several weeks and sometimes months before sub-underwriters are asked to participate'.[11] However, even if the underwriter covers its risks quickly, the syndicate itself is still likely to be exposed for some weeks: with rights issues, ten weeks is not uncommon.

This time frame is in marked contrast to countries like the United States where the final draft prospectus can be circulated to clients with all information but the end price. While the price is finalized only at the last minute, this is informally known in the market and thus potential purchasers are ready to place their orders when the issue opens. If structured properly, the issue is typically closed within a matter of hours.

Types of Underwriting Agreements

Underwritings can be conducted on a firm, standby, contingent, or best effort basis, but in Australia a firm commitment is the most common.

Under a firm underwriting, the offeror[12] is guaranteed the money in question. This may involve the underwriter buying the shares directly and reselling them to the public (the margin representing the underwriter's fee) or acting as an agent receiving commission on the shares sold and buying those that remain. Both methods offer full 'insurance' for the offeror.

At the other extreme is the 'best effort' agreement whereby the underwriter provides no insurance and acts solely as a distributor. Indeed, in the Australian context, the AASE rulings preclude such an arrangement even being called an underwriting: it is technically a placement. The 'underwriter' simply sells what securities it can in return for a commission: the more securities sold the greater the total fee. The offeror receives only the proceeds from these sales.

A standby commitment is somewhere between a 'firm' and 'best effort' underwriting agreement. It is generally arranged only when the underwriting support is thought unnecessary and is most common with rights issues—securities offered to the firm's existing shareholders. As these investors are already familiar with the company and securities normally offered at a discount from the normal market price, the likelihood of a shortfall is less than with a public issue.

Though a shortfall is normally considered in a negative sense (not selling all the shares), in a rights issue a so-called 'technical shortfall' is actually desired. This occurs where, despite attractive terms, not all shareholders (often due to holidays or change of address) exercise their rights. The underwriter then buys these shares at the offer price without having to buy the rights themselves.

The final form of underwriting agreement, a contingent commitment, is the least common and, as the name implies, depends on a particular event. An 'all or none' commitment is a variation of this method and commonly found in offerings relating to mineral development, new ventures, takeovers, or major expansions. These are often rather speculative activities and thus exceedingly expensive if underwritten on a firm basis. On the other hand, raising only half the money would be insufficient to commence business. Thus agreement has the proviso that once a certain proportion of the shares are sold, the underwriter will guarantee selling the rest. Nowadays it is the stock exchange rather than the underwriter that will impose the contingency level, and 60 per cent is not uncommon. If this is not met, all the monies are refunded to the subscribers. This protects the underwriter if the market rejects the offering but still gives some assurance to the offeror.

It should also be mentioned that even under a firm underwriting agreement an issuer may not always raise the funds desired. This is due to the so-called 'escape' clauses in virtually every underwriting contract. At one time such clauses were all-encompassing and could technically allow the underwriter to walk away from the agreement without substantial reasons: the underwriter really had only a moral obligation. More recently the stock exchanges have tightened these terms and now, with the exception of war, misleading information, or external events which significantly affect the company's business, most underwriting agreements are difficult to break. One example of an escape clause used was in mid-1985, when Morgan Grenfell Australia cancelled its underwriting of the $15 million Centralia Property Trust issue when the government White Paper on taxation suggested major changes in trust taxation. Some other issues' escape clauses were exercised by underwriters when the price of gold dropped below US$400 an ounce.

Obviously the fewer the escape clauses, the better the underwriting agreement for the offeror but in return the underwriter would expect a greater fee. At present a normal new issue would have a commission of 2 to 3 per cent while a more speculative issue could be 5 per cent or higher. Recent second board and high tech issues have entailed even higher effective fees.

Film Underwriting

In addition to securities, merchant banks are also active in underwriting film participations. Some firms, such as CCF Australia, have been active in film financing since 1980, but most merchant banks entered the industry only after 1981, when changes in the Income Tax Assessment Act made film investment particularly attractive to high income earners.

Under these provisions an investor in a qualifying Australian film (under Division 10BA of the Income Tax Assessment Act) was allowed a deduction of 133 per cent (initially 150 per cent) of eligible expenses incurred in producing the film as well as a tax exemption on income from the film up to an amount equal to 33 per cent (initially 50 per cent) of these eligible deductions.

Initially, film investments were not popular with investors due to the relatively few Australian box office successes. Through the use of presales and distribution advances, though, most offerings in 1984 and 1985 could guarantee potential investors a minimum 40 per cent return on their investment. Thus investors in the 60 per cent tax bracket could profit even if the 40 per cent was the only money earned. The other change was to raise funds for television movies, series, and documentaries. These productions proved easier to pre-sell, could be completed with fewer difficulties than a feature film, and involved much less money. Besides limiting the potential risk for the underwriter, films with budgets of less than $3.5 million are treated differently by the National Companies & Securities Commission and do not require as detailed a prospectus.

These new tax incentives, guarantees, and fewer administrative requirements saw most major merchant banks with at least some film business over 1984–85. The more active firms included Australian European Finance Corporation, BA Australia, Barclays, BT Australia, Capel Court Corporation, CCF Australia, Hill Samuel (Macquarie), Rothschild Australia, and Sanwa Australia.

For the merchant banks, their 1984–85 raisings were particularly profitable with commissions of at least 5 to 7 per cent of the amount raised. For its *Burke & Wills* film, for example, Rothschild received a fee equal to 6 per cent of the film's budget less its underwriting fee. It will also receive a payment equal to 1 per cent of the film's returns after all investors have fully recouped their investment. Its risk of any shortfall was limited as well, first by the selection process itself—only underwriting saleable films—and second by requiring a minimum subscription level, commonly 35 per cent, before the underwriting liability took effect. The future of this business, however, is less certain since the government in late 1985 reduced the benefit on new underwritings to a 120 per cent initial deduction and a 20 per cent exemption income shelter.

FINANCIAL ADVISORY WORK

As with underwriting, financial and management consulting is an important but often undependable source of merchant bank revenue. It also requires a substantial investment in staff and equipment, experts not just in corporate finance and financial modelling but in accounting, commercial law, and engineering as well. Unfortunately, there is no guarantee that the resulting advisory business will cover these costs. Thus, traditionally, merchant banks have entered this area in conjunction with other business. As an AMBA Campbell Committee submission explained, 'merchant banks, by the nature of their operations, tend to maintain a close and continuing advisory relationship with their clients, regularly reviewing cash flows and projected growth, balance sheets and borrowing capacities, expected future borrowing requirements, and developments within clients' industries'.[13] Initially such advice is simply part of their other services with no extra charge. However over time, as the advice becomes more complex and time consuming, separate consultancy arrangements are made. Eventually, these contracts are sufficient to transform advisory work from simply a marketing and lending service to an independent profit centre.

Given the expected pressures of the new foreign bank entries, most merchant banks consider fee income will eventually provide the bulk of merchant bank revenue and in anticipation are either entering or expanding their corporate advisory work. This business, though, is difficult to establish and often takes some six to seven years before a newly-established corporate finance division repays its establishment costs. As a result, many new entries buy existing corporate business from more established competitors by hiring away their better staff. This escalates corporate finance salaries and has added to the potential cost of entry. Another alternative, adopted by a few firms, is to acquire a firm of advisers rather than individuals. Lloyds International's acquisition of David Block and Associates in 1980–81, for example, gained it Australia's top corporate advisory team, thus placing Lloyds ahead of the previous market leaders, Hill Samuel Australia and BT Australia.[14] Morgan Grenfell Australia followed a similar approach when they acquired Bancorp Limited (Geoff Hill's corporate advisory team) which traditionally handled Adelaide Steamship's takeovers. Another somewhat different entry is that of Australian European Finance which in May 1984 formed a joint venture, AEFC Advisory Services Limited, with Geoff Mullins' Corporate Advisory Services Pty Ltd. Societe Generale, too, first entered the area indirectly in 1983 by an informal arrangement with the corporate advisory firm Bato Reid under which the former would support the latter via its local and international funding power—an arrangement which one assumes ended after Bato and Reid themselves joined with another new merchant bank, Scandinavia Pacific.

It is not just competition from other merchant banks that will affect potential fee income. The same stockbrokers, accountancy firms, and independent consultants who traditionally dominated the advisory field are still as active and if anything are expanding their involvement. With the Price Waterhouse 1984 merger with management consultants Urwicks, and Deloitte Haskins & Sells' joint venture with the IBIS Group, the major accounting firms should also be much more effective competitors for such business than in the past. The trading banks, too, see project finance and other corporate advisory work as a profitable supplement to their lending business. The ANZ Bank, for example, in rationalizing its merchant banking interests, merged its own corporate advisory services division with that of Development Finance Corporation under the name Delfin Corporate Services Limited. According to the Bank, this arrangement gives the new section a 'certain independence' from the Bank's own activities.[15] The company will offer advisory business from the top companies down to the small business level.

In terms of the fees, each merchant bank has its own charging system. As Lloyds explains, 'a retainer relationship is maintained with most of its clients whereby it provides continuing financial advice based upon a detailed knowledge of the client's financial structure and requirements, and a thorough understanding of its management and business policies'.[16] Typically, most firms charge between $140 to $180 per hour with up to $250 per hour in a major takeover defence. Valuation work would have an additional charge of $20 000 to $50 000 if the firm's name was used publicly. Traditionally, merchant bankers have preferred not to discuss 'fees' as such and, as Anthony Sampson commented, have 'invented elaborate euphemisms—compensation, remunerations, advice or even close personal relationship, meaning very high fees. [Indeed] British merchant bankers take their delicacy to the point of not mentioning fees until they send their huge bill'.[17]

The real money in the advisory area is not in the hourly charges but in contingency fees—money paid if the action proves successful. In the recent Allied Mills takeover attempt, for example, Baring Brothers Halkerston and Partners would have received a minimum of $225 000 including a $150 000 'success' fee for its efforts.[18] Such bonuses are subject to negotiation but can easily amount to as much as 0.5 to 1.5 per cent of the transaction in question. Occasionally this can result in huge fees, and in the process some merchant bankers, as *Euromoney* complained, 'have earned themselves in a year more than most company chairmen for doing very little in the frenzy of reorganization and rationalization of companies'.[19] The position is even more impressive when some of these contingency fees are calculated on a per hour basis. Using a large overseas example, in the Texaco–Getty Oil takeover, the main US investment bank, First Boston, reportedly received some $12 million or an effective charge of US$150 000 per hour for the seventy-nine hours worked.[20] Within Australia, too, the end fees can be impressive. Wardley Australia, for example, reportedly earned $2 million from the Bond Corporation for its successful advice and assistance in its Castlemaine Tooheys takeover.[21]

Not surprisingly, clients are beginning to question these charges and at least some now request corporate advisory people to bid for work in advance rather than simply accept an end bill. In response some firms, not already active in corporate advisory work, may gain business at the expense of the established competitors. As yet there are no 'discount' corporate advisers but the Commonwealth Bank controlled Australian European Finance Corporation has specifically priced the services of its new AEFC Advisory Services Pty Ltd joint venture at the lower end of the market in an attempt to gain a market share. Discounting, though, is unlikely to prove significant in the more important advisory contracts, particularly in takeovers.

Mergers and Takeovers

Mergers and takeovers advice is perhaps the best-known merchant bank activity and is important as these skills are also useful in other areas. For example, though press reports concentrate on the 'battle', mergers and takeovers are considerably more complex. Initially, as advisers, merchant banks usually help select likely takeover targets, often maintaining a register of companies wishing to buy or sell out to other firms. Indeed, aggressive marketing of 'list companies' has caused complaints that some merchant bankers have become little more than used car salesmen trying to sell unwanted business to corporate Australia. Merchant banks may also evaluate suitable candidates, consider the financial implications of the acquisitions, recommend the appropriate pricing and bid strategy, help negotiate the terms, prepare the documentation, shareholders' communications and press releases, seek the appropriate government approval (where necessary), arrange or provide the finance required, and then assist in the planning and implementation of the attack. They will also help co-ordinate roles of various agents involved in a takeover to include the lawyers, accountants, and valuers. Such takeovers often provide employment for other merchant banks, as an unwilling takeover candidate will quickly appoint its own merchant banker to advise a defence strategy. If other companies enter the bidding or an independent evaluation[22] is sought, still other merchant banks become involved.

Most firms initially entered this area by providing takeover finance rather than advice, but over the years certain merchant banks developed reputations as effective merger advisers and their financial evaluations and strategies carry considerable weight. Frequent exposure, too, has helped them assemble teams of independent professionals, not unlike in underwriting, which allows them to work effectively and on short notice. Finally, knowing the competition is also valuable and most firms can advise their clients as to the opposition's probable actions. This personal knowledge cannot be over-emphasized as psychology plays as important a role as finance in most takeovers.

The growing complexity of takeover regulations—such as the Companies Act, Securities Industry Act, Companies (Acquisition of Shares) Code, Australian Associated Stock Exchange Listing Requirements, Foreign Takeovers Act, Trade Practices Act, and foreign investment guidelines—has also helped the industry as few bidders will now act without advisers. As one merchant banker complained, while deregulation is the current catchcry in our financial sector, 'one area of the market is subject to increasing and constantly changing regulation. It is the conduct of company takeovers and it has been fundamentally changed by regulation over the past several years'.[23] This emphasis on legal matters has seen an increasing proportion of corporate finance staff recruited from the legal profession and then trained in finance.[24]

This legal and financial expertise has created an informal takeover club whose members continue to gain the bulk of the business. On the legal side, some law firms most noted for takeover work would include: Allen Allen & Hemsley; Baker & McKenzie; Arnold Bloch Leibler; Blake & Riggall; Clayton Utz; Corrs Parry Whiting & Byrne; Daravall McCutcheon; Dawson Waldron; Freehill Hollingdale & Page; Mallesons; Arthur Robinson Hedderwicks; and Stephen Jaques Stone James.[25] On the merchant banking side, the field is even tighter and if anything is becoming more rather than less so. As the financial press commented, while the 'M & A' advisory business is booming, 'there are clear signs that the business is increasingly directed to a few specialists, notably the houses of Macquarie Hill Samuel, Barings and Lloyds'.[26] Taking the latter firm as an example, David Block and Associates, before being acquired by Lloyds in 1982, had handled some $1.5 billion worth of takeovers[27] and more recently, as part of Lloyds, has advised the Packer group's bid for NAPCO; ACI on Alex Harvey; Repco on the Ariadne; Arnotts on Allied and its defence against Bond; Rothmans on Allen's Confectionery; and the Bank of Queensland on the SGIO's offer. Other firms with a significant client basis include Australis Securities (Australian Bank), BA Australia, BT Australia, Capel Court, Morgan Grenfell Australia, Schroder Australia, and Wardley Australia.

Project Finance Work

With the mineral development boom of the late 1970s, project finance became an important potential income source and many larger, international bank affiliated firms have subsequently added 'project finance' to their list of services. In practice, however, by mid-1985 only a few merchant banks had a major commitment in this area: Rothschild Australia's Natural Resources Services division, BA Australia Corporate and Resource Finance Group, Societe Generale Australia's Project Finance Division, Schroder Australia's Project Services Team and AEFC's Project Finance Group as well as Hill Samuel (Macquarie Bank), Morgan Grenfell Australia, and Partnership Pacific.

As the name implies, project finance work relates to structuring the appropriate financial package for a specific project but involves considerably more. Besides the normal credit, cash flow, and collateral considerations, one must evaluate the venture's commercial and engineering viability, its construction costs, the operator's experience and abilities, the quality of future sales contracts, the project's payback period, structure joint ventures, assist in finding partners, prepare the financing plan, present the information memorandums to lenders and investors, arrange the finance, and negotiate the terms. The 'Natural Resource Services' mentioned earlier takes this work a step further with more emphasis on the resources themselves and their marketing. These skills can also be used with effect in other areas. BA Australia's work in forest products, oil and gas, aluminium, coal, and base and precious metals provided the basis for its recent oil and gas unit trust operation. Similarly, its forest product work for Australian Paper Manufacturers gave BA Australia staff work, in conjunction with other Bank of America staff, in project finance in Sabah, Malaysia.

Because of the complexity of project finance, various professional disciplines such as accountants, lawyers, and engineers are employed as a project team. Computer modelling is also important in the evaluation. Indeed financial packages such as BA Australia's 'Profimo' financial model, Hill Samuel's IMPACTS and Schroder Darling's EVA, once gave certain firms a major advantage in this business, but today most work can be accomplished on personal computers through modified commercial packages.

The key difference between project finance and other lending is that security is taken only over the project itself and the repayment depends on the project's cash flows. This limits the borrower's risk largely to the project itself as the borrower's other assets are not pledged as security. Similarly, if structured properly, the borrower can often exclude the project's liabilities from its own balance sheet. While the above conditions make the financing more time-consuming and costly to construct and the overall financing generally more expensive than a normal loan, the resulting funding package is tailored to the project's cash flow.

Investor Relations

Over 1980–81 another financial advisory specialty became apparent with the establishment of investor relations sections within both BT Australia and Hill Samuel Australia's corporate finance departments. These firms had developed skills in handling the financial press and generally communicating with shareholders as a result of their take-over work and eventually realized this service could be marketed in its own right. Today these services include advising clients on the form and content of their annual reports, other communications with shareholders and the stock exchange, presentations to institutional investors and stockbrokers, and relations with the financial press. Investor relations have long been a significant business in the United States but as yet in Australia relatively few companies have actively engaged in such activities. As a result, this business is still devoted largely to takeover-related work. It is also there that the impact of investor relations is most evident. Rather than just lobbying major shareholders and institutional investors, more recent takeovers now include extensive marketing research work on shareholder attitudes, personalized letters, newspaper and radio advertisements, pre-paid envelopes for acceptance, and toll-free advisory hotlines. Even video cassettes are now used to deliver one's message.

GENERAL FINANCIAL ADVICE

Besides the three areas just discussed, merchant banks provide a wide range of consultancy services (often in support of their other operations) ranging from specific financial analysis and corporate restructuring to more general management consulting. Over time, however, some have become important in their own right. These include assistance with government submissions, taxation matters, and economic advice.

With the prolific growth in regulations since the mid-1970s, submissions have become a common part of day-to-day Australian business. As merchant banks were already actively involved with regulations like the Trade Practices Act, Foreign Takeovers Act, and stock exchange listing requirements, they soon became involved with client work on other government-related matters too. These include submissions to the Foreign Investment Review Board, Reserve Bank, Trade Practices Commission, and a variety of government inquiries. As one merchant bank explained, 'continued contact with Canberra in these matters, and the specialist knowledge of the working of these Government departments has enabled us to assist clients successfully in their representations'.[28] Indeed, the realization of specialist knowledge is such that Baring Brothers Halkerston were hired by Bank of Tokyo, Citibank, and Midland Bank to help prepare their trading bank applications even though each bank had long had its own merchant banking affiliates in Australia. The reason for Barings' selection was simply that the advice of one of its key executives, Keith Halkerston (a Campbell Committee member) was considered well worth the added expense.

As many merchant bank activities such as leverage leasing, super-annuation, and film underwriting owe much of their initial success to their tax advantages, many firms established their own in-house expertise to ensure these products met all of the technical require-ments. Later these same skills were developed further and tax planning is now another consultancy service offered by at least a few merchant banks. More firms can be expected to provide similar services as part of their expansion into more retail oriented financial products. Indeed one has hired the former tax partner of a 'big eight' accountancy firm to head a five-man professional team to advise corporate customers and to help in financial product development.

As with taxation matters, most merchant bank economists have also developed from in-house economic forecasting into fee-generated work for clients.

13 Investment Management

As with underwriting, investment management is a relatively new activity for most merchant banks in Australia. Only the older firms—those with previous sharebroker affiliations[1]—had much involvement and this was generally confined to unit trust management. The problem was that following the crash of the Poseidon boom in the early 1970s, share investing lost much of its popularity in Australia and most corporations used life insurance companies to manage their pension or superannuation fund portfolios.

Thus the prospects for merchant bank investment management through the mid-1970s were not particularly good and in any event most of the newer firms had only a passing interest in investment management. Most were owned by a consortium of international banks and, as such, initially directed and staffed by seconded commercial bankers. They generally had little experience with 'merchant banking' and so concentrated on the activities they knew the best—funding and lending; the corporate finance and investment management business could be developed later. Furthermore, there were a number of problems with starting an investment management department. First, as with corporate finance work, experienced staff were not readily available and in any event demanded costly salary packages and support services. Second, substantial funds under management were required. As one merchant banker admitted, 'one has to have continuity of well over $50 million under management to make the activity profitable ... [and] to get $50 to $100 million under management is a tremendous task in the Australian context',[2] and by late 1985 this was probably $100 to $200 million. Third, the market was then virtually dominated by the life companies and would require a long time to penetrate. Finally, there was some concern that under the insider trading provisions of the Securities Industries Act, investment management work might conflict with the firm's lending and corporate finance business.

In more recent years, the industry's attitude towards investment management has changed and since the late 1970s most firms have attempted to initiate or expand their involvement. The reasons are twofold. First, the firms have matured to the point where they could not only subsidize the initial costs but also felt they must offer investment management services. Second, inflation and investment management surveys have made investors realize that not all fund managers produce the same results and that they should 'shop around' with their business. This combination proved favourable for the merchant banking industry and by mid-1985 more than a dozen firms had significant funds under management.

As shown in Table 13.1, BT Australia has traditionally been the industry's market leader due primarily to its success in gaining superannuation business, but now many of its funds come from non-superannuation business too. Similarly, a major portion of Rothschild and Schroder funds, for example, came from publicly marketed unit trusts. Macquarie Acceptance in contrast gained the bulk of its funds via its cash management trust operations. Others, such as PNC International, have succeeded mainly through gaining investment work from insurance companies. Nevertheless, BT Australia remains significantly in front and given its multitude of new investment products is likely to retain its leadership. Nationally, however, it is unlikely to retain its 1984 fourth place status after AMP's $10 billion, National Mutual's $6 billion, and Westpac's $3 billion. Both the ANZ and National Australia banks are expanding in this area, as are a host of others, all of which should cause further fragmentation and growth at the expense of less well-represented firms.

Table 13.1 Selected Merchant Bank Funds under Management

Firm	Date	$m
ANZ Capital Markets	mid-1985	200
Barclays	mid-1985	100
BT Australia	mid-1984	2 300
Macquarie Acceptance	mid-1985	572
Morgan Grenfell Australia	mid-1984	200
Morgan Guaranty Australia	mid-1985	140
PNC International	mid-1984	200
Rothschild Australia	mid-1985	600
SBC Australia	mid-1985	10
Schroder Australia	early 1984	850
Tricontinental	1984	60
Wardley Australia	1984	700

Source: Correspondence with the respective firms, 1985.

As with other aspects of merchant bank market positions, individual investment managers or management teams have strong followings within the market and so when a successful fund manager leaves one company for another, at least some business will move to the new employer. As a result it is becoming less common to enter the industry by acquiring an investment firm—such as Wardley's purchase of John D.G. Robinson & Associates in 1981. Instead, most firms hire away staff from those already in the market. Some recent examples include Morgan Grenfell from BT Australia; AIFC (now ANZ Capital Markets) from Capel Court; and Barclays from Westpac. Further changes can be anticipated as the demand for good managers continues to grow.

Another reflection of the importance of investment management staff was the move by Security Pacific Australia in 1985. In addition to a salary package, Security Pacific offered its new investment management head a 'piece of the action' and expanded into funds management through a subsidiary company owned two-thirds by the merchant bank and one-third by the firm's new investment chief, Steve Sedgman.

Today, merchant bank investment work could be best divided between superannuation business, equity trusts, property trusts, cash management trusts, other trusts, and other investment business. It should be stressed though that such a division is not quite so clear. Most smaller superannuation business, for example, is pooled through a unit trust structure. Similarly, some merchant bank property trusts are marketed almost exclusively to superannuation funds rather than to the general public.

SUPERANNUATION

Most merchant bank investment management is for corporate superannuation or pension funds and this will remain their most important investment activity. Though once the preserve of life companies, their poor investment performance in the mid-1970s made many corporate superannuation and pension fund trustees dissatisfied. They were thus receptive to merchant bank marketing and many split their portfolios, giving the merchant banks part of the money to manage. Good performance brought more business and resulted in splitting of superannuation business into its three component parts: actuarial services, administration, and investment management. Whereas the life offices once performed all three, it is now not uncommon for a different firm to perform each function.

The use of independent rather than life office actuaries was particularly important to merchant banks as in the past life office actuaries ensured that, where possible, the resulting superannuation fund was managed by their life company. In contrast, most independent actuaries now normally prepare a 'short list' of investment managers from which the superannuation fund's trustees select. As these lists normally include at least a few merchant banks, the merchant bankers as well as life companies can now obtain this business.

Another important reason for merchant bank success is the increased publicity given to investment performance surveys such as those by Mercer Campbell Cook & Knight and Investment Measurement Services. Although the former has been in existence since 1973, only in recent years have the results been published in the financial press and they now appear on a monthly basis. Corporate boards are now aware of the managers' differing results and compare these against their own fund's performance. Substantial differences have thus caused many previously self-managed funds under professional management or otherwise to change managers.

As a result, merchant banks have made significant inroads into Australia's $35 to $40 billion superannuation fund market. As shown in Table 13.2, BT Australia with some $2000 million in superannuation funds under management is surpassed only by the AMP Society, Westpac, and National Mutual.

In response, life offices have become much more aggressive investors and ironically this has sometimes worked to the merchant banks' advantage. Colonial Mutual, for example, responded by transferring its superannuation business to a new subsidiary and markets these services separately from its other business, so that customers can purchase actuarial services, documentation, and administration of funds and investment management separately. Kleinwort Benson Australia, a merchant bank partly owned by CML, manages the offshore equity portion of CML's portfolio, and other life companies are likely to make similar arrangements in the future.

In terms of business, merchant banks initially managed only larger, individual superannuation funds. This allowed them to concentrate their service on just a few clients who of course represented the most profitable part of the business. Nevertheless, there are economies of scale in investment management and most firms have eventually bid aggressively for additional portfolios. Similarly, to compete, most firms place a new emphasis on customer service; client contact and reporting are more frequent and in greater depth. The major merchant banks are also now marketing their services to much smaller firms by using pooled superannuation funds to service

Table 13.2 Superannuation Managers: Relative Size and Charges per Firm, 1985

| Manager | Assets Managed | Number Professionals | Investment Management Charges as % of Assets | | |
			PF $1m	PF $10m	IF $10m
ANZ Capital	150	5	1.000	n.a.	0.440
AMP	4 150	21	0.240	0.200	neg.
AUC	589	9	0.625	0.625	0.450
Barclays	70	3	0.600	0.600	0.540
BT Australia	1 800	21	0.600	0.600	0.6
City Mutual	173	5	0.215	0.025	n.a.
CML	660	15	0.454	0.091	0.438
Delfin	100	4	0.700	0.700	0.530
Eagle	155	4	1.200	1.200	n.a.
Equitilink	5	5	0.975	0.975	0.975
First National	20	2	0.600	0.600	neg.
GIO (NSW)	55	3	0.270	0.220	0.410
INVIA	100	3	1.000	1.000	0.500
L & G	115	5	0.600	0.600	0.480
MLC	693	n.a.	0.300	0.155	n.a.
Morgan	80	6	0.600	0.600	0.750
National Mutual	2 000	27	0.240	0.156	0.156
NNPM	370	5	0.500	0.500	0.380
PNC	75	3	0.500	0.500	0.380
Prudential	350	16	0.652	0.515	0.450
Rothschild	389	9	0.625	0.625	0.500
Scottish Amicable	47	3	0.780	0.510	n.a.
Schroder	844	7	0.625	0.625	0.370
SAL	42	1	0.550	0.463	n.a.
Wardley	650	7	0.875	0.480	0.480
Westpac	2 900	20	0.660	0.660	0.440
Zurich	150	4	0.600	0.350	0.500

Source: Catherine Doherty and John Evans, 'The Super Performers', *Australian Business*, 10 July 1985, p. 110.

n.a.—not available, neg.—negotiable, PF—pooled fund, IF—individual fund.

clients whose portfolios of less than $1 or $2 million are uneconomic to handle separately. This difference in administration costs is also generally reflected in the higher management fees for the pooled fund business, as was shown in Table 13.2.

Pooled funds have also been important in improving the firms' viability in the market because it is on their results that the previously mentioned published investment surveys are based. Merchant banks are well represented in these surveys, comprising twelve of the twenty-seven firms listed in Table 13.3, and other

Table 13.3 Investment Linked, Pooled Superannuation Fund Performances by Super Fund Managers (percentage rates of return for periods ended 31 May 1985)

Manager	3 mths	12 mths	3 yrs	5 yrs	Size
ANZ Capital*	7.5 (15)	19.3 (24)	23.3 (8)	16.9 (8)	S
AMP	5.9 (23)	21.2 (21)	18.3 (20)	15.1 (12)	L
ANZ	6.8 (17)	24.5 (15)	19.9 (15)	14.4 (13)	S
Australian Eagle	10.0 (4)	38.4 (3)	28.9 (2)	25.9 (1)	L
Barclays*	7.8 (14)	n.a.	n.a.	n.a.	S
BT Australia*	7.9 (11)	21.2 (21)	22.1 (11)	19.3 (4)	L
City Mutual	9.8 (5)	26.2 (12)	19.5 (16)	14.0 (15)	L
Colonial Mutual	6.5 (20)	22.6 (19)	18.4 (19)	14.1 (14)	L
Delfin*	9.4 (7)	31.5 (5)	28.5 (4)	18.8 (5)	S
Equitilink	25.1 (1)	n.a.	n.a.	n.a.	S
First National*	9.3 (8)	29.6 (7)	23.2 (9)	13.3 (18)	S
Legal & General	9.3 (8)	27.7 (10)	n.a.	n.a.	S
MLC	4.9 (27)	20.3 (23)	19.4 (17)	n.a.	L
Morgan Grenfell*	19.4 (2)	47.5 (1)	n.a.	n.a.	M
Morgan Guaranty*	5.5 (25)	25.0 (14)	20.4 (14)	15.5 (11)	M
National Mutual	6.5 (20	23.5 (17)	17.4 (21)	13.8 (17)	L
NMPM	7.7 (13)	28.0 (9)	18.8 (18)	n.a.	S
Norwich	7.4 (16)	24.3 (16)	n.a.	n.a.	S
PNC Intl*	14.2 (3)	38.9 (2)	29.8 (1)	n.a.	M
Prudential	6.3 (22)	23.5 (17)	21.7 (12)	n.a.	M
Rothschild*	6.8 (17)	26.8 (11)	23.5 (7)	17.5 (7)	S
Schroder Darling*	6.8 (17)	21.3 (20)	16.6 (22)	14.0 (15)	M
Scot. Amicable	7.9 (11)	29.5 (8)	24.2 (6)	16.9 (8)	M
Sun Alliance	5.7 (24)	25.8 (13)	22.7 (10)	18.7 (6)	M
Wardley*	9.6 (6)	31.2 (6)	28.7 (3)	20.7 (3)	M
Westpac	5.0 (26)	17.5 (25)	21.2 (13)	16.6 (10)	L
Zurich	9.3 (8)	32.3 (4)	27.2 (5)	24.3 (2)	M

Source: Mercer-Campbell & Cook Pty Ltd as cited in *Business Review Weekly*, 5 July 1985, p. 86.

Note: reflection of the pool's size at the end of the performance period:
S Assets less than $15 million.
M Assets between $15 and $100 million.
L Assets greater than $100 million.
* Merchant bank.

merchant banks (County Australia, Hambros Australia, and Security Pacific Australia) have also agreed to join the survey.

In the pool competition many merchant banks have had the advantage of their overseas parents' investment resources and since the freeing of most overseas investment controls, have been active offshore investors. Morgan Grenfell's impressive 47.5 per cent return for the twelve months ended May 1985, for example, was due to its heavy overseas investment at the time of a weak Australian dollar. Some suggest merchant banks also have the advantage of relatively smaller pool funds compared with their life office competitors and more flexibility as a result. Others suggest that new entrants may also benefit from initial subsidies from their parents and indeed question the survey results as a true indication of sustainable performance. This view has since been reinforced by the dropping of the traditional market leader, BT Australia, from a first or second rating down to twenty-first place on the last twelve months' performance. Besides the loss of a few key investment managers, the press also blamed its too rapid growth of funds under management over 1983 and early 1984 for the decline and suggested it was refusing additional new fund management.[3] The plan of Security Pacific to initially operate its new super fund with a $200 million funds under management ceiling (viewed by some as the minimum economic size) also supports this view.

Approved Deposit Funds (ADFs) are the newest area of super-annuation management. They developed from changes to super-annuation lump sum settlements taxation. Whereas previously only 5 per cent of such benefits was taxable, contributions and earnings accrued after 30 June 1983 are taxed at 15 per cent on the first $50 000 and 30 per cent on any additional amounts. The 30 per cent rate also applies to all such monies received by recipients under fifty-five years old. This tax, however, can be avoided within ninety days of receipt by using the proceeds to purchase an annuity or postponed by investing the funds in an Approved Deposit Fund. This can defer the normal taxes payable on such monies up until age sixty-five. In addition, any investment income earned on these funds and retained within the ADF is free of income tax. One can normally withdraw these monies on short notice, usually around ten days.

Initially, this business was confined to the life companies which could offer retirees the choice of a deferred annuity or an ADF. In December 1984, however, Hill Samuel (Macquarie) became the first non-life office to launch an ADF. Since then a number of other merchant banks have entered the ADF business and there is now a wide choice of investment options.

The most recent innovation has been the split fund. Sanwa Austra-lia's so-called Prime ADF is one such fund with Transit Units for short-term investment and Investment Units for longer-term ADF investors. There is a 1.5 per cent up-front charge on Transit pur-chases and a 4 per cent charge on the Investment Units as well as an annual management charge equal to 1.5 per cent of the funds under management. In contrast, Wardley charges a straight 2 per cent entry fee regardless of which of its Super Shelter funds are chosen. Further details and fee structures are shown in Table 13.4. As at May 1985 the nineteen ADFs had attracted some $150 million in funds.

While initially ADFs were only available through large centrally administered life companies and merchant bank funds, Hill Samuel (Macquarie) has since allowed individuals to establish their own ADF funds as well. The advantage of a 'personal' ADF is that it does

Table 13.4 Selected Approved Deposit Funds' Terms and Charges

Company	Entry Fee	Exit Fee	Annual Fee	Investment Medium/ Capital Guaranteed	Net Return % p.a.	Minimum Deposit $
AMP Society	nil	nil	excess	FI/No	11.5[a]	1 000
Australian Bank	nil	nil	0.5%	FI/No	10.8[b]	5 000
BT Australia	4%	nil	1.5%	FI,E,U/No	n.a.	5 000
Capital Building Society	nil	nil	excess	FI/Yes	12[a]	nil
Colonial Mutual	nil	nil	excess	FI,E/No	9[a]	nil
Commercial Continental						
Primary Transit	1.5%	$25	1.5%	FI,U/No	n.a.	4 000
Primary Investment	4%	$25	1.5%	E,U/No	n.a.	4 000
Commonwealth Bank	nil	nil	1%	FI,E/Yes	10.5[a]	nil
GIO (NSW)	Note 1	1%	Note 1	FI,E,U/Yes	14.3[c]	nil
Hill Samuel	0.5%	nil	1%	FI/Yes	11.8[a]	5 000
Schroder Darling	nil	nil	1.625%	FI,E/No	n.a.	nil
State Bank (NSW)	nil	nil	1%	FI,E/Yes	10.5	nil
State Bank (SA)	nil	nil	1%	FI/Yes	11[a]	nil
State Bank (Vic.)	nil	nil	Note 2	FI,E/Yes	12[a]	nil
Wardley Australia						
Trustee Investment	2%	nil	1.25%	FI,U/No	n.a.	1 000
Capital Growth	2%	nil	1.25%	FI,E,U/No	n.a.	1 000

Source: *The Weekend Australian*, 16–17 February 1985, p. 21.

FI   Fixed Interest
E   Equity
U   Unit Linked
Note 1   Entry fee for GIO (NSW) is $25 plus 5 per cent of the first $4000 plus 4 per cent of the next $4000–$8000 plus 3 per cent of $8000–$12 000 plus 2 per cent of $12 000–$16 000 plus 0.5 per cent on excess over $20 000. The annual fee is $50 for the first two years and $10 thereafter.
Note 2   Annual fee for State Bank (Vic.) is 6 per cent of earnings of the fund plus 1 per cent of assets of the fund.
Excess   Some funds have a guaranteed investment return, and the manager is entitled to any return in excess of the guarantee.
[a] Yield since inception, fund in operation for less than one year.
[b] Yield for week ended 29 January 1985
[c] Most recent declared average compound investment return over three years.

not require a prospectus, only a trust deed. It is an area well placed for merchant banks as individual ADFs will appeal more to larger individual investors than to the average person. Thus these plans, generally in the $100 000 plus range, are undoubtedly the type of business merchant banks hope to obtain.

EQUITY TRUSTS

Unlike those in the United Kingdom or the United States, unit trusts, mutual funds, and managed investment companies failed to gain much popularity among small investors and as a result were not a significant source of institutional investment within the Australian market until the industry's resurgence in the early 1980s. As one study concluded in 1954, 'Australian trusts had an unfortunate start in that the slump of 1931 hit the first of them before some had found their feet; this is probably one reason why little progress has since been made in Sydney in particular'.[4] Another study in 1974 similarly found that 'the growth of unit trusts and mutual funds has been disappointingly slow compared with overseas experience'[5] and in 1979 much the same could be said.[6] By mid-1981, however, the industry had begun its expansion, increasing from assets of $488.3 million in mid-1978 to some $1300 million. This growth continued, reaching $2773.6 million by mid-1983 and $4749.3 million in mid-1984. As at 30 June 1985, equity, mortgage, and property trust assets stood at an estimated $6872 million.[7]

An indication of the fairly recent growth of unit trusts is that the industry body, the Unit Trust Association of Australia (the UTA) was only established in February 1983. As yet a number of major unit trust operators, in particular General Property Trust, have not joined the UTA and it has only been over 1984–85 that merchant bankers have found it desirable to join. It can be expected that more merchant banks, particularly firms like BT Australia, Elders, Rothschild, Schroder Darling and Wardley, will eventually be added to the current list of members shown in Table 13.5, a process which will be hastened through the planned merger of the UTA with the Cash Management Trust Association.

Besides the economies of scale these additional funds under management provide, unit trust operations produce much higher fees than superannuation business. This is partly because of the higher administrative costs associated with handling the larger number of small investors, but also because investors seemingly have been unconcerned about the increasingly higher fees the newer funds have charged. As a rule, unit trust managers receive two types of compensation, first by a once only initial sales charge as a percentage of the

Table 13.5 Unit Trust Association of Australia Members, 1985

AFT Limited*
Armstrong Jones Management Ltd
BA Investment Management Ltd
Brick Securities Ltd
Clayton Robard Management Ltd
D.F. Johnson Syndicate Corporation Ltd
Equitable Group Ltd
Estate Mortgage Managers Ltd
Growth Equities Mutual Ltd
GT Unit Managers
Heine Management Limited
Hooker Property Funds Management Ltd
Jardine Fleming Australia Management Ltd
Macquarie Counsellors Holdings Ltd
Mirvac Funds Ltd
National Mutual Assets Management
NSW Asset Management Ltd
Oceanic Property Management Ltd
PP Management Ltd
Telford Property Fund Ltd
Westpac Financial Services Ltd

* A subsidiary of Development Finance Corporation/ANZ Bank.

amount invested, and second from an annual management fee calculated on the amount of funds under management. Depending on the trust deed and management agreement, the manager may also receive a redemption fee as well as a refund of certain expenses incurred on the trust's behalf. In return for these monies, the merchant bank manages the trust's investment portfolio and, in the case of an unlisted trust, sells and repurchases the trust's units following a daily formula-determined price related to the trust's underlying assets.

At one time these initial sales charges were not dissimilar to those charged to small investors for normal share transactions, with 2.5 to 5 per cent or lower being commonplace at least among merchant bank run funds. Similarly, the annual management fee was traditionally 0.5 per cent of the trust's net assets. A personal survey in 1981 found only one merchant bank, BT Australia, charging more but then only 0.63 per cent rather than 0.5 per cent. Today, however, there has been a marked increase in the level of charges, with 4 to 8 per cent being the common front-end charge and 1.25 to 1.5 per cent per annum now more common for the management. The industry's most recent entry, SBC Australia's Swiss International Fund, for example, had a 6.5 per cent front-end charge and an annual management fee of 1.5 per cent of the trust's net assets. The recently released

Rothschild Resource Trust and Rothschild International Equity Trusts also reflect these higher charges: a 4 per cent initial charge and a 1.25 per cent per annum management fee.

At least one reason for the higher sales charges is the greater marketing effort used by unit trust managers to sell their products. SBC Australia, for example, took a series of large full-spread advertisements in the *Australian Financial Review* and other journals and arranged for the sale of units through the Commonwealth Bank's branch network. It, as did other managers, also used stockbrokers and even certain building societies. In SBC's case, the retailer would typically keep 3 per cent of any units sold as commission. Unfortunately, many non-merchant banks already offer sharebrokers and investment advisers much higher fees; with Equitilink's Growthlink Trust, for example, they can keep 5.7 per cent of the 8 per cent front-end fee charged. As BT Australia was recently recruiting a 'financial services marketer' to help expand its position with sharebrokers and investment advisers, future merchant bank retail financial products are likely to have higher front-end fees.

At present merchant banks already manage a number of equity unit trusts, with the ANZ Capital Market's Australian Fixed Trusts (AFT), Rothschild Australia, Schroder Australia, and BT Australia accounting for the bulk of these holdings (see Table 13.6). An increasing portion of other merchant banks will also soon enter the business (particularly with international oriented funds) to utilize their parent company's expertise or some specialized area of investment knowledge as discussed in the 'other' unit trust section.

PROPERTY TRUSTS

As part of their superannuation work most merchant banks have some property investments: sometimes directly but more often through listed or private property trusts. As this work has become more important, some merchant banks have established their own in-house or affiliated property management–investment operation. As with the equity trusts, ANZ Capital Market's Australian Fixed Trust has been the traditional leader in this area, with Schroder Australia's Schroder Darling Property Fund number two. This latter fund, established in 1972, was once Australia's largest property trust and in 1985 would still rate a fifth place in size among the listed property trusts.

Of the trusts shown in Table 13.7, some of the more recent merchant bank property entries include BA Australia, which acquired a syndicated property trust run by the Balance Property Trust Group, BA Property Syndicate Trust, and Sanwa Australia, which

Table 13.6 Selected Merchant Bank Equity Unit Trust Connections

Merchant Bank	Unit Trust	Date Trust Established	Fund's Assets 30 June 1985	Sales Charge	Mgt Fee p.a.
BT Australia	Share Australia Fund*	Oct. 1970	1 170 000	4.0%	0.63%
	BT Split Fund	Mar. 1984	90 000 000	5.0%	1.25%
Rothschild Australia	Five Arrows International Equity Trust	Mar. 1984	21 905 383	4.0%	1.25%
	Five Arrows Australia Resources Trust	May 1984	2 245 932	4.0%	1.25%
	Five Arrows Australian Equity Trust	15 Dec. 1974	65 911 724	4.0%	0.5%
SBC Australia	Swiss International Trust	12 June 1985	1 000 000	6.5%	1.5%
Schroder Darling	Australis Fund	Nov. 1984	7 693 126	$5 fee	0.5%
	Schroder Darling Fund		—	—	0.5%
Wardley Australia	Wardley Australia International Trust	Apr. 1964	9 382 392	3.5%	2.5%
			n.a.		

* A mutual fund rather than unit trust.

Table 13.7 Merchant Bank Property Trusts, 1985

Merchant Bank	Property Trust
BA Australia	BA Property Syndicate Trust
	BA New World Trust
	BA Property Investment Trust
BT Australia	BTA Property Trust
Sanwa Australia	Master Fund Property Investment
Schroder Australia	Schroder Darling Property Fund*

* Stock exchange listed fund.

acquired the Equitable Group's Equitable Property Trust No. 3. This trend towards acquisition is understandable, for in addition to the management income from the property trust itself, the manager gains access to the unit holder addresses for marketing other financial products. Had Wardley Australia succeeded in gaining the management rights to the Telford Property Group trusts, for example, it would have added some 30 000 unit holders to its potential client base.

As with the equity trusts, property trust managers of unlisted trusts gain a front-end fee on the sale of units, plus an annual management fee and reimbursement of expenses. Some managers also collect additional fees by acting as the estate agent on the sales of trust assets and as managing agents for the properties.

As the superannuation management requires in-house professional property management expertise, merchant banks will undoubtedly make use of these skills via more general property trust management as well as other fee-generating activities such as valuations, sales, mortgage broking, and property management.

CASH MANAGEMENT TRUSTS

Undoubtedly the most important merchant bank development in investment management was Hill Samuel's introduction on 15 December 1980 of Australia's first money market investment fund, the Hill Samuel Cash Management Trust (now Macquarie Hill Samuel Cash Management Trust). Investors were attracted to the trust's liquidity, safety of investment, and relatively high interest rates and Hill Samuel found its initial expectations of reaching $50 million after the first year achieved within three months, some $170 million within the first six months, and by October 1982 the fund had assets of some $828 million. Hill Samuel's success soon attracted others (see Table 13.8), and some estimate a potential market of over $17 billion for these securities.[8] The only drawback was the Reserve

Table 13.8 Cash Management Trusts in Australia by Establishment Date and Investment Policy

Name	Date Commenced	Invests in Bank and Govt Securities only
Macquarie Hill Samuel Cash Management Trust[a]	15 Dec. 1980	Yes
BA Equitable Group Cash Management Trust[a]	1 July 1981	Yes
AFT Money Market Trust	13 Aug. 1981	Yes
BA Cash Management Trust[a]	30 Sept. 1981	Yes[d]
Australian Liquid Assets Trust[a]	9 Nov. 1981	Yes[d]
Five Arrows Cash Management Trust[c]	20 Nov. 1981	Yes
Australian Ready Cash Trust	25 Nov. 1981	No
Ordmin Cash Management Trusts	15 Jan. 1982	Yes
PP Cash Management Trust	22 Jan. 1981	Yes
AUC Cash Guarantee Trust[ab]	25 Feb. 1982	No
Tricontinental Management Trust	29 Mar. 1982	No
Royal Aust. Cash Management Trust[b]	29 Mar. 1982	Yes
Tricontinental[a]	Apr. 1982	No
Schroder Darling Cash Management Trust[b]	15 June 1982	Yes
Were Securities Cash Trust	July 1982	Yes[b]
City Mutual Cash Management Trust	18 Oct. 1982	Yes
BT Australia High Yield[a]	Nov. 1982	Yes[b]
AFT Government Trust	Dec. 1983	Yes
ALAT Prime Fund	Apr. 1984	Yes

[a] Parent company guarantee.
[b] Since merged or ceased business.
[c] Formerly the International Pacific Corporation Cash Investors' Fund.
[d] Also invests in securities issued by wholly- or partly-owned bank subsidiaries.

Bank's initial policy that firms with trading bank shareholders could not offer cash management funds. This was later modified to exclude only fully-owned trading bank subsidiaries.[9]

Today cash management trusts accept initial deposits of generally $1000 to $5000 and subsequent deposits of lesser amounts. The proceeds then are invested in money market securities with generally less than 180 days maturity. The early funds restricted their investments to government and bank-related securities but some later entrants allow non-bank bills of exchange and corporate promissory notes investment as well, often up to a certain maximum. As shown in Table 13.9, bank bills, deposits with FCA corporations, and promissory notes account for the bulk of industry assets. By limiting their investment to quality securities and maintaining portfolios with an average maturity of 90 days or less (the average maturity was 58.2

Table 13.9 Cash Management Trust Assets by Type, April 1985

	$m
Cash and bank deposits	106.3
Deposits with FCA corporations	239.4
Deposits with others	74.9
Bank accepted/endorsed bills	742.2
Other bills	68.9
Prom. notes—public authorities	136.3
Prom. notes—FCA corporations	84.4
Prom. notes—other	31.2
Treasury notes	3.0
Other Commonwealth government securities	22.0
Other government securities	1.6
Accrued interest	15.1
Total Assets	**1 525.2**

Source: Australian Bureau of Statistics, *Cash Management Trusts, Australia,* April 1985, p. 3.

days in July 1985 and ranged from 30 to 93 days), most funds offer redemption on twenty-four hours and, in some cases, same-day notice. There is also generally no commission involved with buying the units and only a small charge if the redemption is within thirty days of purchase.

In return for managing the fund's portfolio and handling the unit's sales and redemptions, the managers generally receive a fee stated as a percentage of the funds under management, often calculated daily. This commonly amounts to a daily charge at 0.002055 per cent or approximately 0.75 per cent per annum. The manager is also generally reimbursed for the administrative and other expenses incurred on behalf of the fund,[10] which are expected not to exceed 0.25 per cent per annum and, like the management fees, are payable quarterly.

Cash management trusts initially had the advantage that there were few other outlets for high-yielding, twenty-four-hour notice withdrawal within the Australian financial sector. Most merchant banks and authorized money market dealers would accept funds on this basis but required deposits of at least $20 000 and $50 000 respectively. The cash management trusts, then, gave small investors access to the short-term money market yields normally afforded only larger or corporate investors. The trusts grew rapidly as a result and by 1982 had reached $2000 million in assets. Subsequent growth proved more difficult and although the industry generally improved its marketing and investment conditions, the industry high, reached in

May 1983, stood at only $2297.2 million. Their assets have since declined, falling to $1800 million by the end of 1983 and to a low of $1438.4 million in June 1984. They have since remained around $1500 to $1600 million and stood at $1644.3 million in July 1985.

The reason for the cash management trusts' slower growth and then decline was to a large extent due to their great success. The cash management trusts showed the obvious demand by investors for high-yield short-term investments and, as deregulation permitted, other financial institutions introduced their own money market yield-related accounts. Building societies and credit unions were particularly aggressive in marketing these new products and soon the major building societies had substantial funds under management. St George's Flexi Rate Plan had assets of $330 million; NSW Building Society's (Advance Bank) $235 million; and United Permanent's $220 million, at a time when Hill Samuel ($421 million), ALAT ($304 million), and BA Australia ($125 million) were the only trusts with assets over $100 million. In addition, many life companies began to offer a similar deposit facility, and the AMP is believed to have the largest equivalent operation.

The industry's rapid growth, particularly at the expense of the politically sensitive home lending institutions (building societies and savings banks) also concerned the government and in February 1982 the then Prime Minister, Malcolm Fraser, suggested state governments consider controlling this growth. There were also Labor Party suggestions to require that trusts lend for housing or control their interest rates under Part IV of the Financial Corporations Act. Such comments in September 1982 caused the formation of the Australian Cash Management Trust Association. This body has since acted as the industry voice in government and public affairs matters and made submissions to a range of government inquiries. As with the industry itself, merchant bank affiliates dominate its membership list shown in Table 13.10. In late 1985 it announced plans to merge with the Unit Trust Association of Australia.

In response to competition, cash management trusts changed their initial deposit and withdrawal conditions (see Table 13.11), generally reducing the amounts required for initial and subsequent investments–withdrawals and the withdrawal notice. They now also offer a telephone withdrawal service and many provide third party cheques, periodic payments and withdrawals, postage-paid correspondence, and toll-free telephone service numbers. More recently, two trading bank–merchant bank affiliated funds, the Australian Bank's Australian Liquid Assets Trusts and the Macquarie Bank's Macquarie Hill Samuel Cash Management Trust, have also offered

Table 13.10 Cash Management Trust Association Members, 1985

AFT-Delfin Management Limited*
BA Cash Management Trust*
City Mutual Cash Management Trust*
Rothschild Five Arrows Cash Management Trust*
Macquarie Hill Samuel Cash Management Trust*
Ordmin Cash Management Trust
PP Cash Management Trust
Tricontinental Cash Management Trust*
Were Securities Cash Management Trust

* Directly or indirectly merchant bank affiliated.

cheque account facilities. With ALAT, for example, one can arrange an Australian Bank cheque account so that any deposit held in excess of one's working balance is automatically placed in ALAT. This money is then returned to the cheque account when required. As a result of this facility, ALAT has since become second only to Macquarie Hill Samuel in asset size. Macquarie, since gaining bank status in early 1985, now offers a Cash Manager Cheque Account Facility whereby unit holders pay $5 for twenty cheques and eight deposit forms so that they can use their trust much like a normal cheque account while receiving daily money market rate-related interest.

Another withdrawal innovation is that at the BT Australia's High Yield Trust which allows its unit holders to withdraw their savings by a low cost Diners' Club card as well as the more traditional methods. Besides the marketing appeal, the Diners' Club connection also gave BT access to Diners' Club's 200 000 members in Australia.

Another result of increased competition has been some rationalization within the industry. Estimates suggest that an asset base of $125 million is probably required to operate a cash management trust profitably,[11] and many shown in Table 13.12 have been unable to reach this size. As a result some original entries have since left the industry, with their trusts being acquired by other operators. BA Australia has been the most active in growth by acquisition and acquired control of the Equitable Cash Management Trust in February 1983, control of the AUC Cash Management Trust in August 1983, and Schroder Darling's CMT in November 1983. More recently, RBC Australia has also sold its RoyAust CMT to City Mutual.

Another competitive response has been to develop specialist funds. The most recent trusts differ from their predecessors in that they were designed to appeal to superannuation funds trying to fulfil the

Table 13.11 Cash Management Trusts Sales and Withdrawal Conditions

Fund	Initial Investment $	Subsequent Investment $	Minimum Withdrawal $	Withdrawal Notice
AFT Government	2 000	1 000	1 000	24 hrs–3 p.m.
AFT Money Market Trust	2 000	1 000	1 000	24 hrs–3 p.m.
Australian Liquid Assets Trust	5 000	500	500	Same day–3 p.m.
Australian Prime	25 000	5 000	5 000	24 hrs–4 p.m.
BA Cash Management Trust	1 000	500	Any	Same day–5 p.m.
BT Hi-Yield Trust	5 000	1 000	1 000	24 hrs–2 p.m.
BA Equitable Cash Management Trust	1 000	500	Any	Same day–noon
City Mutual Cash Management Trust	2 000	100	500	24 hrs–2 p.m.
Five Arrows Cash Management Trust	2 000	500	500	Same day–noon
Macquarie Hill Samuel CMT	5 000	1 000	1 000	Same day–noon
Ordmin Cash Management Trust	2 000	Any	Any	24 hrs–noon
PP Cash Management Trust	500	Any	Any	24 hrs–noon
Tricontinental Cash Management Trust	1 000	300	300	24 hrs–3 p.m.
Were Securities Cash Trust	1 000	Any	Any	24 hrs–3 p.m.

Table 13.12 Money Market Trusts by Parent Companies and Total Assets, 12 July 1985

Parent	Unit Trust	Total Assets $m
AFT/Delfin BNY[a]	AFT Money Market Trust	157.80
AFT/Delfin BNY[a]	AFT Government Trust	6.90
Australis Securities[a]	Australian Liquid Assets Trust[b]	356.50
Australis Securities[a]	Prime Fund	26.90
BA Australia[a]	The BA Cash Management Trust[b]	163.30
BA Australia[a]	BA Equitable Cash Management Trust	17.80
BT Australia[a]	BT High Yield	30.40
Brick Securities	Australia Ready Cash Trust	1.63
City Mutual Life/Trans City[a]	City Mutual Cash Trust	90.96
Macquarie Acceptances[a]	Macquarie Hill Samuel Cash Management Trust[b]	429.00
Rothschild Australia[a]	Five Arrows Cash Management Fund	33.50
Ord Minnett	Ordmin Cash Management Trust	64.90
Potter Partners	PP Cash Management Trust	125.00
Tricontinental[a]	Tricontinental Cash Management Trust[b]	76.51
J.B. Were	Were Securities Cash Management Trust[b]	63.20
Total Assets		**$1 644.3**

Source: *Business Review Weekly*, 19 July 1985, p. 129.

[a] Merchant bank affiliated.
[b] Parent company guarantee.

old 30:20 ratio requirement. Both Hill Samuel's Public Securities Trust and AFT's Government Securities Trust were designed primarily for this purpose. While the removal of the 30:20 ratio in late 1984 has detracted from their appeal, they never the less still attract funds from investors wishing the utmost security.

Given the trading banks' new regulatory freedoms to pay daily interest on demand deposits, cash management trusts are unlikely to regain their 1980–82 growth but they should retain an important role in the 'retail' funds management side of merchant banking. Even if only marginally profitable, the money market funds under management give greater flexibility to merchant bank money market dealers particularly with bank paper and semi-government promissory notes. On the corporate side, the client lists are a valuable commodity in themselves. With the Hill Samuel underwriting of the Westfield Trust, for example, its cash management trust clients received an unsolicited Westfield prospectus with the invitation to subscribe. Similarly, old Westfield Property Trust unitholders, who did not transfer their holdings to the new Trust, received invitations to place their money with Hill Samuel's Cash Management Fund; the $5000 minimum deposit was waived in this case. In short, cash management trusts fit well within the industry's broadening financial service base and will be put to more such uses in the future.

OTHER UNIT TRUSTS

Besides the more traditional areas of equity, property, and cash management trusts, merchant banks have actively developed investment trusts or investment companies specializing in other areas of investment. Two recent entries by Rothschild Australia and what was formerly Hill Samuel, for example, invest in basically gold, and gold and silver respectively, while a new BA trust is in oil and gas exploration.

Of the three, Rothschild Australia's Gold Securities Australia Ltd is most straightforward. It is a listed investment company created to invest in local and foreign company gold shares, gold bullion, futures, coins, and other gold objects. Rothschild manages the equity side of the portfolio, with others handling the remainder. For its services Rothchild receives a monthly fee of 0.75 per cent per annum on the market value of the fund's equity portfolio plus a performance fee each year equal to 1 per cent of the gross increase in the portfolio's market value.

The Hill Samuel Gold and Silver Trust offers a different means of investing in gold and/or silver. The trust is comprised of two classes of units, gold units and silver units, with each representing one ounce of the respective commodities. It also differs from other trusts in that one can purchase or sell the units with quantities of gold or silver as well as Australian dollars. In addition, Hill Samuel has tied this fund to its cash management fund so that one can move between the two via phone notification or automatically by nominating a price at which the commodity could be sold. The funds will then be deposited directly into the cash management fund. There is an entry and exit fee of 1.5 per cent of the dollar amount in gold transactions and a 2 per cent charge for silver as well as an annual management fee of $25 plus 1 per cent of the fund's value.

BA Australia's BA Petroleum Explorer Trust is another different investment area. It was established to develop exploration permits in the Surat and Eromanga Basin areas and is managed by BA Oil and

Gas Management (60 per cent owned by BA Australia and 40 per cent by CU Nominees on behalf of interests of the law firm of Layton Utz and Mr D.F. Libling). As manager, it receives a fee equal to 3 per cent of all exploration expenses as well as an annual fee, indexed to the CPI, of one quarter of a cent on each unit in the trust outstanding and a reimbursement of expenses. In addition, it receives a royalty of 1.5 per cent of the gross well-head value of all petroleum derived or 5 per cent on the sale of any properties in which it has this royalty interest. Interests associated with the managers also received 7 800 000 capital units in the trust at the special price of 1 cent per unit compared with the 20 cents paid by public subscribers.

Other specialist trusts can be expected. Elders, for example, has announced plans for an agricultural trust, property, commodity, and a high-tech fund, and Wardley for an international commodities futures trust and an open-end property trust.

OTHER INVESTMENT BUSINESS

In addition to superannuation funds, merchant banks also manage other investment portfolios for both corporate and private clients. These involve generally at least $100 000 and are subject to the same fee schedules as the superannuation funds, with a charge of at least 0.6 per cent per annum. Those firms with strong overseas investment connections have been most successful in this area as many of these portfolios are invested into international fixed interest and equity securities.

These overseas connections have also been important in gaining management work from foreign-sourced investment. Wardley Australia, for example, is the manager for the Hongkong and Shanghai Banking Corporation's Australia Unit Trust. Hambros Australia, too, is responsible for the Australian portion of its parent's international portfolio.

Merchant banks are also active in an advisory rather than a management capacity. This advice may be offered either under a specific contract or in support of the firm's other operations. Often this advice makes use of the merchant bank's other specialists. For example, some use their money market dealing expertise to advise clients on short-term investment strategies. Their international department's knowledge in foreign exchange, and connections with overseas investment bankers, can similarly be utilized. Indeed, some firms publish monthly or quarterly market reports on one or both subjects.

14 The Futures Business

For most merchant banks the futures market is a relatively new business and most of the industry has become either floor or associate member of the Sydney Futures Exchange only since 1980. The earliest to become a floor member, AML Finance (now part of Elders Finance) joined on 7 July 1977, no doubt due to its pastoral wool-broking connections. With the introduction of 90-day bank bill futures in 1979, however, many merchant banks became floor members. These included BT Australia, Elders, Hill Samuel (Macquarie), Trans City, Capel Court, Schroder Darling (Schroder Australia) and the Bill Acceptance Corporation. But for Bill Acceptance, which sold its seat to its indirect parent company, the Westpac Banking Corporation in 1985, these firms are all still floor members.

The futures market, represented by the Sydney Futures Exchange, trades in futures contracts rather than the underlying commodities they represent.[1] Basically, a futures contract is the right to buy or sell a certain quantity of a specific item on a set date in the future at a pre-arranged price. It differs from an option in that the contract must be completed (either by making or taking delivery of the underlying item) unless the obligation is offset by the purchase or sale of another similar contract, netting out one's exposure (the contract to buy cancelling out a contract to sell). Where the obligation is not offset, completion is by way of physical delivery, except for certain contracts where a cash settlement is required instead.

The Sydney Futures Exchange was established in 1959 for the trading of greasy wool futures contracts. It has since expanded to cover other contracts but, as shown in Table 14.1, only a few have proved successful; the others have been withdrawn. Over time financial futures contracts have come to dominate the Exchange's trading activity (see Table 14.2). The introduction of exchange traded options (shown in Table 14.3) over mid-1985, all of which are financial related, has further reinforced this trend. In the process,

Table 14.1 Sydney Futures Exchange Contracts

Contracts	Commenced	Suspended
Greasy wool	11 May 1960	Still traded
Trade steer[a]	16 July 1975	Still traded
Gold[b]	19 Apr. 1978	Exp. Mar. 1986
Bank bills	17 Oct. 1979	Still traded
Boneless beef	19 Apr. 1979	16 Jan. 1981
Pound sterling*	26 Nov. 1980	16 Feb. 1982
Fat lamb[c]	21 May 1981	May 1985
Silver	15 Oct. 1981	Dec. 1985
Export bullocks	17 May 1982	Sept. 1982
US dollars*	19 Mar. 1980	Still traded
Japanese yen*	19 Mar. 1980	16 Jan. 1981
Two-year Treasury bonds*	29 Feb. 1984	Exp. Dec. 1985
All Ordinaries Share Price Index*	16 Feb. 1983	Still traded
All Industrials Share Price Index*	3 Apr. 1984	Aug. 1984
Metal and Minerals Share Price Index*	3 Apr. 1984	Aug. 1984
Ten-year Treasury bonds*	5 Dec. 1984	Still traded
Gold—Comex	Expected 1986	n.a.

Source: Sydney Futures Exchange, 1985.

[a] Initially known as live cattle contracts.
[b] The suspension relates to a new contract with Comex specifications.
[c] The initial contract specifications were revised in October 1983.
* Cash settlement required rather than physical delivery.

Table 14.2 Sydney Futures Exchange Trading by Type of Contract

Type of Contract	Number of Contracts		
	1983	1984	1985
Wool	22 309	9 257	6 792
Trade steer	37 895	20 788	14 280
Gold	27 099	2 299	307
Ninety-day bank bills	161 324	172 607	594 086
US dollars	43 065	60 131	59 154
Fat lamb	383	477	–
Silver	17 407	1 741	155
All Ordinaries Index	180 014	237 011	282 317
Two-year Treasury bonds	–	10 788	560
Ten-year Treasury bonds	–	1 917	242 282

Source: Sydney Futures Exchange, 1986.

Table 14.3 Sydney Futures Exchange Traded Options

Type of Option	Commenced	Trading to end Dec. 1985
Bank bills	10 May 1985	13 024
US dollars	1 June 1985	390
All Ordinaries	18 June 1985	3 720
Ten-year Treasury bonds	10 Oct. 1985	6 249

Source: Sydney Futures Exchange, 1986.

many traditional commodity or sharebroking firms have either sold their floor membership or were acquired by other financial institutions, mainly banks and merchant banks. Indeed almost a quarter of the seats changed hands over 1984. A full list of the present floor members, shown in Table 14.4, shows that these institutions now account directly or indirectly for at least ten of the now twenty-nine members. Significantly, each of Australia's four major trading banks is now a floor member. The Commonwealth gained its floor membership in 1983 and Westpac, the most recent addition, only in 1985. A similar trend among associate members over 1983–85 has seen many previously unrepresented merchant banks and stockbrokers acquire associate membership in one or more of the contract markets.

The major difference in the membership categories is that floor members, as the name implies, have direct access to the trading floor and can trade on their own behalf as well as that of their clients. Associate members trading through a floor member in the days of fixed commission rates, were entitled to a 50 per cent discount from the scheduled rates. Associate members could in turn be either full associate members (entitled to the discount on all transactions) or simply market associates for a specific contract. Today, with dealers free to negotiate their own rates, there is no longer a direct price advantage with associate membership. A full associate member, however, is entitled to join the Exchange's clearing house and this may result in some administrative savings. There is also some status in a marketing sense with both the associate and clearing house membership. As with the floor members they can deal either on their own account or for clients. The final category, a local member, was introduced on 1 June 1984. It allows direct access to the trading floor but only dealing on one's own account or for a floor member; no client business is permitted. As at 16 December 1985, there were 29 floor members, 143 full associate members, 119 market associate members, and 71 local members. All floor members must be

Table 14.4 Sydney Futures Exchange Floor Members

All-States Futures Pty Ltd
Australian Bank Ltd
Bain & Company
Barclays Australia Ltd
C.A. & L. Bell Commodities Corporation Pty Ltd
Bisley Commodity Brokers Ltd
BT Australia Ltd
Capel Court Corporation Ltd
Citicorp Capital Markets Australia Ltd
Commonwealth Bank of Australia
Darlington Futures Australia Pty Ltd
A. Dewavrin Futures Pty Ltd
Edgley Mutual & General
Elders Drexel Australia Ltd
Global Futures Pty Ltd
C. Itoh & Co. (Aust.) Ltd
Jackson Securities Ltd
Macquarie Bank
McCaughan Dyson Futures Ltd
McIntosh Hamson Hoare Govett
Merrill Lynch, Pierce, Fenner & Smith
Morgan Guaranty Australia Ltd
National Australia Bank Ltd
Ord Minnett Futures Pty Ltd
Rouse Woodstock Pty Ltd
Schroder Darling & Company Ltd
Trans City Holdings Ltd
Wardley-ACLI Commodities Ltd
Westpac Futures Ltd

Source: Sydney Futures Exchange, 1985.

members of International Commodities Clearing House Ltd. This body handles the Exchange's clearing activities and monitors the deposits on outstanding contracts. The more active associate members are usually clearing house members.

In terms of business, membership was probably more beneficial in the early 1980s. Since then low commodity prices coupled with the crash of a few major commodity (admittedly non-exchange member) brokers has dampened the overall trading levels. Similarly, the introduction of negotiated commission rates in December 1984, coupled with the transformation of previously major customers into floor members and competitors, has also worked against high profits from futures broking. Nevertheless, in the financial area merchant banks still have good potential to trade for their own account as well as for clients.

In the long run, most members consider an international trading link with the Commodity Exchange of New York (Comex) and possibly a European futures market will do much to increase trading levels. The lifting of restrictions on non-resident trading in Australian futures as well as other exchange controls has certainly opened the potential for a greater international linkage between the Sydney Futures Exchange and overseas markets. In addition to the twenty-four hour clock trading concept in which Sydney would fill the partial vacuum between the US closing and the British opening, there is also more potential for trading between the Australian and Asian markets and standardization of contracts between most futures markets should result.

To attract international trading, the Sydney Futures Exchange signed an agreement with Comex on 7 March 1985 for a trading link between the two exchanges in the Comex gold futures contract. Under the agreement a special communication and clearing link will be established whereby all Comex gold contracts traded on the Sydney exchange will be handled via the Comex Clearing Association in New York. This will thus allow a Sydney contract to offset any outstanding sell positions in New York. As of late 1985, the trading and administrative support systems were still being finalized, with the first trading expected some time in 1986. Among other matters, the previous contract specifications on gold futures needed raising from 50 to 100 ounces and of course needed to be quoted in US rather than Australian dollars. Following the successful trading of the gold contract, silver futures is the next contract planned for a Comex linkage.

Another international contract in the planning stage involves a linkage with the London International Financial Futures Exchange (LIFFE). It will involve an offset agreement similar to Comex on this Exchange's Euro-dollar time deposit contracts. Other international contracts and exchange linkages are also planned. In the meantime contracts for bank bill, Treasury bonds, and US dollars remain the most important for the merchant banking industry.

CURRENCY FUTURES

The currency futures were the first new contracts considered when the Sydney Futures Exchange assumed its present name in 1972 and tried to diversify its greasy wool operations. Unfortunately, the government was largely undecided over the Exchange's proposal. Worse still, there was a legal question as to whether the resulting futures transactions, related directly to money rather than physical commodities, might be illegal under the New South Wales state government's Gambling and Betting Act. Fortunately, on 15 January 1979, the Federal Treasurer, while not allowing non-resident participation, did indicate that he had 'no objection' to the concept.[2] On that basis the New South Wales state government also lent its support and, in December 1979, resolved the remaining problems with the passage of the Futures Market Act 1979.

A currency futures contract, like other of the Exchange's contracts, is a legally binding agreement to purchase a specific quantity and quality of a commodity at a future date and price. In the case of US dollars, each contract is for US$100 000 and, depending on the maturity and trade date, delivery can be set from less than one to over eighteen months; Table 14.5 provides the other specifications.

Initially, due to exchange control restrictions, physical delivery, that is the provision of US$100 000 for settlement, was not allowed and the equivalent amount of Australian dollars was paid instead. With the removal of foreign exchange controls, there is no longer the same legal restriction but physical delivery is still not permitted.

Table 14.5 US Dollar Currency Futures Contract Specifications

---

Contract Unit
One hundred thousand United States dollars (US$100 000).

Rate of Exchange for Mandatory Close Out
The rate of exchange for mandatory close out shall be the mid-rate for the US dollar as quoted by the Reserve Bank of Australia on the morning of the last permitted day for trading and shall be calculated to the nearest 0.0001 Australian dollar per US dollar.

Mandatory Cash Settlement
All bought and sold contracts in existence at the close of trading on the last permitted day for trading in the delivery month shall be settled by the Clearing House at the rate of exchange for mandatory close out.

Quotations
Prices shall be quoted in Australian dollar per US dollar in multiples of 0.0001 dollars.

Deposit
As determined by the Clearing House from time to time.

Delivery Months
Spot months plus next five consecutive months then financial quarters out to eighteen months.

Termination of Trading
The third Wednesday of the delivery month or such other day as the Board may determine. Trading ceases at 12.00 noon.

Source: Sydney Futures Exchange, 1985.

BANK BILL CONTRACTS

As mentioned, bank-accepted bills of exchange futures were the first of interest-rate-related futures contracts as well as the first financial futures contract on the Sydney Futures Exchange. When they began trading on 17 October 1979, the Exchange was the first outside the United States to trade in interest-rate-related contracts. Each contract is based on five $100 000 face value bank-accepted bills with a minimum of 85 and a maximum of 95 days to maturity and traded with the yield quoted in so much per $100 in multiples of 0.01 per cent; further details are shown in Table 14.6. Each contract is a legal

Table 14.6 Bank Bill Futures Contract Specifications

Contract Unit
$500 000 face value 90-day bank-accepted bills of exchange.

Tenderable Bills
5 × $100 000 face value bank-accepted bills of exchange maturing 85 to 95 days from settlement day.

Contract Price
Yield per annum per cent (to two decimal places).

Quotes
One-hundred minus price.

Deposit
As determined by the clearing house, and subject to change from time to time.

Delivery Months
Spot month plus next six consecutive months then financial quarters out to two years.

Termination of Trading
Wednesday prior to the second Friday of the month.

Settlement Day
Second Friday of the month.

Approved Acceptors
Australia and New Zealand Banking Group Ltd
Australian Bank
Bank of New Zealand
Banque National De Paris
Commonwealth Bank of Australia
National Australia Bank
State Bank of New South Wales
State Bank of Victoria
Westpac Banking Corporation

Approved Settlement Facility
Commonwealth Bank of Australia

Source: Sydney Futures Exchange, 1985.

agreement to make or take delivery of the specified securities at a predetermined price and future date.

As with other contracts, the trading can be divided into three major types: traders, speculators, and hedgers. In its initial years these contracts were used primarily by financial institutions, professional money market dealers, and traders rather than corporate borrowers or speculators. For example, dealers wishing either to hedge against interest rate rises or to benefit from falls find futures contracts of significant assistance. Though the contracts are for bank bills, they could also help hedge against risks in other securities (i.e. cross hedging), as there is a direct correlation between bank bill rates and most other money market securities. Dealers also often conduct 'cash and carry' transactions in the futures market. These involve the simultaneous purchase of longer maturity bills on the physical market and sale of a shorter-term futures contract covering the same amount; the bills are then delivered, closing out the contract when they reach a suitable maturity. For example, a dealer could purchase 180-day bills in the physical market and sell a 90-day bill future contract for delivery three months later. In three months, the physical bills would have a three-month maturity and so could be delivered against the contract, cancelling out the position. In trying to profit from the difference between the physical and future market rates, dealers help ensure that prices remain in line. Finally, by buying a series of forward bank bill contracts, a dealer can create a synthetic security with up to a two-year maturity even though that maturity may be unavailable in a 'real security'.[3]

An increasing number of hedgers—both lenders and borrowers— now also use the market to fix their borrowing rates in advance and several banks also encourage customers to insure against interest rate changes by this means. Similarly, some lenders will now offer to buy customers' bills at a fixed price in the future by simply covering the risk exposure on the futures market (see Table 14.7). This business grew so quickly that by late 1981 one writer concluded that 'the interest rate futures market has changed from the finance world's gambling casino to an integrated part of the money market'.[4]

TEN-YEAR AUSTRALIAN TREASURY BOND FUTURES

December 1984 saw the introduction of another financial future, the contracts for ten-year maturity Australian Treasury Bonds (whose specifications are shown in Table 14.8). As Treasury bonds are among the most actively traded money market securities, these futures can help hedge portfolios as well as to arbitrage or position for expected interest rate movements. Of course, this can be done

Table 14.7 Ninety-day Bank Bill Futures Quotes

Date	Asked	Bid
December 1985	81.80	81.75
January 1986	84.00	81.00
February 1986	84.00	81.00
March 1986	82.68	82.66
April 1986	84.00	81.00
May 1986	84.00	81.00
June 1986	83.85	83.50
September 1986	85.00	84.75
December 1986	85.50	84.75
March 1987	85.45	84.00
June 1987	85.00	84.00
September 1987	85.50	84.50

Source: Sydney Futures Exchange, 29 November 1985.

Table 14.8 Ten-Year Treasury Bond Futures Contract Specifications

Contract Unit
Commonwealth Government Treasury Bonds with a face value of $100 000, a nominal coupon rate of 12 per cent per annum, and a term to maturity of ten years, no tax rebate allowed.

Cash Settlement Price
The arithmetic mean on the last day of trading of yields to two decimal places provided by twelve dealers, brokers, and banks, at which they would buy and sell Treasury bonds as described in the contract specifications, excluding the two highest-buying and the two lowest-selling quotations.

Mandatory Cash Settlement
All bought and sold contracts in existence as at the close of trading in the contract month shall be settled by the Clearing House at the cash settlement price.

Quotations
Prices shall be quoted in yield per annum per 100 dollars face value in multiples of 0.01 per cent. For quotation purposes the yield shall be deducted from 100.00. (The minimum fluctuation of 0.01 per cent equals approximately $60 per contract, varying with the level of interest rates.)

Contract Months
March, June, September and December, up to twelve months ahead.

Termination of Trading
The fifteenth day of the cash settlement month (or the next succeeding business day where the fifteenth day is not a business day). Trading ceases at 12.00 noon.

Source: Sydney Futures Exchange, 1985.

with a bank bill contract, but as interest rates often move differently at the longer end of the market, these contracts are more helpful when hedging against similar longer-termed exposures. The price movements at the longer end of the market for any given change in interest rates are also much greater than those on short-term fixed interest securities. This greater potential for trading profits appeals to dealers and speculators alike. Furthermore, as only cash settlement is allowed, the trader is spared the brokerage costs of buying the bonds if the contract is held to maturity. This contract has proved very popular, as have the exchange trade options on these futures contracts.

15 Foreign Exchange Business

The merchant banks' foreign exchange business is probably both the industry's newest and most significant área of expansion. It was originally confined to providing informal advice on foreign exchange matters to customers when arranging for their overseas borrowings. Eventually these activities developed into a separate source of fee income and then gradually expanded into currency hedging, currency futures, and finally in 1984 to actual foreign exchange dealing. In 1984 most merchant bank foreign exchange business was conducted through its international division. As mentioned in Chapter 8, this division is also typically in charge of the firm's offshore operations as well as trade financing and offshore capital raisings. Though both areas are closely tied to foreign exchange operations they are discussed separately in the domestic lending and offshore financing chapters; currency futures have been addressed in Chapter 14.

More recently, with their strong dependence on overseas funding, many merchant banks have integrated their foreign exchange operations with their domestic money market business to form a Treasury division. An increasing portion of the industry is likely to follow this example.

CURRENCY HEDGING

Although the merchant banking industry cannot take credit for initiating Australia's currency hedge market, there is little question that it developed it into a significant market. Starting in February 1978 with Hill Samuel Australia, an increasing number of merchant banks entered the hedge market business, initially as brokers (matching clients with foreign exchange receivables with others having foreign exchange liabilities) and then dealing as principal. As more firms entered the business, both the size of the market and its transactions increased and finally, on 11 June 1979, as a reflection of its competition, the trading banks commenced their own inter-bank foreign currency hedge market operations.

It was thought that the trading bank hedge market might mean an end to most merchant bank business. Instead the reverse happened. As the merchant banks could also trade with the trading banks, it gave them a new place to offload their foreign exchange positions and so, at a price, merchant banks could suddenly handle much larger transactions than before. The inter-bank hedge market also gave hedging more creditability in the local market and firms which once thought it speculative began to reconsider hedge cover. Furthermore, over time what was once the inter-bank hedge market and the inter-merchant bank hedge market began to merge and by mid-1982 industry estimates placed its combined size at the $10 to $12 billion in outstandings. It has grown rapidly since and as at July 1985, the market had some $60 033 million outstanding in hedge contracts.[1]

In terms of the market itself, it is difficult to estimate the relative size of the trading banks versus non-banks and customers or the size of the individual firms. Some estimates, such as shown in Table 15.1, suggest that as the market developed, both bank and non-bank dealers became increasingly important as they assumed more and more of the work as principals. Indeed, it was soon easy to obtain competitive immediate quotes of up to $10 million for up to twelve months.

In terms of actual firms, by late 1983 the hedge market had over thirty major participants. The larger merchant bank hedge dealers included such firms as Hill Samuel, Citicorp, BA Australia, Barclays, BT Australia, and Elders Finance; Elders in 1982, for example, claimed over 30 per cent of the hedge market.[2] Over 1984, Capel Court, Lloyds International, Partnership Pacific, and Schroder Darling were also important in this market.

In addition to matching customer foreign exchange exposures, merchant banks also attracted business through parallel loans and offshore currency exchanges for hedging cover of up to twelve years.

Table 15.1 Foreign Currency Hedge Market Turnover

Year	Turnover $m	Clients %	Banks %	Other Principals %
1980–81	20 000	60	20	20
1981–82	35 000	40	25	35

Source: David Fallon, 'Foreign Exchange Developing into Key Area', *Australian Financial Review*, 1 November 1982, p. 21.

Simulated foreign currency loans and deposits, dating from 1982, were another development. Though the interest paid on these accounts and the currency exchange risk involved are a result of the overseas market in that currency (mainly US dollars), the actual payment of interest and redemption of the deposit on maturity are accomplished in Australian currency—again eliminating the need for foreign exchange control approval as no money leaves Australia.

The major change in merchant bank operations and the future of the hedge market resulted from a number of regulatory changes in Australia over 1983–84. First, on 28 October 1983, came the removal of the requirement that bank forward cover be provided only for trade-related transactions and then only within seven days of the liability being incurred. Previously the many foreign exchange obligations which did not comply with these requirements provided the major transaction base for the hedge market. With the end of these restrictions, as the Treasurer, Paul Keating, explained, 'the present distinction between the foreign exchange and currency hedge markets' was removed.[3] These measures, coupled with the Reserve Bank's withdrawal from the official forward exchange market on 31 October, the floating of the Australian dollar, and the freeing of most foreign exchange controls in December 1983 brought an end to many of the previous potential price advantages that the hedge market could provide. Finally, in June 1984, the foreign exchange market itself was greatly expanded with a list of forty firms authorized to obtain foreign exchange dealer licences.

Initially it was suggested that the hedge market would disappear as the new dealers, previously the market's major players, transferred their hedge business to the foreign exchange side of the market. While this did occur, the impact on the hedge market was slower than perhaps expected. A survey of participants in mid-1985, though, indicates that a degree of uncertainty remains, with 44 out of 148 dealers suggesting the hedge market will not remain viable. Interestingly, 76 felt that the hedge market could remain viable even with turnovers of less than $200 million.[4] At least one reason for its continuance in the short term is that not all dealers granted licences were able to trade immediately and thus had to rely on hedging in the meantime. BT Australia, for example, found that while hedge market transactions still accounted for around half of its foreign exchange turnover in 1984, this importance had dropped to 25 per cent over 1985 and was expected to account for only 10 per cent over 1986. Likewise, not all firms active in the hedge market, notably Repco, obtained authorization for a licence. Even those firms with licences, however, may still find the hedge market affords certain opportunities. For example, the new dealers will have relatively low overnight and inter-bank exposure limits and so they may be forced to use the hedge market once these limits are reached. The hedge market may also still offer some advantages with third currencies. These involve hedging between non-Australian dollar currencies rather than the traditional US–Australian dollar coverage. Originally provided mainly in US dollars–Japanese yen, this market now covers limited amounts of US dollar–German mark and US dollar–British pound sterling transactions and will probably move to more exotic currencies as the forward market absorbs the more active ones.

Despite these more specialist areas, there seems little question that as the hedge market trading becomes thinner, its competitive position should likewise deteriorate and further reinforce the trend now favouring the spot and forward markets. Profits from hedge market operations should decline as a result and there seems little question that margins today are much thinner as a result of the 1983–84 changes.

The Reserve Bank's withdrawal from its traditional announcement of the US–Australian dollar mid-rate at 9.30 a.m. on each trading day has also adversely affected the hedge market for it was on this rate that most hedge contracts were settled. Instead, the settlement rate is now calculated based on the average of the inter-bank quotes on the Reuter Screen at 9:48 a.m. on the day in question, less the highest and lowest quote. The problem is that customers find some dealers are subsequently unwilling to deal at these rates. This has raised suggestions that the hedge market settlement rate is now subject to dealer manipulation and some now avoid the market accordingly.

FOREIGN EXCHANGE ADVISORY WORK

As mentioned, merchant banks first entered the foreign exchange business as advisers. This position was normally due to the firm's association with offshore lending work. It would seek local clients for offshore loans and receive a finders' fee from overseas institutions. As other than US dollar loans became commonplace in the Euro-markets, customers began to seek advice not only on the terms and conditions but also the currency options available. In the process, merchant banks had to examine the customer's overall foreign exchange exposure. Eventually this developed into a business in its own right and most major merchant banks today provide a full range of foreign-exchange-related advisory services. These commonly include identifying customer currency risk exposures; advising on the management of foreign exchange, interest rate, liquidity and liability exposures; providing information on expected international currency and interest rate movements; selecting and installing computer-based foreign-currency-exposure management software; and advising on the taxation implications of foreign exchange. In addition to any direct fees, good foreign exchange advice generally means that clients will give at least part of their foreign exchange business to the firm concerned.

Besides the normal advisory work, training in foreign exchange management has also been a high profile source of revenue for some merchant banks. Since 1980, for example, BA Australia has conducted courses for over 700 corporate treasury and commercial managers on identifying foreign exchange risks and analysing the best means to minimize these exposures. In addition, BA has also provided customized foreign exchange workshops and more advanced specialist courses.[5]

As part of their advisory work, some merchant banks have developed computer software for their customers and actively market these packages. Midland International Australia Ltd, for example, utilizes its Midland Bank parent's ITC Momentum Model to predict currency trends and provide clients with daily buy and sell recommendations on the Australian dollar against fourteen other currencies. BA Australia's 'Position Watch' is another computer software package designed to keep an exact record of a client's foreign exchange exposure, and other firms such as Citicorp and Hill Samuel have similar foreign exchange software packages available.

In addition to strictly advice and training, some merchant banks also manage their clients' interest rate and foreign exchange exposure to obtain their borrowings at the lowest effective interest cost. This management feature is particularly attractive to medium-size companies with an active foreign currency exposure too small to justify the personnel and computer costs for an in-house foreign exchange operation.

In terms of the quality of foreign exchange advice, merchant banks have rated well but not necessarily better than the major trading banks. *Business Review Weekly*'s 1985 survey, for example, ranked Westpac first on strategic foreign exchange advice, but shared this first place position with Citicorp. BT Australia and Capel Court ranked second and third place respectively. The other firms and their relative ratings are shown in Table 15.2. For the purposes of the survey, strategic advice included such matters as exposure management and long-term positions in foreign exchange.

Table 15.2 Foreign Exchange Dealers with the Best Strategic Advice

Institution	Responders' Foreign Exchange Turnover			
	Under $100 m	$100–$199 m	$200–$499 m	Over $500 m
ANZ Bank	18	8	4	–
BA Australia	10	4	11	2
Barclays Australia	10	5	8	4
BNP	29	4	–	10
BT Australia	13	4	4	18
Capel Court	23	7	8	12
Commonwealth Bank	17	3	7	7
Citicorp	30	21	12	15
DBSM	5	3	4	–
Elders	35	6	6	3
Lloyds	14	8	4	5
Macquarie Bank	25	11	8	9
Michell NBD	11	–	–	–
National Aust. Bank	34	4	2	10
Partnership Pacific	25	–	–	–
Schroder Darling	12	9	1	5
Societe Generale	9	–	–	2
Westpac Banking	43	16	15	13

Source: 'The BRW foreign exchange poll', *Business Review Weekly*, 24 May 1985, p. 50.

Note: The scoring gave a first choice mention, 3 pts; a second place, 2 pts; and a third place, 1 pt. The results were then weighted to reflect the importance of the responder: those with a turnover of more than $500 million receiving 7.5 per point; $200 to $499 million, 3.5 per point; those with $100 to $199 million, 1.5 per point; and those with less than $100 million, 0.33 per point.

FOREIGN EXCHANGE DEALING

As part of deregulation following the lifting of most foreign exchange controls and the floating of the Australian dollar, the Reserve Bank in January 1984 invited foreign exchange licence submissions. These licences were at least in part designed to bridge the gap between the removal of most foreign exchange control restrictions and the licensing of new trading banks for the local market. The applicants required a minimum capital of $10 million and certain staffing and administrative conditions as well. Most internationally affiliated firms had little difficulty in supporting such applications. Unlike trading bank licences, however, these new licences have no lender of last resort or other Reserve Bank support.

On 10 April 1984, the Treasurer confirmed the decision to increase the number of foreign exchange dealer licences and on 19 June 1984 announced that forty companies had been authorized as foreign exchange dealers; the actual licensing would be handled through negotiation with the Reserve Bank. The number of approvals surprised most market participants who had expected a fairly restricted number (only ten to twelve) of new licences.[6] Instead, the Treasurer licensed most major applicants and thus, as with the later foreign bank applications, many were surprised at their success. As a result, only eighteen of the forty operators formally commenced operations on 25 June 1984. The remainder had to arrange for the increased capital, staffing, and equipment. Other institutions have since been added to the list and the position as at late 1985 is shown in Table 15.3; all but three of the new firms were merchant banks.

The extensive merchant bank foreign exchange licensing is at least partly a result of heavy lobbying by the Australian Merchant Bankers Association and some suggest the licences were also in part compensation to the industry for the removal of the 14-day interest rule on bank deposits.[7] In support of this view, not all those active in the hedge market received licences. Repco, a non-merchant bank which had applied unsuccessfully for a licence, was a very active dealer in the currency hedge market and despite the lack of a licence has never the less continued quoting hedge prices in the local foreign exchange market for German marks, Japanese yen, and a number of more exotic currencies like Austrian shillings and Maltese pounds; understandably, without a licence it cannot quote in the physical (deliverable) foreign exchange market.

In terms of operations, the new dealers will generally provide spot and forward cover in major currencies for periods of up to one month for amounts of up to $10 million. Obviously some firms are more active than others in this regard as well as in the range of currencies covered. Elders Finance, for example, now claims that it 'deals in more than twenty currencies, ten of them actively ... [with] a 24 hour dealing capability through our offices in Australia, Hong Kong, London and New York' as well as being Australia's largest dealer in third currencies.[8] Partnership Pacific, too, has taken advantage of its knowledge of regional currencies and was the first merchant bank to list screen prices on the Malaysian ringgit and the Singapore dollar as well as the US dollar, German mark, and Japanese yen.

Since floating the dollar in December 1983, a forward market has developed between major currencies and the Australian dollar where

Table 15.3 New Foreign Exchange Dealers in Australia

ABN Australia Ltd
AMP Acceptances Ltd
Amro Australia Ltd
Midland International Australia Ltd
AUC Holdings
Australian International Finance Corporation Ltd
BA Australia Ltd
Barclays Australia Ltd
BBL Australia Ltd
BT Australia Ltd
Capel Court Corporation
Chase-NBA Group Ltd
Chemical All-States Ltd
CIBIC Australia Ltd
Citicorp Australia Holdings Ltd
Commercial Continental Ltd
Dominguez Barry Samuel Montagu Ltd
Elder's Finance and Investment Co. Ltd
European Asian of Australia Ltd
Euro-Pacific Finance Corporation Ltd
First Chicago Australia Ltd
Grindlays Securities Australia Ltd
Hambros Australia Ltd
Hill Samuel Australia Ltd
Indosuez Australia Ltd
Kleinwort Benson Australia Ltd
Lloyds International Ltd
Marac Australia Ltd
Mitchell NBD Ltd
Midland International Australia Ltd
National Westminster Finance Australia Ltd
Partnership Pacific Ltd
RBC Australia Ltd
Rothschild Australia Ltd
SBC Australia Ltd
Schroder Darling and Co. Ltd
Security Pacific Australia Ltd
Societe Generale Australia Ltd
Standard Chartered Australia Ltd
Trans City Holdings Ltd
Tricontinental Corporation Ltd
Wardley Australia Ltd

Source: Commonwealth of Australia, *Gazette, No. S540*, 21 December 1984, p. 2.

the forward premium is simply due to interest rate differentials. While the interest rate differential was certainly a major factor in the pre-float market, it was but one factor, as foreign exchange controls limited the market's ability to arbitrage rate differentials. A pure forward market should operate on finer margins as the exact rates should become very much easier to calculate and generally enhance the dealers' trading abilities.

At present the non-bank dealers must take full advantage of such trading as their local capitalization, generally only $10 million, places them at a marked disadvantage vis-à-vis their much larger trading bank competitors. Furthermore, given their capitalization, any major expansion into foreign exchange could work against other merchant bank operations, for the liabilities created in foreign exchange would limit a firm's balance sheet potential to support other areas.

In the money market, for example, most corporate lenders place a dollar limit on their overall exposure to each merchant bank as well as other corporate players. To the extent that foreign exchange exposure causes corporate depositors to limit their deposit levels further, this should also impact on the industry. Given their lower limits, those merchant banks affected will need more customers to raise the same level of deposit funds, and the customers will now have to spread their deposits over a larger number of firms.

In mid-1984, shortly after the licences were granted, Australian Ratings conducted a study, simply deducting some $5 million from the capital position of each of the new licensees in an effort to show the impact that the potential foreign exchange exposure might have on overall gearing levels. The results, shown in Table 15.4 and which are subject to a number of assumptions and qualifications, nevertheless illustrate the potential problem that an active foreign exchange business could have on the industry as a whole. Needless to say, the smaller the initial capital base, the greater the gearing impact on those actively entering the foreign exchange business. Martin Corporation (now CIBC), for example, would see its gearing rise from 20.9 to some 33.1. Thus there is a strong argument for the shareholders to increase their equity considerably more than the $10 million required. Alternatively, the firm would need to keep its overall exposure in foreign exchange at a low level. This problem of course will affect foreign exchange dealing as well. Indeed, trading in actual currencies rather than hedge contracts may limit some merchant banks' previous turnover as prudential restraints could mean lower inter-market limits between dealers.

To the extent that wholly-foreign-bank-owned merchant banks are considered on their parents' merits in foreign exchange dealings,

Table 15.4 Selected Foreign Exchange Licensees and their Potential Gearing Positions, 1984

Group	Shareholders' Funds ($m)	Gearing (times)
Natwest Finance	96.0	5.9
Security Pacific Australia	8.2	13.6
Capel Court	25.3	14.4
Hambro Australia	12.0	14.7
Wardley Australia	45.8	15.5
RBC Australia	5.7	15.8
Amro Australia	6.2	16.4
Partnership Pacific	53.0	19.8
Barclays Australia	27.1	21.9
BT Australia	26.1	22.4
Kleinwort Benson	6.4	22.6
Lloyds International	24.6	23.8
AIFC	21.6	24.3
Schroder Darling	10.3	24.8
BA Australia	16.8	25.8
Societe Generale	15.2	25.6
Elders Finance	20.7	26.0
Chase-NBA	27.2	28.6
Grindlays Securities	5.7	29.1
Standard Chartered	10.4	29.3
Rothschild	5.0	30.0
Euro Pacific	16.9	30.2
SBC Australia	5.0	30.5
Martin Corp.	8.6	33.1
Tricontinental (ex TFC)	20.7	33.5
AUC (ex AUC Discount)	6.1	37.9
AMP Acceptances	6.3	45.6
First Chicago	5.2	49.2
Trans City (ex TC Discount)	1.7	121.8
Commercial Continental (ex LIF)	0.6	289.3

Source: Australian Ratings as cited in the *Australian Financial Review*, 24 July 1984, p. 59.

Note: These gearing figures are calculated based on the firms' then reported shareholders' funds less an arbitrary $5 million of their then liabilities. The exercise is simply to show the potential impact and does not reflect their actual positions.

they could have a considerable advantage over their consortium or locally-owned competition. These latter firms would then require much larger capital bases to provide the same degree of security. Thus the recent spate of shareholder rationalizations, by which most foreign-owned merchant banks have become wholly-owned subsidiaries of their overseas parents, was very timely.

EFFECTS OF THE NEW LICENCES

Whether the operations of the new dealers have done much to improve the foreign exchange market remains an open question. At the time of the licensing, for example, the *Australian Financial Review* predicted that 'the additional licences will not significantly add to the depth of the foreign exchange market in the short term'.[9] Indeed, rather than improve the market, at least some suggest that the reverse has happened. As one observer commented, 'there are now probably fewer really active players than there were in those good old days' before the floating of the dollar and the new licences.[10] Many merchant banks are really price-takers rather than market-makers in foreign exchange. They quotes prices and otherwise deal with clients and then offset these positions with other firms via the inter-bank market. They do not take positions in the currencies themselves. Most merchant banks are price-takers; BT Australia, Capel Court, and Elders would be among the few exceptions. Similarly, even by the end of 1984, only an estimated twelve of the some forty newly-authorized foreign exchange dealers were trading in the physical foreign exchange market.[11]

Looking more specifically at the quality of service, a survey of 157 corporate treasurers (conducted by Australian Industrial Research in 1985), ranked none of the major trading banks among the top five dealers providing the best service; the specific positions for this survey are shown in Table 15.5. Interestingly, these results directly contrasted the *Business Review Weekly*'s 1985 survey which showed the major trading banks holding the top rankings, with Westpac holding first place, followed by the ANZ Bank, the Commonwealth, BNP, and National Australia. It also differed from previous *Business Review Weekly* surveys where merchant banks like Hill Samuel

Table 15.5 Foreign Exchange Dealers Ranked by Quality of Service

First Place	BT Australia
	AMP Acceptances
Second Place	Capel Court
Third Place	Macquarie Bank
Fourth Place	Schroder Darling
Fifth Place	Lloyds

Source: Australian Industrial Research Pty Limited as cited in Peter Starr, 'Major trading banks lose in FX rankings', *Australian Financial Review*, 11 September 1985, p. 1.

(now Macquarie Bank), BA Australia, Citicorp and Barclays stood out as the dominant factors in the hedge market in 1983 and where Hill Samuel, Citicorp, and Capel Court rated similarly in 1984.[12]

The impact of these dealers to date though is still limited to certain segments of the market. For example, among those responding to the *Business Review Weekly*'s 1985 foreign exchange survey, 53 per cent of smaller companies reported no benefit from the increased licences while only 28 per cent of larger companies felt similarly.[13] In time the new dealers will no doubt expand their services to the smaller companies but for the immediate future the trading banks will seemingly dominate this sector.

Besides insufficient marketing power to reach smaller clients, merchant banks have found the trading banks often unwilling to lose this business. Besides normal price competition, it is rumoured that some trading banks might even suggest that a potential client's overall financial arrangements need reviewing if too much foreign exchange business is placed elsewhere—a deadly form of moral suasion. The financial press has even reported rumours that 'Westpac has allocated $2 million, supposedly from advertising budgets, to loss leading quotes in the foreign exchange market', a practice understandably denied by Westpac.[14]

The merchant banks are also at a disadvantage vis-à-vis the banks as many firms are only now entering the business and there is much additional paper-work as well as the cost of foreign exchange control screening which is not required in hedge market transactions. Similarly, rather than just settlements in Australian dollars, licensed merchant banks must now settle through overseas bank accounts in the countries concerned. Their whole administrative systems need revision. This is particularly true for those firms now only actively entering the business. Not only are there substantial salary bills in hiring dealers but there is also a major capital equipment investment, an estimated $1 to $2 million to equip a quality foreign exchange trading desk.[15] As a result, many new entrants have found brokers more economic than adding additional dealers and communication facilities. In addition, with so many participants, searching directly is more difficult to justify compared with a brokerage cost of around $30 for a $1 million Australian dollar spot and $40 for each US$1 million of third currency transactions. Many firms now conduct most foreign exchange business through brokers and some estimate they now handle 40 per cent or more of Australia's total foreign exchange volume.[16]

The most visible sign that a foreign exchange licence is not 'a permit to print money' was the announcement by BOT Australia on

13 August 1985 that it had withdrawn from the spot and forward market in Australian dollars. Significantly, the firm had only commenced dealing on 1 August. According to local press reports, it 'had been prepared to do business in quite large parcels, unusual for a bank of BOT's size, experience and lack of corporate base, and that this may have contributed to its sudden withdrawal'.[17] BOT continues to trade in yen and German marks. As one writer concluded, 'foreign exchange is not the easy money spinner it was once reputed to be'.[18]

16 Overseas Expansion

As with their diversification efforts, Australia's merchant banks have limited their expansion overseas mainly because of their parents' operations in these countries. This has particularly been the case with consortium-owned operations.

In the early days, the major incentive for overseas expansion was to avoid the withholding tax provisions on foreign-controlled domestic companies on-lending to local borrowers. Thus many foreign-controlled merchant banks established their own overseas subsidiaries. This allowed them to raise their funds offshore and then, by relending the money directly to their client borrowers, they avoided this tax problem. Besides these specific borrowing and on-lending operations, such booking operations also proved useful for accepting foreign currency deposits; negotiating and issuing letters of credit; foreign exchange and money market dealings; providing investment management, trustee, nominee, and custodian services; and participating in Asian and Euro-currency loan and bond syndications.

Most early subsidiaries were 'telex machine' operations where the firm had no full-time staff overseas but rather used the offices of another, often a parent, company. This is sometimes still the case, as with Australian International Finance's Australian International Limited in Vanuatu and Euro-Pacific Finance Corporation's branch office in Vanuatu. The trend, however, is for a staffed operational presence. In recent years a number of firms have accomplished this by using their parent company's facilities in places like Hong Kong or by acquiring an existing operation. Elders Finance, for example, expanded its operations in early 1983 by purchasing the Girard Bank's local deposit-taking company subsidiary in Hong Kong and in 1984 purchasing the Private Investment Company for Asia or PICA. Capel Court similarly acquired a Hong Kong deposit-taking company (Ever Finance) in 1984.

Besides helping to fund and on-lend foreign currency to Australian customers, these offshore subsidiary operations may also be active in merchant banking in their own right. Commonly these firms borrow in Asian and Euro-currency markets on the strength of their parent company's guarantee and on-lend the funds through international loan syndications and direct lending. As Euro-Pacific reported, its British operation 'has developed, and now maintains, an extensive portfolio of Euro-currency syndication loans—in the majority of cases lending is on a sovereign risk basis', particularly to Southeast Asia.[1] Today, funding and lending is just part of these operations as their overseas location makes them ideally suited to assist their parents' trade financing and foreign exchange dealing. Many firms have also entered the corporate advisory business, taking advantage of their position to advise Asian and other overseas investors on Australian conditions and vice versa. This provides not only direct revenue but also possible spin-off work for the subsidiary, its parent, and its shareholders.

Another overseas area for Australian merchant banks is elsewhere in the Southwest Pacific region. Many international banks considered Sydney the appropriate headquarters for matters concerning such countries as New Zealand, Papua New Guinea, Fiji, and the smaller Pacific island countries. Thus in some cases, Australian merchant banks are tasked by their parents to provide regional merchant banking services. Lloyds International, for example, actively provides international merchant banking services to clients in Australia, New Zealand, Papua New Guinea, and the Pacific Islands on its parent's behalf. This Australasian-styled thinking occasionally has made Australian merchant banks responsible for establishing their parents' New Zealand operation too. This is sometimes reflected in terms of ownership as well. Hill Samuel Australia (Macquarie Bank), rather than Hill Samuel of the United Kingdom, for example, owned Hill Samuel New Zealand (now FAS Macquarie Ltd).

Australian-owned companies have been active in New Zealand too, with All-States Capital, for example, having 100 per cent ownership of a New Zealand money market corporation, Rediscount (offices in Auckland, Christchurch, and Wellington), and a major shareholding in a New Zealand official dealer, APA Discount Corporation.

The most impressive overseas expansion by an Australian merchant banking group unfortunately is no longer in existence. This was the overseas office and subsidiary network established by the Nugan Hand Group. Some may question whether this firm was a merchant bank and the findings of the Royal Commission into its operations suggest it lacked many of the definitional requirements suggested in Chapter 2. Even so, its overseas network was impressive, at least on paper, and is presented in Table 16.1. Such companies were established primarily in the mid to late 1970s, and for a

Table 16.1 Nugan Hand Group's Overseas Representation

Subsidiaries	
Argentina	Nugan Hand (Argentina) Inc.
Cayman Islands	The Nugan Hand Bank
	Swiss Pacific Holdings Ltd
Chile	Nugan Hand (Chile) Inc.
West Germany	F.A. Neubauer Bank
Great Britain	Nugan Hand (UK) Ltd
Hawaii	Nugan Hand, Inc. (Hawaii)
Hong Kong	F.A. Neubauer Management (Hong Kong) Ltd
	Nugan Hand (Hong Kong) Ltd
	Nugan Hand Insurance Brokers Ltd
	Nugan Hand International Holdings Ltd
	Nugan Hand Management Services Ltd
	Nugan Hand Nominees Ltd
	Nugan Hand Trade Asia Ltd
	Nugan Hand Travel Ltd
Malaysia	Nugan Hand Holdings Sdn. Bhd.
	Nugan Hand (Malaysia) Sdn. Bhd.
Panama	Nugan Hand Inc. Panama
Philippines	Nugan Hand International (Manila)
Singapore	Nugan Hand Singapore (Pte) Ltd
	Nugan Hand Management Services (Pte) Ltd
	F.A. Neubauer Management (Pte) Ltd
Thailand	F.A. Neubauer Management Ltd
	Nugan Hand (Thailand) Ltd
United States	Nugan Hand International Inc. (United States)
	Nugan Hand (NY) Inc.
Nugan Hand Bank Representative Offices	
Hong Kong	
Saudi Arabia	
Nugan Hand International Representatives–Agents	
Brazil	
Chile	
Italy	
Korea	
Mexico	
Taiwan	

Source: Royal Commission of Inquiry into the Activities of the Nugan Hand Group, *Final Report*, Canberra: Australian Government Publishing Service, 1985, pp. 1123–4.

brief period Nugan Hand advertisements featured prominently in a wide range of business publications, mainly in Asia, Australia, and the Middle East. However, the group experienced difficulties and its operations effectively came to an end with the death of Frank Nugan in January 1980 and the disappearance of Michael Hand in June 1980.[2]

Of the continuing businesses, the most notable merchant bank overseas operation, listed in Table 16.2, has traditionally been that of Partnership Pacific's offshore bank, Partnership Pacific Bank NV. Incorporated in Curaçao, the Netherland Antilles, this firm is a major offshore operator. In 1983 it raised some US$50 million through a floating rate certificate of deposit issue on the international market. For many years it has proved a major contributor to its parent's overall profits. The generally lower tax position of these overseas earnings is an important reason why these subsidiaries provide a major portion of their group's earnings. In 1983, for example, BA Australia attributed some 52.7 per cent of its group earnings to its Hong Kong operation.[3] BT Australia similarly earned close to 38 per cent of its net earnings from Hong Kong[4] and Australian European Finance earned some 23.2 per cent of its group earnings through its Netherland Antilles subsidiary's US$187 million loan portfolio.[5]

Another interesting area of overseas expansion was the Spedley Group's 1982–83 acquisition of the United Kingdom based Kirkland-Whittaker Group Limited. This firm, which has branches in Jersey, Luxembourg, Amsterdam, and Bahrain, is a licensed member of the Foreign Exchange Brokers Association and one of twelve licensed by the Bank of England as an Interbank Foreign Exchange and Eurocurrency Deposit Market dealer.[6]

The leadership in offshore operations in 1985, however, belongs unquestionably to Elders Finance. Prior to 1984, it had already established the most extensive network of overseas offices, with representation in Bahrain, Hong Kong, London, and New York, and had become a floor member of the London International Financial Futures Exchange. In mid-1984 this network expanded considerably with the acquisition of the Asian-based investment company, the Private Investment Company for Asia (PICA) SA.

PICA was a unique operation among Asia's financial institutions as it was one of the few true multinationals, with 234 shareholders from some twenty different countries and a professional staff of 62 comprised of seventeen different nationalities.[7] It also differed in that each of its shareholders held less than 0.5 per cent and had invested more for philosophical reasons—the promotion of private

Table 16.2 Selected Australian Merchant Banks and their Overseas Affiliates

Merchant Bank	Overseas Firm	Location
AEFC	Australian European Finance Corporation NV	Netherland Antilles
AFIC	Australian International Ltd	Vanuatu
BA Australia	BA (Australia) HK Ltd	Hong Kong
Barclays Australia	Office with parent	Singapore
Bill Acceptance Corp.	Representative office	London
BT Australia	Office with parent	Hong Kong
Commercial Continental[a]	Commercial Continental (South East Asia) Ltd	Hong Kong
Elders Finance	Elders Pacific Limited	Hong Kong
	Elders Australia (Finance) Ltd	Hong Kong
	Elders PICA SA	Panama
	Elders Pacific (Bahrain) Ltd	Bahrain
	Elders Finance (Overseas) Ltd	Hong Kong
	Elders Finance Limited	UK
Euro-Pacific[b]	Branch office	Hong Kong
	Branch office	Vanuatu
	Euro-Pacific (Overseas) Ltd	England
First National Ltd	CNG International Ltd[c]	Hong Kong
Hambro Australia	HAL Investments	Singapore
	Halasia Limited	Hong Kong
Hill Samuel Australia[d]	FAS Macquarie Ltd	New Zealand
	HSA Overseas Ltd	Hong Kong
Partnership Pacific	Partnership Pacific Bank NV	Netherland Antilles
SBC Australia	SBCA (Hongkong) Ltd	Hong Kong
Tricontinental[b]	Tricontinental Finance (HK) Ltd[e]	Hong Kong
Wardley Australia Ltd	Wardley Australia Overseas Ltd	Hong Kong

[a] Now Sanwa Australia.
[b] Now Toronto-Dominion Australia.
[c] Soon to be First National of Australia Limited.
[d] Now Macquarie Acceptances.
[e] Tricontinental shares its subsidiary, with the State Bank of Victoria and the Rural and Industries Bank of Western Australia holding 39 and 10 per cent respectively.

enterprise in Asia—than for financial gain. Since its founding in 1969, PICA had become a venture-capital-styled merchant bank which often made equity investments as well as providing loan capital to clients within the region. In the process it developed a regional branch network with representation in Indonesia, Hong Kong, Japan, Malaysia, the Philippines, Singapore, South Korea, Taiwan, and Thailand; minority equity investments in a range of different companies; an Asian Currency Unit (offshore banking) licensed subsidiary in Singapore; an extensive $354.4 million loan portfolio spread over twelve Asian countries[8] and perhaps most importantly, a trained and experienced professional multinational banking staff.

Now known as Elders PICA SA, the company will gradually be restructured so that Elders' other international business operations will also profit from this new office network. In particular, PICA's offices should help expand Elders' own trade finance and trading opportunities within the region as well as provide more comprehensive service to its clients. It is expected that Elders PICA will also expand its foreign exchange dealing and funding operations in line with Elders' international expansion in that area. Finally, PICA's Singapore subsidiary, PICA (Pte) Ltd, also provides Elders with a direct participation in Singapore's Asian Dollar Market, a position not yet shared by any other Australian merchant bank.

In early 1985, Elders' overseas position was further strengthened by the announcement of a financial co-operation agreement with Yasuda Trust and Banking Company of Japan, an affiliate of the Fuyo industrial group. This co-operation is expected mainly in Southeast Asia and may assist Elders in developing an offshore investment management operation. Its new Elders PICA operations should prove of particular assistance in that respect. In addition, Elders also announced plans in 1985 to establish a merchant bank in New Zealand in co-operation with New Zealand's Goodman Group Ltd.

While it would be incorrect to view Elders' expansion as typical for the industry, there is little question that most Australian merchant bankers can see what overseas representation offers in the way of potential Australian business. Foreign investment advisory work, particularly from Asia, is already an important source of local corporate finance work and it is interesting that some firms, such as Barclays Australia and Bill Acceptance Corporation, are now actively developing Asian business. It seems certain that other firms will follow; even though one's foreign parents can refer the business, having a direct Australian presence to discuss matters in person is an unquestionable advantage. The expansion of merchant bank foreign exchange dealing also argues for more Asian offices, as a Hong Kong or Singapore dealing operation provides more trading flexibility for its Australian parent. In addition, such offices might provide a useful training and recruitment facility for their Australian dealing operations. Elsewhere there is also the matter of other South Pacific representation. New Zealand merchant banking already has an Australian presence and, if the Australian–New Zealand Closer Economic Relations (CER) agreement proves successful, there may be a greater two-way flow of financial institution representation. There is also some limited potential in places such as Papua New Guinea and Vanuatu, which presently have a one-firm merchant banking industry, and Fiji, which has long wished for local merchant banks to be established.[9] In short, merchant bank overseas representation can be expected to grow and, if past experiences are a good indication, prove a very profitable part of the industry's future operations.

17 Other Activities

In contrast to other financial institutions in Australia, most merchant banks have developed as an arm of an existing, often foreign, financial institution or as a consortium of local and overseas financial institutions rather than as separate institutions in their own right. As a result, Australian merchant banks have tended to be part of an existing financial group rather than developing as a financial group themselves. Thus most Australian merchant bank subsidiaries were established for administrative, regulatory, and tax reasons (securities dealers, discount companies, investment companies, nominee companies, and fund management firms), rather than for diversification. Even so, given the industry's tendency for exploiting new market opportunities, merchant banks will no doubt expand into other fields and already some firms are active in areas as yet not commonly associated with Australian merchant banking. This chapter discusses a selection of these activities.

COMMODITIES

As mentioned in Chapter 14, some merchant banks are active dealers in commodity as well as financial futures. This full service concept fits well with the industry's general expansion into sharebroking. In addition to commodity futures, some firms also deal in physical commodities. Probably the best example is Hill Samuel (Macquarie) whose Commodity Division in 1983 was Australia's leading gold and silver bullion dealer and conducted business both for immediate delivery or on a spot deferred or forward basis. Its trading position was such that it agreed to buy the production of several gold producers for up to twelve months with a guaranteed minimum price. Mase-Westpac, Darlington, Dominguez Barry Samuel Montagu, Wardley-ACLI, and Capel Court have also been active in the bullion market. With the removal of most foreign exchange controls, Hill Samuel has since expanded its bullion dealing to overseas markets as well, particularly to Southeast Asia.

Given Australia's position as a gold producer and its time zone location between the United States closing (7.00 a.m. in Sydney) and the Hong Kong market's opening (12.30 p.m. in Sydney), bullion and other physical metal trading, like futures contracts, may develop into one of Australia's international financial activities.

COMPUTERS

Because of their computer requirements, some merchant banks have developed their own programming work into saleable products within the industry or have otherwise found an affiliated computer software firm of assistance. Here Hill Samuel (Macquarie) is again probably the most notable with its ownership of Business House Systems Australia Pty Ltd. This firm sells and supports the so-called HOUSE system, an integrated software package for banks. Chemical All-States Ltd is also involved in software sales, but on a direct basis. These relate to its Chemical Bank parent's BankLink computerized cash management system which, since mid-1983, has been sold to the Commonwealth Bank, National Australia Bank, State Bank of Victoria, and the Australian Bank. Finally, both Citicorp Capital and Development Finance Corporation are shareholders, with 18 and 25 per cent respectively, in another local computer financial software company, Computations.

FINANCE COMPANIES

As most merchant banks' parents already have their own interests in non-bank financial institutions, few merchant banks have established their own finance company subsidiaries. Two major exceptions are Tricontinental, which has its own Tricontinental Finance Corporation Limited subsidiary (formerly Ampol-Repco Finance Ltd), and First National Ltd's First National Finance Corporation (formerly Managed Deposits). Both companies serve as a useful fund-raising vehicle, particularly with public, long-term deposit raisings. First National Finance, for example, raises amounts of $100 or more on terms up to five years through the sale of debentures. Tricontinental Finance, too, raised medium-term funds through debenture sales and as of early 1985 had some $46 million in debentures outstanding: $37 million from sales to individual investors and $9 million from corporate placements.[1]

INSURANCE

In the United Kingdom many merchant banks have traditionally had strong links with the insurance industry. As yet there has been no such movement in Australia. Nevertheless, insurance seems an appropriate area for merchant bank diversification, particularly given the importance that investment bonds play in funds management and the potential that annuities have under the new superannuation taxation system.

As with these other diversification areas, insurance is conducted by subsidiary or affiliated companies. Hill Samuel Australia's wholly-owned Lowndes Lambert Australia Insurances Limited, for example, provide corporate insurance broking. This seems the most common type of merchant bank involvement and one which supports merchant banks' lending activities. As another firm, Commercial Continental (now Sanwa) explains, its Hogg Robinson CCL Pty Ltd subsidiary offers insurance brokering services and its Credit Insurance Association (Australia) Pty Ltd arranges credit insurance against debtors' failure in both Australia and overseas.[2]

MANAGEMENT AND INVESTMENT COMPANIES

As mentioned elsewhere, some merchant banks provide equity finance in addition to their normal lending activities. For the most part this is generally through redeemable preference shares and of a short to medium term. A few firms, however, sometimes invest in a client's ordinary shares; a few of these investments are considered elsewhere within this chapter. A more specialized venture capital is also provided through a new investment vehicle, the investment and management company (MIC). These firms are licensed under the Management and Investment Company Act 1983 and afford special tax advantages to their initial shareholders. Basically those investors subscribing to new shares in a MIC can deduct the full amount of the purchase in the year in question provided they do not subsequently resell the securities for at least four years. The MICs in return must invest primarily in a specified range of enterprises and gain approval from the MIC Licensing Board for each investment. As the MICs are to encourage small export-oriented, innovative Australian business, their client companies should have no more than 100 employees nor a net worth of more than $6 million. They should also be less than ten years old and have prospects for an average growth in sales of more than 20 per cent over the next three years.

As of 1985, merchant banks were major shareholders in two of the then ten licensed MICs: BT Australia in BT Innovation Limited and Hambro Australia in Hambro-Grantham (MIC) Limited. Since its initial $10 million capital raising, BT Innovation in mid-1985 raised an additional $2.5 million in equity funds. This made it the largest MIC and it had shareholdings in companies such as Cybergraphics Pty Ltd, Memtec Ltd, and Scitec Pty Ltd.

One would have thought that this venture capital would appeal to other firms in the industry and be a logical part of the much discussed expansion into investment banking. Outside of Tricontinental's 10 per cent shareholding in the recently listed Australia Venture Capital Ltd, though, there seems little other direct merchant bank involvement in venture capital. It could be, however, that many executives still recall the serious losses experienced by a couple of merchant banks in the mid-1970s through direct equity participations in client firms.

SPECIALIST NON-FINANCIAL CONSULTING

Most merchant bank corporate finance divisions have a fairly wide range of consulting activities, but some have established specialist subsidiary companies for this purpose. Hill Samuel, for example, through Noble Lowndes Australia Ltd and Cullen Egan Dell Australia Pty Ltd affiliates, are active in employee remuneration and benefits planning and administration. Trans City now also owns Marshall's Reports, an industry and market research consulting firm which in addition to its regular industry reports also produces a weekly newsletter providing a précis of related articles in a range of local and overseas financial publications.

PROPERTY SERVICES

As with many diversification activities, few merchant banks have entered the property business directly. With Schroder Australia, for example, its unit trust operations gradually expanded into property trusts in 1972, and from the staff required for property trust management came other property skills as well. Others have entered due to their lending activities, others from mortgage-backed money market securities, and still others from their financial advisory work.

As a result, many merchant banks, such as ANZ Capital Markets, CIBC Australia, Hambros Australia, Partnership Pacific and Schroder Australia, have separate property divisions within their operations offering a fairly wide range of services. These include first mortgage funding via a cash advance or bill line facility, property development, guarantees and performance bonds, construction finance, valuations, project assessment, sales, investment advice, packaging joint venture proposals, property management, market analysis, and arranging finance.

STOCKBROKERS

In the long term, the industry's move into the brokerage industry is probably the most important of these other activities. As discussed in Chapter 12, membership of the stock exchange would considerably help merchant banks compete for new underwritings and it was only an internal exchange rule (one precluding corporate members) that kept the merchant banks out. This practice was finally prohibited by the Trade Practices Commission and on 1 April 1984 corporate memberships were allowed on Australia's major stock exchanges. Even so, the ownership was restricted to a maximum of 50 per cent holding by previously non-exchange members. In other words, merchant banks at most can purchase a 50 per cent interest now; they must wait until 1 April 1987 before purchasing the remainder.

The choice of 1 April (April Fool's Day) seems appropriate as this action marked the partial removal of a practice which should never have been allowed and in any case had effectively been illegal since the passage of the Trade Practices Act in 1974. Even then the 1984 implementation came about only because the Australian Merchant Bankers Association had served a writ of mandamus on the Trade Practices Commission to enforce the law.

With the removal of the corporate ownership limitations, most major financial institutions, including the major trading banks, sought affiliations with local stockbrokers, and the merchant banks have been particularly active in this area.

Elders Finance established the first merchant bank broker affiliation, in this case with the Melbourne brokers Roach, Tilley, Grice and Company. As with most early acquisitions, the key partners will stay to form the basis for Elders' expansion into a full stockbroking operation interlinked with its other financial activities. Indeed with the computerization of its rural office network, Elders should eventually provide local access to share-trading facilities in most rural areas. Most other firms have taken a similar approach and view these potential acquisitions not as simply a means of entry into the stockbroking business, but rather as the start of a whole new field of business.

The present affiliation, shown in Table 17.1, reflects only part of what will be an extensive rationalization of stockbroking and merchant banking operations, as some earlier arrangements were hampered by a government announcement on 18 April 1984 that instead of the 50 per cent foreign ownership limitation applied to most non-bank financial institutions, a maximum limit of 15 per cent per foreign owner with a total foreign ownership limit of 40 per cent would be applied to stockbrokers. Thus Morgan Grenfell Australia, instead of purchasing its shareholdings in Horden, Utz and Bode directly, did so through a 50 per cent owned joint venture with three of the broker's key partners. This company in turn owned 50 per cent of the broker—a position that foreign-owned Morgan Grenfell could not hold directly. These later acquisitions were generally

Table 17.1 Selected Merchant Bank Stockbroker Affiliations

Merchant Bank	Broker	Exchange	Percentage
Barclays[a]	Meares and Philips Ltd	S	50.0
Citicorp	Clarke & Co.	M	50.0
Dominguez Barry Samuel Montagu	Dominguez Barry Samuel Montagu Securities Ltd	M	50.0
Elders Finance	Roach Tilley, Grice	M	40.0
Jardine Fleming	Valder, Elmslie, Jardine Fleming Ltd	S	50.0
Kleinwort Benson	Hattersley, Maxwell Noall Ltd	S	50.0
Macquarie	Macquarie Davis	S	50.0
Morgan Grenfell	Horden, Utz & Bode Ltd	S	50.0
Security Pacific[b]	McIntosh, Hamson, Hoare & Govett		4.5
Standard Chartered	Pring, Dean & Co	S	50.0
Trans City[c]	Trans City Securities	S	50.0
Wardley Australia[d]	Rivkin Ltd	S	50.0

[a] Barclays' 50 per cent ownership in this case is held by Barclays de Zoete Wedd Ltd, a British firm formed from a merger between Barclays Merchant Bank Ltd, British jobber Webb Durlacher Mordaunt & Co., and British broker de Zoete & Devan. This holding, however, under Reserve Bank guidelines, may have to be transferred to Barclays Australia when it commences local trading bank operations.

[b] The holding is rather indirect via Security Pacific's parent bank's 30 per cent holding in the London brokers Hoare & Govett who in turn own 14.9 per cent of McIntosh Hamson.

[c] Sydney broker R.F. Arthur is the exchange partner in this instance.

[d] Twenty-five per cent of Rivkin is held by London stockbrokers James Capel & Co., but it in turn is owned 29.9 per cent by Wardley's parent, the Hongkong and Shanghai Banking Corporation, who will soon acquire a full 100 per cent.

completed in the understanding that if the government later raised its ownership restrictions to 50 per cent the merchant bank could increase its share accordingly. As discussed in Chapter 7, new foreign investment policies have since allowed full foreign ownership of most non-banking institutions. At present, then, only the 50 per cent non-member limitation established by the stock exchanges themselves has precluded the merchant banks from gaining 100 per cent ownership. Come 1 April 1987 many of these present joint ventures will become wholly-owned merchant bank subsidiaries. Likewise, those merchant banks not already listed in Table 17.1 are likely to establish stockbroking operations themselves and then join the exchange.

18 Staffing

As mentioned previously, a merchant bank's reputation depends directly on the quality of its employees. A firm with a good reputation for a particular service, for example, can quickly lose its lead position with the loss of only a few key personnel. This is because a merchant bank can afford only so much management depth and certain people, due to their skill and market reputations, are impossible to replace.

This relationship between good staff and success has been a major obstacle to rationalization within the Australian merchant banking industry. One can certainly acquire a merchant bank's corporate structure and office network, but retaining the bank's expertise is another matter. Employment contracts will do little to ensure the good staff stay and for the most part, particularly in corporate finance, a merchant bank's customers are customers of individual staff members first, and customers of the firm second. If those staff leave then, all too often, so does the firm's business.

The importance of quality staff is of course nothing new for the industry but it has become a growing problem as many new merchant banks have attempted to buy their way into certain areas by hiring key executives from other firms. Perhaps the most recent example of full-scale staff bidding was by National Westminster's new merchant bank, County Australia Holdings. Over 1985 it obtained a six-man fixed interest team from broker McCaughn Dysons and two key investment management people from Wardley Australia. The fixed interest 'acquisition', according to press reports, was for market value plus performance bonuses: the former would mean at least some $100 000 to $150 000 per person. Other investment management staffing raids include Commercial Continental (Sanwa Australia) hiring from Schroder Darling (Schroder Australia) and Barclays from Westpac and the brokerage industry.

Previously it was perhaps more common to purchase an existing business within the same area. Lloyds International is probably the best example of staffing by corporate acquisition with its purchase of David Block & Associates; Lloyds' position in corporate finance moved up from close to bottom to the very top. Morgan Grenfell similarly expanded its corporate advisory business through the acquisition of Geoff Hill's Bancorp. Corporate acquisitions have also been common in investment management. Wardley, for example, acquired its initial investment operations in 1981 by purchasing the superannuation fund managers John D.J. Robinson and Associates.

Staffing, then, is a major problem facing most merchant banks and even in 1984 one writer was complaining that 'merchant banking has the highest executive turnover rate in the finance industry'.[1] With the continued entry of new merchant banks and the expansion of existing firms into new areas, staff turnover will certainly increase. Each new area requires additional professional and support staff and as a result the average number of merchant bank employees has increased year after year and, as shown in Table 18.1, now stands at 145 employees per firm. The specific staffing for individual firms is listed in Table 18.9 at the end of this chapter. This staffing demand is also due to increased representation within the industry, with most firms expanding from what was initially just a Sydney–Melbourne structure to offices in the other capital cities. While Sydney in 1985 accounted for 59.7 per cent of all merchant banking staff, up from the 58.7 per cent figure shown in Table 18.2, this dominance should gradually decline as existing merchant banks open offices in other states. The opening of new merchant banks in Sydney and, to a lesser extent, Melbourne, should ensure that these cities continue together to account for almost 90 per cent of employees.

Given the potential for increased staff turnover, merchant banks now face the problem of whether to consider their own staff more as

Table 18.1 AMBA Merchant Bank Employee Numbers, 1980–85 (year ending 30 June)

Year	No. of Firms	No. of Employees	Percentage Increase	Average No. of Staff
1980	24	1 768	–	74
1981	25	2 402	35.86	92
1982	25	2 928	21.90	117
1983	26	3 372	15.16	130
1984	27	3 742	10.97	139
1985	28	4 073	8.85	145

Source: Australian Merchant Bankers Association, *Annual Report*, 1985, p. 21.

Table 18.2 AMBA Merchant Bank Employment by City, 30 June 1984

City	No. of Employees	No. of Firm Offices	Per cent of Total Staff
Sydney	2 195	27	58.7
Melbourne	1 104	27	29.5
Brisbane[a]	217	23	5.8
Adelaide	64	10	1.7
Perth	124	19	3.3
Other[b]	38	8	1.0
Total	**3 742**	**114**	**100.0**

Source: Australian Merchant Bankers Association, *Annual Report*, 1984, p. 5.
[a] Includes Townsville.
[b] Includes Hobart, Darwin, and Canberra.

temporary workers, soon to leave for greener pastures, or to try and encourage their current people to stay. Of course they have no choice for if a firm treats its employees as transient, they will almost certainly become so. The answer then is to try to retain quality people.

One means to keep key staff is to pay high salaries. As a result, merchant banking staff have experienced very good rises over recent years with, as shown in Table 18.3, double digit increases commonplace.

As suggested in Table 18.3, a large portion of these rises have not been in base salary but rather in a wide range of fringe benefits. Thus in 1985 a typical merchant banking remuneration package included at least a below market rate housing loan, a superannuation scheme, a potentially sizable annual bonus, a car and a 'hostess' or representation allowance.[2] The wide range of other fringe benefits commonly available as at March 1985 is shown in Table 18.4.

Table 18.3 Average Merchant Banker's Remuneration Increases, 1981–85 (percentage figures for the year ending 31 March)

	1980	1981	1982	1983	1984	1985
Base salary	12.9	15.3	16.9	13.0	7.4	9.5
Total cash	15.0	17.0	22.2	13.7	9.0	12.9
Total remuneration	16.7	17.0	31.6	16.2	7.9	13.4

Source: *Key Remuneration Issues for Financial Intermediaries*, Sydney: Cullen Egan Dell Australia, 16 July 1985, p. 1.4.

Note: The above percentages include only those employees who have remained in the same job with the same company from one year to the next.

Table 18.4 Merchant Bank Fringe Benefits by Type and Frequency, 1985

Benefit	Percentage of Companies
Vehicle	100
Home loan	100
Personal loan	56
Representation allowance	100
Expense reimbursement	65
Vehicle allowance	65
Club subscriptions	91
Professional associations	91
Other subscriptions	50
Telephone payments	91
Home working facilities	24
Employer superannuation	100
Additional superannuation	47
Deferred remuneration	6
Overseas travel	65
Local travel	56
Daily travel rate	18
Subsidized health insurance	41
Children's education	24
Spouse allowance	47
Bonus/incentive plan	50
Share plans	15
Offshore directorates	9

Source: *Key Remuneration Issues for Financial Intermediaries*, Sydney: Cullen Egan Dell Australia, 16 July 1985, p. 1.10.

Australia's taxation system was largely responsible for the growth in fringe benefits as most were a deductible expense for the employer but in many cases not taxable in the hands of the employee. From the employer's viewpoint, fringe benefits increased their employees' after-tax income at much less cost than a direct salary increase. This was particularly true as employee base salaries moved into higher and higher marginal tax brackets. Thus, as shown in Table 18.5, the larger the base salary level, the more such fringe benefits comprised an employee's total remuneration; the change around the $100 000 level reflects the importance of incentive payment schemes to key executives. Following the Treasurer, Paul Keating's 19 September 1985 announced tax measures on fringe benefits, some changes should be expected in their relative importance. Under his plan, entertainment expenses were no longer a deductible expense for taxation purposes after 19 September 1985 and the employers would be subjected (effective 1 July 1986) to an additional tax at the then

Table 18.5 Merchant Bank Fringe Benefits as a Percentage of Remuneration, 1985

Salary Group	Fringe Benefits as a Percentage of Total
Less than $20 000	21.2
$20 000 to less than $25 000	27.8
$25 000 to less than $30 000	32.7
$30 000 to less than $35 000	37.6
$35 000 to less than $40 000	37.1
$40 000 to less than $50 000	39.4
$50 000 to less than $60 000	40.7
$60 000 to less than $70 000	45.0
$75 000 to less than $100 000	43.9
$100 000 and above	34.5

Source: *Key Remuneration Issues for Financial Intermediaries*, Sydney. Cullen Egan Dell Australia, 16 July 1985, p. 1.6.

corporate tax raté on all non-cash fringe benefits provided to employees as well as payments to non-employees. Non-cash fringe benefits would still not be taxable in the employee's hands, but the employer would now effectively pay the tax. In other words, where the employer could previously deduct these benefits for tax purposes, many would no longer be deductible and be subject to an added tax as well. Thus, instead of costing 54 cents on each dollar spent (the after tax cost at the 46 per cent corporate tax rate), these benefits would cost $1.49 for every dollar provided.

Not too surprisingly, many employers have expressed concern over these fringe benefit and entertainment expenses changes and, while there is still some doubt whether the proposals will be fully implemented, some changes in the remuneration system can be expected; there will possibly be a greater reliance on performance-related bonuses and employer-funded (still deductible) superannuation. Until the various tax measures are put into law, most employers plan only nominal changes in their present remuneration packages, with the possible exception of entertainment allowances. Already, though, tax consultants are devising means (such as two-person luncheon seminars, expanded use of in-house dining facilities, and advertising in nearby business restaurants) to counter the loss of entertainment expenses and no doubt other fringe benefits may well be reconstructed in response to the end legislation.

Just as the level of fringe benefits differs as one rises up the salary scale, so the remuneration levels vary considerably depending on the person's area of expertise and the particular market demand for these services. Traditionally, as shown in Table 18.6, corporate finance executives have received the largest salary levels and this still remains the case. Indeed, in 1984 (see Table 18.7) corporate finance executives' salaries increased more than those for any other job category including that for senior management.

Though their average percentage increase over 1984 might have been low, not all chief executives were badly treated. Indeed, a survey of chief executive salaries at the end of 1984 found David Clarke, Chairman of what was then Hill Samuel Australia, reputed to be the highest paid within the industry with a salary package of $450 000 per year, up from only $250 000 in 1983. Chris Corrigan, then Managing Director of BT Australia, was similarly reported to

Table 18.6 Merchant Banking Remuneration by Position, 1983

	$
Chief Executive	120 000–250 000
Executive Director, Corporate Finance	90 000–150 000
Executive Director, Lending	70 000–150 000
Executive Director, Money Market	80 000–120 000
Executive Director, International	80 000–150 000
Senior Foreign Exchange Dealer	40 000–50 000
Foreign Exchange Manager	50 000–70 000
Trainee Money Market Dealer	17 000

Source: Helen Dalley, 'Money Men Lead Pack', *Australian Business*, 10 August 1983, p. 79.

Note: Figures exclude bonus payments.

Table 18.7 Merchant Bankers' Salary Increases, 1985 (year ending 31 March)

Job	Percentage Increase
Senior management	11.4
Corporate advice	19.2
Lending	10.5
Money market—domestic	11.9
Money market—international	13.6
Investment management	16.5
Accounting	13.3
Average increase	13.4

Source: Noble Lowndes Cullen Egan Dell, as cited in Peter Hartcher, 'Merchant bankers' pay rises outstrip the average', *Sydney Morning Herald*, 26 June 1985.

Note: Figures based on those employees occupying the same position this year as in the previous sample.

be earning \$450000, up from \$200000 in 1983. Third on the list was Tony Berg, then Hill Samuel's Managing Director, with \$350000, up from \$200000 in 1983. The other chief executives listed earned a meagre \$300000 or less.[3]

These salary levels need to be considered in light of the monies paid in other parts of industry. Another survey of the highest paid 125 executives in Australia, published in early 1984, found merchant bankers accounting for twenty-three or 18.3 per cent of the total. Significantly, of those executives listed in Table 18.8, only one Australian trading bank chief executive, Westpac Banking Corporation's Bob White (\$175000) was included. The other three, the ANZ Bank's John Milne (\$145000), National Australia's Jack Booth (\$125000), and the Commonwealth's Vern Christie (\$80572), had salaries reportedly too low to qualify a mention.[4]

Table 18.8 Merchant Bankers Among Australia's Top 125 Executives

Salary	Executive	Position	Firm
\$250000	David Clarke	Managing Director	Hill Samuel Australia
\$220000	David Block	Executive Director	Lloyds International Ltd
\$220000	Peter Mason	Executive Director	Lloyds International Ltd
\$200000	Tony Berg	Deputy Man. Dir.	Hill Samuel Australia Ltd
\$200000	Chris Corrigan	Managing Director	BT Australia Ltd
\$200000	Neil MacLachlan	Managing Director	Wardley Australia Ltd
\$200000	Arthur Charles	Executive Director	Lloyds International Ltd
\$200000	Tony Parkes	Executive Director	Lloyds International Ltd
\$200000	James Graham	Managing Director	Rothschild Australia Ltd
\$190000	Bill Gurry	Managing Director	Capel Court Corp. Ltd
\$180000	Rob Ferguson	Deputy Man. Dir.	BT Australia Ltd
\$180000	Paul Espie	Managing Director	BA Australia Ltd
\$170000	Graeme Samuel	Executive Director	Hill Samuel Australia Ltd
\$170000	James Yonge	Executive Director	Wardley Australia Ltd
\$170000	Tony McGrath	Executive Director	Wardley Australia Ltd
\$160000	Bill Moyle	Managing Director	First National Ltd
\$160000	Olev Rahn	Executive Director	BT Australia Ltd
\$160000	Barry Brownjohn	Executive Director	BA Australia Ltd
\$160000	John Ormandy	Managing Director	Societe Generale Australia Ltd
\$160000	John Tomkins	Executive Director	Wardley Australia Ltd
\$160000	Ken Mackay	Executive Director	Wardley Australia Ltd
\$160000	John Mitchell	Chief Executive	Lloyds International Ltd
\$150000	Brian Gatfield	Chief Executive	Schroder Darling and Co.

Source: 'Top Executives What They Earn', *Australian Business*, 15 February 1984, pp. 34–6.

Note: The survey listing included direct salary and other payments but excluded superannuation and retirement benefits.

The point is that top merchant bankers already receive among the top salaries within Australian finance. It is perhaps then not so surprising that it is not simply the salary or package size that has influenced many recent staff changes. Of equal, if not greater importance, are non-financial matters such as increased responsibilities, exposure to new areas, prestige, and frankly just a greater challenge.[5]

While delegation of authority has always been a key facet of successful merchant banking, some executives would like to broaden their exposure and take a greater part in their firm's overall operations. One means to retain top executives, then, is to provide board of director positions either on the firm's overall holding company or on subsidiaries.

Keeping one's chief executives, however, is just part of the staffing problem. Pressures at the lower levels have forced changes there too. For example, when merchant banks were first established, many relied mainly on experts serving on secondment from their parent shareholders. Many older consortium merchant banks relied fairly heavily on seconded staff up until fairly recently. Australian European Finance Corp., for example, only began hiring staff on the open market in 1984; secondments from the Commonwealth Bank and other shareholders had previously provided the bulk of their professional people.

Another industry response to these staffing pressures has been to change merchant bank attitudes towards recruitment. At one time, it was unusual for a new graduate to be hired by a merchant bank, an honours graduate in finance being the possible exception. This policy, however, has changed in recent years with some merchant banks conducting campus interviews and virtually all firms interviewing at least some students approaching them directly. This in turn has produced management trainee programmes and it is interesting to see the difference in approach between firms. BT Australia, for example, places new graduates in a functional area for at least eighteen months before reassigning them. In contrast, Barclays' trainees first spend three weeks in each division to get a feel for the firm's overall operations and then receive a six-month training period within each.[6] Most others also ensure exposure to the firm as a whole but leave the time-frame for discussion.

Overseas hirings is another source of merchant bank staffing actively being considered. Australia has traditionally paid well compared with its Commonwealth counterparts and on that basis may be able to attract experienced foreign personnel. In 1984, for example, a senior foreign exchange dealer in London earned around

$45 000 per year, while someone with the same qualifications in Australia received $80 000 to $90 000 a year.[7] In support of such hirings, the Australian Merchant Bankers Association has requested special government consideration in employer-nominated immigration visas, temporary visas, and extensions of existing temporary visas. The Australian Merchant Bankers Association has subsequently obtained approval for a Group Employer Nomination Scheme which allows more liberal immigration treatment for importing the foreign staff necessary for the industry's new foreign exchange and potential banking licences. Indeed, AMBA lobbying efforts over 1984–85 resulted in 46 migration places, 55 temporary residents, and 24 extensions of temporary resident permits.[8]

Such importation will certainly be helpful but overall should do relatively little towards offsetting the industry's current salary pressures. Staff shortages were already a problem before the granting of over forty foreign exchange licences fostered a major demand for dealers. The recent licensing of sixteen new trading banks will further add to the competition. All Australian-born chief executives of these new entries (as of May 1985) were at one time Australian merchant bank executives. In the long term, competition may eventually force some long-awaited rationalization within the industry and in the process put a damper on further salary rises, but there will always continue to be a strong demand for good people, and at the higher levels merchant banking salaries will continue to reflect this.

Though not really a part of the industry's staffing problems, some mention should be made of the union movement within merchant banking. As yet unions have not had a major impact on the merchant banking industry, but as the industry itself continues to grow in numbers so will the pressures for union recognition. At present the major pressure from the union side is from the Australian Bank Employees Union and the Federated Clerks' Union. In August 1984, for example, the Australian Bank Employees Union served a log of claims on the industry to establish a new Bank Official (Merchant Banks) Award which would cover all merchant bank staff. Rationally, given the employees' salary success to date, it seems doubtful that many professional staff would wish union representation and by the very nature of their work, the support staff are more appropriately covered under the Federated Clerks' awards.

In conclusion, staffing remains a problem and at least for the immediate future, shows no sign of being resolved. The large number of new merchant banks as well as the new trading banks should ensure that an active market remains for finance industry staff over at least 1986–87. One problem, though, for those seeking larger

Table 18.9 Selected Merchant Bank Staff Size by Firm, 1984

Firm	Total Staff
ABN Australia Ltd	32
All-State Capital	50
AMP Securities	120
Amro Australia	47
AUC	150
Aust. Eur. Fin. Corp.	113
Aust. Int. Fin. Corp.	140
Australis Securities	40
BA Australia	195
Banque Bruxelles Lamb.	35
Barclays Australia	142
Baring Bros Halkerston	14
Bill Acceptance Corp.	60
Boston Financial	88
BOT Australia Ltd	25
BT Australia	159
Capel Court Corp.	200
CCF Australia	24
Chemical All-State	110
CIBC Australia Ltd	80
Citicorp Cap. Markets	140
Commercial Continental	76
Delfin-BNY Acceptances	15
Development Fin. Corp.	299
Dominguez Barry Sam. Mont.	120
Elder's Finance & Invest	170
Euro-Pacific Finance	78
European Asian of Aust.	50
First Chicago Australia	39
First National	147
French Australian Fin.	37
Grindlays Australia Ltd	35
Hambros Australia	45
Indosuez Australia	60
Intersuisse-ADF	8
Japan Australia Invest.	10
Kleinwort Benson Aust.	79
Lloyds International	209
Macquarie Acceptances	300
Marac Investments Aust.	120
Midland Inter. Aust.	65
Mitchell NBD	21
Morgan Grenfell Aust.	56
Morgan Guaranty Aust.	133
NCNB Spedley	2

Table 18.9 (cont.)

Firm	Total Staff
NZI Securities Aust.	48
Partnership Pacific	169
PNC Inter. Fin.–Aust.	10
RBC Australia Ltd	45
Rothschild Australia	90
SBC Australia Ltd	29
Scandinavian Pacific Ltd	21
Schroder Darling	140
Security Pacific Aust.	58
Societe Generale Aust.	104
Spedley Securities	26
Standard Chartered Aust.	95
Sumitomo Perpetual Aust.	18
Trans City Holdings	130
Tricontinental	200
Wardley Australia	246

Source: Correspondence and discussions with respective firms.

salaries is that high remuneration can continue only as long as the respective staff members more than cover their costs. The present state of competition alone makes it questionable whether all employees will do so and, with the large number of competitors expected over 1986, there will be even more doubts in the future. Initially, employers may be willing to absorb any differences in an attempt to establish market share, but this process cannot be continued for very long.

19 The Campbell and Martin Reports

A review of the Australian financial sector was conducted, starting in 1979, by the Committee of Inquiry into the Australian Financial System (the Campbell Committee)[1] and then again in 1983–84 by a Review Group on the Australian Financial System (the Martin Review Group).[2] During these deliberations each of Australia's various financial institutions, markets, and instruments was examined and then evaluated in the light of each Committee's terms of reference. The end product in both cases was a report of the findings together with recommendations for improving the system.

THE CAMPBELL REPORT

With the first review of the financial sector for forty-three years, the Campbell Committee understandably received submissions from a wide range of individual financial institutions, professional bodies, government departments, academics, and business people. Australia's merchant banks were no exception and most major firms prepared their own written submissions and gave oral evidence before the Committee as well as assisting the Australian Merchant Bankers Association in its submissions. While the AMBA's initial and subsequent submissions obviously dealt with matters specific to merchant banking, the general emphasis was much broader, with a large number of the AMBA recommendations concerned with improving the financial sector's operations as a whole rather than just the merchant banking industry. Its basic recommendations, at least partially impacting on the industry, are shown in Table 19.1.

Given the number of submissions and the time spent by merchant bankers before the Committee together with the industry's past record of significant market innovations within Australia, one might have expected the Final Report to have included a number of recommendations, if not comments on, the industry's operations. Merchant banks, though, hardly received a mention. Indeed, the

Table 19.1 AMBA Submission to the Campbell Committee: A Summary of Recommendations

- That there be less use by the authorities of direct controls and more reliance on open market operations.
- That all deposit-taking institutions be supervised by the Reserve Bank as the one appropriate authority.
- That Australian foreign exchange markets be developed and the Reserve Bank achieve its exchange rate objectives through market intervention.
- That anomalous tax provisions of the capital markets be amended.
- That restrictions on foreign investment be reviewed.
- That present arrangements relating to the Loan Council be altered.
- That borrowing by major semi-government authorities be on a competitive basis with other public and private sector securities.
- That the extent and frequency of economic and financial information and commentary available to the public from the public sector be improved.

Source: Australian Merchant Bankers Association, *Annual Report*, 1980, p. 7.

only discussion specially on the industry—on page 328—accounts for a grand total of seventy-nine words in an 838-page report:

19.255   Merchant banks and like institutions do not ordinarily take deposits from unsophisticated investors, and are not subject to regulation. However, in recent times, some merchant banks have shown a greater willingness to accept deposits from individual investors. In future, if they solicit small deposits, merchant banks should be subject to the proposed non-bank regulatory framework or issue a prospectus. If, on the other hand, they deal only in 'wholesale' markets, the Committee sees no need for prudential regulations.[3]

It would be an understatement to suggest that merchant bankers were surprised by this treatment (or lack of it). As one complained, 'dinosaurs get more copy in Encyclopaedia Brittanica and they have been extinct for 70 million years'.[4] While the AMBA was perhaps more diplomatic, characterizing the Final Report as 'a logical progression toward the marketing and provision of efficient financial services to the under community',[5] it did note that the Report 'has failed to perceive the significance of the merchant banks' in the financial system.[6] Possibly the industry should have been flattered by this marked lack of attention and taken the view that whereas the Committee had found many potential improvements for other financial institutions, merchant banks were already operating efficiently and hence required no changes.

If the Campbell Report had little to say concerning merchant banks directly, many of its recommendations, as shown in Table 19.2, if adopted, would nevertheless have had a decisive impact on the industry.

Many have since interpreted that the key message from Campbell

Table 19.2 Selected Campbell Committee Final Report Recommendations

- Remove direct interest rate controls from the Banking Act and Financial Corporations Act.
- Remove exchange controls.
- License domestic institutions as trading banks so long as they are of sound standing.
- Restrict new foreign participation Australian banking only by the number of licences granted.
- Banking licences issued to non-residents should carry no different requirements than those held by residents.
- No direct controls on size or growth of lending nor any restrictions on deposit-taking by banks, building societies, credit unions and other deposit-takers.
- Allow exchange rates to be determined by market forces.
- Remove captive market arrangements for financial institutions to hold Government securities or to provide funds to Federal Government or its agencies at less than market rates of interest.
- Provide greater protection for investors and depositors with financial institutions primarily through improved financial and other market information and compliance with prudential controls.

Source: *Australian Financial System: Final Report of the Committee of Inquiry*, Canberra: Australian Government Publishing Service, 1981.

to the merchant banking industry was that there would be two types of financial institutions in a post-Campbell financial sector—those institutions that were banks and those that were not. By also recommending the removal of many past restrictions on new bank entry, those merchant banks who wished to have trading bank status could then apply. Given the level of deregulation proposed, there would be little other choice; the banks would be freed of the bulk of their then restraints but maintain their advantages in terms of the foreign exchange market and the payments system. Unfortunately, at the government level increased foreign participation in the banking sector remained a potential political problem and one which the then government preferred to minimize by allowing entry on a very restricted basis. Thus, where the Campbell Report argued that its various measures should be implemented in a package form, the government opted for a piecemeal approach which allowed trading banks considerable new freedoms but did not allow other institutions the same access to banking licences as Campbell had recommended. Such a strategy was obviously not appreciated by the merchant banking industry and, as it commented on this process in 1981, 'deregulation, without a concomitant increase in competition, is not consistent with the concept of competitive neutrality proposed by the Campbell Committee'.[7]

While the Campbell Committee hearings had already resulted in a number of deregulation measures, a change of government at the federal level in March 1983 postponed any further implementations. Instead, given the political implications of many Campbell recommendations, the new government appointed its own committee to review the Campbell recommendations with regard to 'the government's economic and social objectives, and the need to improve the efficiency of the financial system'.[8] The Committee, headed by a former banking executive, Victor Martin, did not hold public hearings like the Campbell Committee nor did it call for submissions. Nevertheless most major financial institutions made submissions of one kind or another.

Given Mr Martin's past comments to the Campbell Committee and his former long association with the banking industry, most non-bank financial institutions as well as foreign banks generally expected that his report would contain a number of unfavourable recommendations. Though his Final Report did not single out the non-banking sector for special treatment, it did not present a very optimistic future for non-banking institutions. As one observer complained: 'Martin recognises two classes of financial institutions, the banks: solid, good and reliable, decent and desirable; and the motley group of others who needed to be treated with suspicion.'[9]

Most of the Report's recommendations greatly improved the existing banking industry's ability to compete, while at the same time restricting new entries and hence competition. Indeed, as one writer complained, the Martin Report

puts no pressure on the Australian financial system to become competitive, there is no incentive for reform. It is a triumph for the status quo. As well it is a triumph for the major entities of that system, the banks. As the managing director of Westpac, Bob White, stated 'I couldn't have written it better myself'.[10]

While Mr White was pleased, most merchant bankers were not. The Martin Report did not ignore the merchant banks, as did Campbell, and even had some kind words regarding their talents in 'innovations and expertise, especially in corporate financing and international financial services'.[11] The Report also suggested the industry would survive the lifting of the then interest prohibition on trading bank deposits of less than fourteen days. The merchant banks'

capacity to compete with the banks would still be maintained ... by the banks remaining subject to more stringent prudential and other regulatory restraints. Moreover, merchant banks generally provide services (foreign-exchange related services, corporate advice, etc.) additional to the acceptance of deposits and the provision of funds. In the past merchant banks have shown great flexibility and an impressive capacity to innovate. The further they develop the range of services, the better placed they will be to counter any contraction in their role in financial intermediation.[12]

However, despite this brave future, that section closed with the chilling words that 'the Group acknowledges that structural adjustments may be necessary in this sector'.[13]

Martin predictions aside, of most concern to the merchant banking industry was the sudden change in emphasis from Campbell's full co-ordinated deregulation proposals to what appeared to be Martin's deregulation for the banks now and increased competition for them later (see Table 19.3). Even then, the Martin approach took a very restrictive view of new bank entry, greatly limiting the number of institutions as well as the degree of foreign ownership allowed. As one observer commented on the proposed new entries: 'operations would be constrained in several ways, leaving them unable to provide a significant competitive offset to the proposed new scope afforded the few large and powerful Australian banks.'[14] Another merchant banker was not so kind: as he commented on the foreign ownership question, it is 'difficult to understand the logic of limiting ownership to 50% for either foreign or domestic applicants'.[15] In any case the foreign ownership issue is fortunately now largely a moot point following the licensing of sixteen new foreign-affiliated trading banks, many of which are fully foreign-owned, and the lifting of most foreign investment limitations on the merchant banks themselves.[16]

Table 19.3 Selected Martin Review Group Recommendations

- Remove the 14- and 30-day rule restriction on bank deposits.
- Remove the 60 per cent limit on trading bank ownership of merchant banks.
- Give non-bank financial institutions access to the cheque clearing system.
- Do *not* proclaim Part IV of the Financial Corporations Act.
- Remove all interest rate controls on banks.
- Develop a secondary mortgage market.
- Grant four to six banking licences through a one-off tender.
- Consider the possibility of additional foreign exchange dealers.
- Abolish remaining captive market requirements for financial institutions to hold government securities.
- Adopt a more flexible approach to foreign investment particularly for restructuring present ownership.

Source: *Australian Financial System: Report of the Review Group*, Canberra: Australian Government Publishing Service, 1984.

20 The Future

Since its establishment, Australian merchant banking has undergone many role changes. Conceived initially as investment bankers, Australian merchant banks gradually transformed their operations first into the money market, then offshore financing, de facto wholesale banking, and the foreign currency business. Recently, with the overseas and local banks expanding into these areas respectively, the industry is restructuring its operations yet again with a re-emphasis on its initial justification, that of investment banking. Some may question this new orientation and suggest that many of the current or planned market participants will have closed shop before the end of the decade. Certainly the future did seem grim following the Campbell Committee recommendations. Firms appeared to have Hobson's choice of either becoming a bank or quitting their Australian operations. Then the Martin Review Group's recommendations effectively closed the door to most bank entries. Thus as one writer in 1984 predicted, the industry was at 'the start of the biggest shake-out in the Australian finance industry since the Great Depression'.[1] Other comments, such as 'life won't just be tough for merchant bankers, it will be impossible', 'the era of merchant banking is just about over' or 'in five years most of the 41 companies on the list [a list of the then merchant banks] will have disappeared' would hardly have given merchant bankers cause for optimism.[2] To many, too, the recent authorization of sixteen foreign-affiliated trading banks has only confirmed this position, as has the Australian government's continued effort towards deregulation.

Perhaps not surprisingly the words 'doom and gloom' and 'rationalization' now feature prominently in short articles on the industry's future. Such dire predictions, though, are commonplace when considering the future of Australian merchant banks. As R.R. Hirst commented when writing on this topic in the early 1970s, 'it is claimed that the capital market is now over-banked and that the decade will see consolidation. The same predictions were made in 1960'.[3] There were then around forty-eight merchant banks in operation. There are now close to a hundred merchant banks in Australia and by mid-1986 some 120 will be either approved or operational. The expansion over 1984–85 has been such that, as one writer complained (with only some exaggeration), there are now 'something like 2 million merchant banks in Australia. Apart from sacred sites, Pierpont cannot think of any commodity which our nation possesses in such abundance'.[4] Like our sacred sites, most of these companies will still be here in the future. Those rationalizations that do occur will be a product of mergers or acquisitions at the parent bank level rather than any intentional merging of foreign-controlled merchant banks. Admittedly, some companies may be quite different operations than they are today but the numbers of merchant banks are not likely to decline. Indeed it is probable that there will be even more participants. The question to address then in looking at the industry's future is not whether merchant banks will continue to exist or which firms will remain, but rather the way in which these firms will operate.

In considering this future, the deregulation of Australia's trading banks will no doubt continue to be the most serious variable. The banks' freedom to pay interest on call deposits, gained on 1 August 1984, is still having its effects on both the wholesale and retail sides of the money market and matters are unlikely to stabilize until the newly-authorized trading banks have established their own operations in the market.

Since August 1984, the trading banks have been in direct competition for call and overnight deposits, deposits which were previously mainly merchant bank and authorized dealer money. Given their status in the market (due both to their financial power and Reserve Bank support) these institutions can certainly raise funds at lower rates than a merchant bank. However, to date this advantage has not been as large as expected, with the merchant bank generally paying around 0.5 to 0.75 per cent more in per annum terms than a trading bank for the same deposit. Furthermore, this advantage is in turn more than offset by the trading bank's need to place 7 per cent of its deposits in Reserve Bank SRD accounts earning only 5 per cent and to keep 12 per cent of its overall liabilities (used to finance Australian dollar lending) in generally lower-earning prime assets. While up to 3 per cent of the SRD money can be counted against its prime asset requirements, it is not difficult to see that the slight rate advantage presently gained in trading bank funding would be more than offset by the loss of earnings on the SRD monies alone. The trading banks could, of course, always squeeze the merchant banks from the market by bidding up the rates, but paying interest on current accounts is a double-edged sword. By paying high rates trading banks can attract money which might otherwise have gone to the merchant banks or cash management trusts. However, the higher rates are just as likely to attract money from non-interest-bearing accounts within the bank itself. In time, these accounts will probably be replaced with a system of paying market rate interest and fully costing depositors' transactions, but for the present trading banks are still moving carefully. Again the new foreign entries will probably intensify the adjustment problem.

Also of significance in merchant bank deposit raisings is the use of parent company guarantees or letters of credit. In recent years, Boston Australia, Wardley, and, most recently, BT Australia, among others, have issued money market securities with such backing. The ability to fund their local lending on the offshore market, again with parent-company support, has also raised funds on terms comparable to their banking counterparts who of course, if used in Australia, must keep at least 12 per cent in prime assets. Within Australia, too, parent-bank guarantees over all borrowings are also becoming more common.

Thus as of late 1985 the major crisis had still not come and if anything merchant banks still have a slight advantage due to regulations: the supposed lower funding costs of the trading banks, due to their higher credit status, non-interest-bearing deposits, and the payments float, are no longer the same advantages as some initially perceived.[5] As one successful banking applicant admitted, 'as the regulations stand today, there are advantages to being a merchant bank'.[6] Some have even suggested that those firms who failed to gain a trading bank licence in 1985 were the winners and not the losers. As *Euromoney* commented, the 'first prize is a merchant bank; second prize is a commercial bank'.[7]

Whether this favourable position will continue, of course, is quite another matter. Already the margins on merchant bank acceptance business have dropped from 1.0 to less than 0.5 per cent and some firms have questioned the economics of writing business under these conditions. At least one firm, Schroder Australia, has already sold off its basic lending operations in order to concentrate on its securities trading and investment banking. Others, such as Dominguez Barry Samuel Montagu, Kleinwort Benson Australia, Morgan Grenfell Australia, and Wardley Australia, have all indicated a similar intention to restructure their operations more along US investment bank lines. The others to a lesser extent may follow but this, as one merchant bank predicts, 'is not to say merchant banks will vacate the corporate lending market'.[8] They will simply become more competitive and place even greater emphasis on financial product development and credit assessment in order to reverse the declining margins in more traditional areas.

In considering this new emphasis on investment banking the industry is better placed today than ever before for success. This is due to the consolidation of shareholdings leaving most merchant banks the wholly-owned subsidiary of a major international financial institution and, through the foreign exchange licence requirements, with a substantially larger paid-up capital. This improved financial stature will be important if these firms wish to be aggressive bidders for local underwritings. Most larger firms have already established ownership affiliations with local stockbrokers so that they can now compete both from outside and from within the stock exchange. These affiliations, which are likely to become eventual mergers, have the further advantage of consolidating corporate advisory work where previously such brokers had been competitors.

In conclusion, then, far from a bleak outlook, Australian merchant banks face an exciting future where all their talents for innovation and resiliency will be tested as never before. In the process, however, this competitive pressure in itself should go a long way towards ensuring the industry's survival. Few, if any, players will quit the field entirely but the industry of the late 1980s will be structured somewhat differently than before. The market could easily have as many as six tiers. The first category would still probably be those merchant banks owned by the four major trading banks as their parents' branch structure and financial standing will continue to provide them with a fairly important advantage at least for the next few years. The next category, of course, are those newly-authorized foreign-affiliated trading banks which chose to restrict their business to much the same services they provided while merchant banks. It is impossible at present to know which banks will actually adopt such policies. Deutsche Bank and Morgan Australia, however, have both indicated a preference for merchant banking styled business and it is difficult to imagine firms like BT Australia or Lloyds leaving an otherwise profitable business in favour of retail banking. Third will be the merchant banking operations of those newly-licensed foreign trading banks planning a strong retail orientation such as Bank of America Australia, Chase AMP, Citibank, and National Mutual Royal Bank. The fourth tier will be those merchant banks wholly owned by a sizable foreign financial institution and active in most aspects of the industry. The fifth category will be those few remaining (if any) foreign consortium ventures or largely locally-owned, non-bank-affiliated companies, and the last grouping would comprise those foreign-owned merchant banks serving mainly as the operational arm of their parent banks' Australian representative office. So rather than our present three layers of merchant banks (local trading-bank-affiliated, foreign-bank-affiliated, and others), the industry will become even more segmented. This should encourage even greater specialization and product development than in the past and through this competition ensure that Australian merchant banks continue as the innovators of Australian finance.

Appendix I
Financial Corporations Act Form 4

FORM 4　　　　　　　　　　　　　　　Regulation 6

COMMONWEALTH OF AUSTRALIA

Financial Corporations Act 1974

MONEY MARKET CORPORATION PERIODICAL STATEMENT OF FINANCIAL OPERATIONS, ASSETS, SELECTED LIABILITIES AND INTEREST RATES

AS AT......./......./19.......

NAME OF REGISTERED CORPORATION..

GENERAL DIRECTIONS

1. For the purposes of preparing this statement
   (a) where registered corporations are related to other registered corporations included in the category Money Market Corporations, *do not* include transactions, or any assets or liabilities arising directly from transactions, between those corporations in this form.
   (b) a reference to a bank is to be read as a reference to—
       (i) a bank within the meaning of the *Banking Act 1959*; or
       (ii) a bank constituted by a State Act;
   (c) a reference to a contingent asset is to be read as a reference to an asset which would, on the happening of a future event that may or may not happen, become an asset of the corporation making this statement;
   (d) a reference to a statistical period shall be read as a reference to the first statistical period, or a successive statistical period, as the case requires, within the meaning of regulation 6;
   (e) a reference to a resident is to be read as a reference to—
       (i) a person, not being a body corporate, who is ordinarily resident in Australia; or
       (ii) a body corporate that is incorporated in Australia;
   (f) where a body corporate that is a resident has a place of business outside Australia, the body corporate shall be deemed not to be resident in relation to the affairs of the body corporate conducted by the body corporate at or through that place of business, including any business carried on, transactions entered into and acts and things done by the body corporate at or through that place of business;
   (g) where a body corporate that is not a resident has a place of business in Australia, the body corporate shall be deemed to be a resident in relation to the affairs of the body corporate conducted by the body corporate at or through that place of business, including any business carried on, transactions entered into and acts and things done by the body corporate at or through that place of business;
   (h) the question whether corporations are related to each other shall be determined in the same manner as the question whether corporations are related to each other is determined under the *Companies Act 1981*.

2. All amounts entered in this statement are to be expressed in Australian currency. If an amount in respect of an overseas line of credit or in respect of an asset or liability realizable or payable in a currency other than Australian currency is to constitute or be included in any amount entered in an item in the statement, the value of the line of credit, asset or liability is to be included in the statement at the equivalent in Australian currency calculated at the rate of exchange used in

233

determining the value of the line of credit, asset or liability for the accounts of the corporation as those accounts stood at the end of the statistical period.

3. For the purpose of completing this statement—
   (a) an amount that would, but for this direction, be shown as an amount of less than $500, shall be disregarded;
   (b) an amount that would, but for this direction, be shown as an odd multiple of $500, shall be shown to the next succeeding multiple of $1,000; and
   (c) other amounts shall be shown to the nearest $1,000.

4. A reference in Part I, II, III, IV, V or VI to a direction shall be read as a reference to a special direction.

5. Separate copies of this statement are to be furnished to the Reserve Bank of Australia, Sydney and the Australian Bureau of Statistics, Canberra.

STATUTORY DECLARATION

I..of...
                    (Name of officer)   (Residential address of officer)

in the..do solemnly and sincerely declare:
            (State or Territory)   (Occupation)

1. that I am the...of...
                (Description of office)   (Name of corporation)

2. that the Periodical Statement of Financial Operations, Assets, Selected Liabilities and Interest Rates dated......../......../........, and lodged herewith, has been prepared in accordance with the directions contained in that statement and is to the best of my knowledge and belief a true statement of the assets, liabilities, financial operations and interest rates of the corporation(s) in respect of which the statement is made as those assets, liabilities, operations and interest rates are shown in the books, accounts and records of the corporation(s).

And I make this solemn declaration by virtue of the *Statutory Declarations Act 1959* and subject to the penalties provided by that Act for the making of false statements in statutory declarations conscientiously believing the statements contained in this declaration to be true in every particular.

....
(Signature of declarant)

Declared at .... the .... day of .... 19........

Before me..

Title...

(A Justice of the Peace or other person before whom a statutory declaration may be made under section 8 of the *Statutory Declarations Act 1959*)

PART I FINANCIAL OPERATIONS

$'000

1. COMMITMENTS TO RESIDENTS (OTHER THAN TO RELATED CORPORATIONS) TO PROVIDE FINANCE INCLUDING COMMITMENTS TO DISCOUNT BILLS OF EXCHANGE (Direction 1)
   (1) Net change during the period (Direction 2)   . . . .
   (2) Lending commitments remaining unused at end of period (Direction 3)   .   ...

2. COMMITMENTS REMAINING UNUSED AT END OF PERIOD TO ACCEPT/ENDORSE BILLS OF EXCHANGE AS PART OF ACCOMMODATION FACILITIES (Direction 4)   . . . .

3. BORROWING LINES AND STANDBY FACILITIES AVAILABLE TO THE CORPORATION AT END OF PERIOD (Direction 5)
   (1) Total (used and unused) made available by:
       (a) Residents   . . . .
       (b) Non-residents   . . . .
   (2) Unused:
       (a) Made available by residents—
           (i) Related corporations that are not banks   . . . .

      (ii) Banks (Direction 6) . . . .
      (iii) Other . . . .
    (b) Made available by non-residents . . . .

4. BILL (ACCEPTANCE/ENDORSEMENT) LINES AVAILABLE TO THE CORPORATION UNDER ACCOMMODATION FACILITIES AT END OF PERIOD (Direction 7)
    (1) Total (used and unused) made available . . . .
    (2) Unused available from:
      (a) Banks . . . .
      (b) Other . . . .

PART II SELECTED LIABILITIES

5. BORROWINGS FROM RESIDENTS (Direction 8)
    (1) Borrowings by the corporation's acceptance of bills of exchange and the issue of promissory notes (Direction 9) . . . .
    (2) Other borrowings from:
      (a) Related corporations that are not banks—
        (i) Registered under the *Financial Corporations Act 1974* . . . .
        (ii) Other . . . .
      (b) Banks—
        (i) Bank accepted bills of exchange (Direction 10) . . . .
        (ii) Other . . . .
      (c) Other . . . .

6. BORROWINGS FROM NON-RESIDENTS . . . .

7. LIABILITIES ARISING FROM THE ACCEPTANCE OF BILLS OF EXCHANGE UNDER ACCOMMODATION FACILITIES (Contra item 17) . . . .

PART III ASSETS (Direction 11)

8. CASH AND BANK DEPOSITS
    (1) Certificates of deposit:
      (a) Negotiable . . . .
      (b) Other . . . .
    (2) Cash and other bank deposits . . . .

9. PLACEMENTS WITH AUTHORISED DEALERS IN THE SHORT TERM MONEY MARKET . . . .

10. OTHER PLACEMENTS AND DEPOSITS (Direction 12)
    (1) Related corporations:
      (a) Registered under the *Financial Corporations Act 1974* . . . .
      (b) Other . . . .
    (2) Other corporations registered under the *Financial Corporations Act 1974*:
      (a) Money market corporations . . . .
      (b) Other . . . .
    (3) Other businesses . . . .

11. BILLS OF EXCHANGE PURCHASED AND HELD (Direction 13)
    (1) Bank accepted/endorsed:
      (a) Public authorities (Direction 14) . . . .
      (b) Corporations registered under the *Financial Corporations Act 1974* (Direction 15) . . . .
      (c) Other . . . .
    (2) Other:
      (a) Public authorities (Direction 14) . . . .
      (b) Bills accepted by corporations registered under the *Financial Corporations Act 1974* . . . .
      (c) Other . . . .

12. PROMISSORY NOTES PURCHASED AND HELD (Direction 16)
    (1) Public authorities (Direction 14) . . . .

     (2) Corporations registered under the *Financial Corporations Act 1974* . . ..

     (3) Other . . . .

13. OTHER GOVERNMENT AND PUBLIC AUTHORITY SECURITIES
    (Direction 17)

     (1) Treasury notes . . . .

     (2) Other Commonwealth Government securities . . . .

     (3) Other . . . .

14. OTHER SECURITIES (Direction 18)

     (1) Shares:

        (a) Related corporations . . . .

        (b) Other corporations . . . .

     (2) Other securities:

        (a) Related corporations . . . .

        (b) Other businesses . . . .

15. FINANCE LEASE RECEIVABLES (Direction 19)

     (1) Leveraged lease (Direction 20) . . . .

     (2) Other (Direction 21) . . . .

16. LOAN OUTSTANDINGS (Direction 22)

     (1) Related corporations:

        (a) Registered under the *Financial Corporations Act 1974* . . . .

        (b) Other . . . .

     (2) Other corporations registered under the *Financial Corporations Act 1974* ....

     (3) Individuals (Direction 23) . . . .

     (4) Other loans and advances . . . .

17. CLIENTS' COMMITMENTS ARISING FROM THE ACCEPTANCE
BY THE CORPORATION OF BILLS OF EXCHANGE UNDER
ACCOMMODATION FACILITIES (Contra item 7) . . . .

18. OTHER ASSETS IN AUSTRALIA . . . .

19. OVERSEAS ASSETS . . . .

20. TOTAL ASSETS . . . .

PART IV   INTEREST RATES

21. BORROWING RATES (Direction 24)

Term to maturity	Value of funds received $'000	Weighted average interest rate (per cent per annum)
(1) At call and up to 24 hours	....	
(2) Exceeding 24 hours but not exceeding 7 days	....	
(3) Exceeding 7 days but not exceeding 3 months	....	

22. BASE LENDING RATE APPLICABLE TO A TERM LOAN ON THE
SECOND LAST WORKING DAY OF THE PERIOD (NOMINAL
INTEREST RATE PER CENT PER ANNUM) . . . .

PART V MATURITY DISSECTION OF BORROWINGS, LOAN OUTSTANDINGS AND
SELECTED SECURITIES AT END OF PERIOD

$'000

23. BORROWINGS FROM RESIDENTS (OTHER THAN BORROWINGS
FROM RELATED CORPORATIONS) CLASSIFIED BY PERIOD OF
NOTICE FOR WITHDRAWAL, OR REMAINING PERIOD TO
MATURITY WHERE A MATURITY DATE IS SPECIFIED

     (1) At call and up to 24 hours . . . .

     (2) Exceeding 24 hours but not exceeding 7 days . . . .

     (3) Exceeding 7 days but not exceeding 3 months . . . .

     (4) Exceeding 3 months but not exceeding 1 year . . . .

(5) Exceeding 1 year . . . .

Total of item 23 (Direction 25) . . . .

24. BILLS OF EXCHANGE AND PROMISSORY NOTES PURCHASED AND HELD CLASSIFIED BY REMAINING PERIOD TO MATURITY

(1) Not exceeding 1 month . . . .
(2) Exceeding 1 month but not exceeding 3 months . . . .
(3) Exceeding 3 months but not exceeding 6 months . . . .
(4) Exceeding 6 months . . . .

Total of item 24 (Direction 26) . . . .

25. OTHER PLACEMENTS AND DEPOSITS (OTHER THAN WITH RELATED CORPORATIONS), FINANCE LEASE RECEIVABLES AND LOAN OUTSTANDINGS (OTHER THAN TO RELATED CORPORATIONS) CLASSIFIED BY REMAINING PERIOD TO MATURITY

(1) Not exceeding 1 month . . . .
(2) Exceeding 1 month but not exceeding 3 months . . . .
(3) Exceeding 3 months but not exceeding 1 year . . . .
(4) Exceeding 1 year but not exceeding 3 years . . . .
(5) Exceeding 3 years . . . .

Total of item 25 (Direction 27) . . . .

PART VI SELECTED LIABILITIES AND ASSETS AT END OF PERIOD
ONLY TO BE COMPLETED FOR THE MONTHS OF SEPTEMBER, DECEMBER, MARCH AND JUNE

26. SHAREHOLDERS' FUNDS AND SUBORDINATED LOANS . . . .

27. BORROWINGS FROM RESIDENTS (OTHER THAN BORROWINGS FROM RELATED CORPORATIONS) AT END OF PERIOD

(1) Secured over assets of the corporation . . . .
(2) Unsecured . . . .

Total of item 27 (Direction 25) . . . .

28. LOAN OUTSTANDINGS (OTHER THAN TO RELATED CORPORATIONS AND INDIVIDUALS) AT END OF PERIOD

(1) That involve or make provision for the issuing of bills of exchange . . . .
(2) Other . . . .

Total of item 28 (Direction 28) . . . .

COMMENTS: Please provide any comments which you consider would assist in interpreting the information supplied in this statement.

_____

_____

_____

_____

_____

_____

_____

Please nominate the officer to be contacted if any queries arise regarding this statement

Name .... Position ....

STD Code .... Telephone No. ....

SPECIAL DIRECTIONS—

1. Include commitments to provide finance that involve or make provision for the issuing of bills of exchange.

2. Show the amounts by which total existing commitments were increased or decreased during the period, and the amount of new commitments made during the period.

3. Include the amount of loan commitments to the extent to which the loan moneys have not been disbursed, and the amount of bill discount facilities to the extent that they have not been drawn upon.

4. Include the amount of facilities made available by the corporation for the acceptance or endorsement of bills of exchange *only* where the arrangements under which the facilities are made available do not involve a commitment by the corporation to provide finance.

5. (1) Include all borrowing lines and standby facilities that involve arrangements to provide finance to the corporation for use in its business in Australia.
   (2) Include all lines which involve commitments to discount bills of exchange, even where such bills are also part of acceptance/endorsement lines available to the corporation.
   (3) Do not include lines that *only* involve commitments to provide accommodation facilities to the corporation. Such facilities should be included in item 4.

6. Include overdrafts *only* to the extent that they have not been drawn upon.

7. Include all lines that involve arrangements by banks or others to provide accommodation facilities to the corporation. Facilities that also involve commitments to discount bills of exchange should be excluded from item 4 and included in item 3.

8. (1) Include interest which has been capitalised.
   (2) Do not include interest that has accrued on borrowings but is not yet paid.

9. Include all bills of exchange payable by the corporation except—
   (a) bills accepted by the corporation and held by it; and
   .(b) bills that have been accepted on behalf of customers under accommodation facilities (liabilities arising from accommodation facilities are to be included in item 7).

10. Include borrowings made by the issue of bills of exchange drawn by the corporation and accepted by a bank.

11. (1) Include *only* the value of assets in Australia in the amounts entered in items 8 to 18 (inclusive).
    (2) Do not include contingent assets.
    (3) Do not include unearned income.
    (4) Corporations that include in their accounts interest that has accrued but is not yet received are to exclude that interest from the amounts entered in items 8 to 17 (inclusive) but are to include it in the amount entered in item 18.

12. Do not include the following, which should be reported in specific items elsewhere—
    (a) deposits with banks;
    (b) placements with authorised dealers in the short term money market;
    (c) holdings of securities issued by government or public authorities;
    (d) moneys payable to the corporation on bills of exchange or promissory notes; and
    (e) holdings of securities such as debentures and unsecured notes.

13. Do not include—
    (a) the amounts of bills held in respect of which the corporation is the acceptor;
    (b) the amounts of bills held where the corporation is the drawer (the amounts of these bills are to be included in the amounts entered in item 16); and
    (c) bills of exchange lodged with the corporation as collateral by a borrower (transactions where the corporation contracts to sell back the securities lodged with the corporation as collateral by a borrower should be treated as loans, and the amounts entered in item 16).

14. Include public marketing authorities with public authorities.

15. Include *only*—
    (a) bills of exchange drawn by registered corporations where they are accepted by a bank; and
    (b) bills of exchange accepted by registered corporations and endorsed by a bank.

16. Do not include promissory notes lodged with the corporation as collateral by a borrower. Transactions where the corporation contracts to sell back the securities lodged with the corporation as collateral by a borrower should be treated as loans, and the amounts entered in item 16.

17. (1) Include securities mortgaged by the corporation as collateral for its borrowings.
    (2) Do not include securities lodged with the corporation as collateral by a borrower. Transactions where the corporation contracts to sell back the securities lodged with the corporation as collateral by a borrower should be treated as loans, and the amounts entered in item 16.

(3)   Do not include bills of exchange and promissory notes issued by public authorities.

18.   Include all forms of securities not elsewhere included and shares of all kinds.

19.   (1)   Include amounts receivable by the corporation as lessor under finance lease agreements (including partnership lease agreements).

   (2)   Finance lease is the leasing or hiring of tangible assets under an agreement, other than a hire purchase agreement, which transfers from the lessor to the lessee substantially all the risks and benefits incident to ownership of the asset without transferring the legal ownership.

   (3)   Do not deduct provisions for doubtful debts. Provisions for doubtful debts should be deducted from item 18.

20.   (1)   Include *only* amounts receivable by the corporation to the extent of the corporation's equity participation in leveraged lease agreements.

   (2)   Do not include lease receivables under lease agreements for land and buildings except where land or buildings form part of a total package of assets included in a lease agreement.

21.   (1)   Include, as finance lease receivables, any residual value of the assets leased.

   (2)   Do not include lease receivables under lease agreements for land and buildings in this item.

22.   (1)   Include all assets arising from the provision of finance that are not elsewhere included.

   (2)   Include the amounts of loans that involve or make provisions for—

   (a)   the issuing of bills of exchange accepted by the corporation whether or not the bills have been sold; and

   (b)   the issuing of bills of exchange drawn and held by the corporation.

   (3)   Include all non-equity (i.e. debt) participation in leveraged lease agreements.

   (4)   Do not include amounts due from trade debtors for the sale of goods or the provision of services where payment in full for the goods or services is required before the expiration of 3 months from the day on which the contract for their sale or provision is entered into. These amounts are to be included in item 18.

   (5)   Do not deduct provisions for doubtful debts. Provisions for doubtful debts should be deducted from item 18.

23.   (1)   Do not include loans or advances made to finance the purchase of land for the purpose of sub-division. The amounts of these loans or advances are to be included in sub-item 16 (4).

   (2)   Do not include finance provided to an individual for use in connection with a business carried on by him. The amounts of such finance are to be included in sub-item 16 (4).

24.   For each of the terms to maturity specified show, for the second last working day of the period, the funds received by the corporation and the weighted average interest rate percent per annum for borrowings of the types described by sub-items 5 (1) and 5 (2) (b) and (c).

25.   The total of this item should equal the sum of sub-items 5 (1) and 5 (2) (b) and (c).

26.   The total of this item should equal the sum of items 11 and 12.

27.   The total of this item should equal the sum of sub-items 10 (2) and (3), 15 (1) and (2) and 16 (2), (3) and (4).

28.   The total of this item should equal the sum of sub-items 16 (2) and (4).

Appendix II
Selected Merchant Banks in Australia and their Shareholders, 1985

Merchant Bank	Shareholders
ABN Australia	100% Algemene Bank Nederland (Holland)
All-States Capital Group	100% All-States Holdings (Australia)
Allied Irish Australia	Allied Irish Bank (Ireland)
Amro Australia	100% Amsterdam-Rotterdam Bank (Holland)
ANZ Capital Market Corp. (Australian International) Finance Corp.)	100% ANZ Banking Group (Australia)
Arab Australia	100% Arab Bank (Jordan)
Australian European Finance Corp.	51% Commonwealth Bank of Australia
	19% Banque Nationale de Paris (France)
	15% Banca Nazionale del Lavoro (Italy)
	15% Dresdner Bank (Germany)
Australis Securities	% Australian Bank Ltd
BA Australia (Mercant. Bill Corp.)	100% Australian Bank Ltd (Aust.–USA)
Barclays Australia	100% Barclays International Australia (UK owned)
Barings Bros Halkerston & Partners	50% Baring Brothers & Co. (UK)
	25% K.W. Halkerston (Australia)
	25% M.D. Burrows (Australia)
BCC Australia	100% BCCI Holdings (Luxemburg)
BBL Australia	100% Banque Bruxelles Lambert (Belgium)

Bill Acceptance Corp.	100% Australian Guarantee Corp. (Australia)
BNP Pacific (Australia) (French-Australian Financial Corp.)	100% Banque Nationale de Paris (France)
BNS (Australia)	100% Bank of Nova Scotia (Canada)
BNZ International (Australia)	100% Bank of New Zealand (New Zealand)
Boston Australia (Boston Financial)	100% First National Bank of Boston (USA)
BOT Australia	100% Bank of Tokyo (Japan)
BT Australia	100% Banker Trust Co. (USA)
BYN Australia	100% Bank of New York (USA)
Capel Court Corporation	100% National Mutual Royal Bank (Aust.–USA)
Cathay Finance	100% Commercial Bank of China (Taiwan)
Credit Commercial de France (Australia) (CCF Australia)	100% Credit Commercial de France (France)
Chase AMP Capital Markets (AMP Acceptances)	100% Chase AMP Bank (Australia–USA)
Chemical Australia (Chemical All-States)	100% Chemical Bank of New York (USA)
CIBC Australia (Martin Corporation)	100% Canadian Imperial Bank of Commerce
Citicorp Capital Markets Australia	100% Citibank Limited (US owned)
County Australia Holdings	100% National Westminster Australia Bank (UK owned)
Credit Lyonnais Australia	100% Credit Lyonnais (France)
Dia-Ichi Kangyo Australia (Japan Australia Acceptances)	100% Dia-Ichi Kangyo Bank (Japan)
Daiwa ANZ International	50% ANZ Bank (Australia) 30% Daiwa Securities (Japan) 20% Nippon Life Insurance (Japan)
Daiwa Finance Australia	100% Daiwa Bank (Japan)
Delfin-BNY Acceptances	100% ANZ Capital Markets (Australia)
Development Finance Corporation	100% ANZ Capital Markets (Australia)

Dominguez Barry Samuel Montagu	100% Samuel Montagu (UK)
Elders Finance	100% Elders IXL (Australia)
Equiticorp Australia	100% Equiticorp Holdings (New Zealand)
European Asian of Australia	100% European Asian Bank (consortium)
First Chicago Australia	100% First National Bank of Chicago (USA)
First National (Chase-NBA)	100% National Australia Bank (Australia)
Fuji Intern. Finance Australia	100% Fuji Bank (Japan)
Grindlays Australia	100% ANZ Banking Group (Australia)
Hambro Australia (Australian Fin. & Invest.)	97% Hambro (UK) 3% local staff
IBJ Australia	100% IBJ Australia Bank (Aust.– Japan)
Indosuez Australia	100% Banque Indosuez (France)
Intersuisse	14.9% First Pacific (Hong Kong) 10.0% Ownes Investment (New Zealand) 75.1% Australian shareholders
KEB Australia	100% Korea Exchange Bank
Kleinwort Benson Australia	100% Kleinwort Benson (UK)
Kuwait Asia Australia	100% Kuwait Asia Bank (Bahrain)
Kyowa Finance Australia	100% Kyowa Bank (Japan)
Lloyds International	100% Lloyds Bank International (UK)
LTCB Australia	100% Long-Term Credit Bank of Japan
Macquarie Acceptances (Hill Samuel Australia)	100% Macquarie Bank
Manufacturers Hanover Australia	100% Manufacturers Hanover (USA)
Marac Australia	100% Marac Holdings (New Zealand)
Mellon Australia	100% Mellon Bank (USA)
Merril Lynch Intern. (Australia)	100% Merril Lynch Intern. (USA)
Michell NBD	50% G.H. Micheli & Sons (Australia)

	50% National Bank of Detroit (USA)
Midland International Australia	100% Midland Bank (UK)
Mitsubishi Trust Australia	100% Mitsubishi Trust & Banking (Japan)
Mitsui Finance Australia	100% Mitsui Bank (Japan)
Mitsui Trust Finance (Australia)	100% Mitsui Trust & Banking (Japan)
Montreal Australia	100% Bank of Montreal (Canada)
Morgan Grenfell Australia	100% Morgan Grenfell (UK)
Morgan Guaranty Australia (Australian United Corp.)	100% J.P. Morgan & Co. (USA)
NCNB Australia (NCNB Spedley)	100% National Bank of North Carolina (USA)
Nikko Securities (Australia) (Oceania Capital Corp.)	100% Nikko Securities (Japan)
Nippon Credit Australia	100% Nippon Credit Bank (Japan)
Nomura Australia	100% Nomura Securities (Japan)
NZI Securities Australia	100% NZI Corporation (New Zealand)
OUB Australia	100% Overseas Union Bank (Singapore)
Partnership Pacific Limited	100% Westpac Banking Corp. (Australia)
PNB Australia	100% Philadelphia National Bank (USA)
PNC Intern. Finance Co. (Australia)	100% PNC International Finance Corp. (USA)
PNC Intern. Financial Services (Pittsburgh National Seldon)	50% PNC Inter. Finance Corp. (USA)
	40% CIC Holdings Ltd (Australia)
	10% Pamsel Investments (Australia)
Rothschild Australia	100% Rothschild (UK)
Saitama Australia Finance	100% Saitama Bank (Japan)
Sanwa Australia (Commercial Continental)	100% Sanwa Bank (Japan)
SBC Australia	100% Swiss Bank Corp. (Switzerland)
Scandinavian Pacific	100% Scandinavian Bank (consortium)
Schroders Australia (Schroder Darling & Co.)	100% Schroders (UK)

Security Pacific Australia	100% Security Pacific National Bank (USA)
Societe Generale Australia	100% Societe Generale (France)
Spedley Securities	100% Spedley Holdings Ltd
Standard Chartered Australia	100% Standard Chartered Bank (UK)
State Street Australia	100% State Street Bank & Trust (USA)
Sumitomo International Finance Australia (Sumitomo Perpetual)	100% Sumitomo Bank (Japan)
Sumitomo Trust Finance (Australia)	100% Sumitomo Trust and Banking (Japan)
Taiyo Kobe Australia	100% Taiẏo Kobe Bank (Japan)
Tokai Australia Finance	100% Tokai Bank (Japan)
Takugin Australia	100% Hokkaido Takushoku Bank (Japan)
Toya Trust Australia	100% Toya Trust & Banking (Japan)
Toronto Dominion Australia (Euro Pacific Finance)	100% Toronto-Dominion Bank (Canada)
Trans City Holdings	50% City Mutual Life Assurance (Australia)
	50% Irving Trust Company (USA)
Tricontinental Corporation	100% State Bank of Victoria (Australia)
UBAF Holdings (Australia)	100% Union de Banque Arabes et Françaises (France)
UBS Australia	100% Union Bank of Switzerland (Switzerland)
UOB Australia	100% United Overseas Bank (Singapore)
Wardley Australia	51% Hongkong Bank of Australia (HK–Australia)
	49% Wardley Limited (Hong Kong)
Yamaichi Australia	100% Yamaichi Securities (Japan)
Yasuda Trust Australia	100% Yasuda Trust and Banking (Japan)

Note: Where a merchant bank had been approved but not yet established by the end of 1985, it has still been listed. Where a merchant bank has adopted a new name, the old name is also provided in brackets.

Notes

1 INTRODUCTION

1 Report to the Colonial Office by Governor Lachlan Macquarie from Sydney in 1810 as cited in *A Brief History of Australian Banking*, Sydney: The Rural Bank of New South Wales, 1936, p. 9.

2 WHAT ARE MERCHANT BANKS?

1 In its 1985 annual report, the Reserve Bank actually used the term on page 23. Similarly, the Federal Treasurer has also used the term merchant bank on some occasions (see Treasurer's Press Release, 10 September 1984). The Australian Merchant Bankers Association is one of the few examples where the term merchant bank is used in a corporate name.

2 The references to 'houses' refers to the accepting houses, a similar name for money market corporation in the United Kingdom. Sir Edward J. Reid, *The Role of the Merchant Banks Today*, London: Institute of Bankers, 1963, p. 1.

3 L.H.L. Cohen (ed.), *Clay and Wheble's Modern Merchant Banking: a guide to the workings of the Accepting Houses of the City of London and their service to industry and commerce*, 2nd edn, Cambridge: Woodhead-Faulkner, 1983, p. 9.

4 Donald T. Brash, 'The role of the merchant banks today', *Accountants Journal*, June 1973, p. 410.

5 The definition was inserted into the Securities Industry Regulations 1971 by the Securities Industry (Exemption) Regulations 1971 as cited in G.F.K. Santow, 'The Role of Merchant Banks in Australia', *Australian Business Law Review*, December 1973, p. 321.

6 The Treasury Press Release, no. 66, 17 October 1975.

7 Nigel Dew, 'Money Market Corporations', B. Comm. (Hons) thesis, James Cook University, 1985, pp. 14–16.
8 *Australian Financial System Interim Report of the Committee of Inquiry*, Canberra: Australian Government Publishing Service, 1980, p. 145.
9 Tan Chwee Huat, *Financial Institutions in Singapore*, Singapore: Singapore University Press, 1978, p. 43.
10 Michael Blanden, 'Why are merchant bankers different?', *The Banker*, August 1981, p. 11.
11 Carol Parker, 'Challenge for The Clearers', *The Banker*, August 1981, p. 49.
12 Blanden, op. cit., p. 11.
13 Anthony Sampson, *The Money Lenders*, London: Hodder and Stoughton, 1981, p. 238.
14 Hans-Peter Bauer, 'What is a merchant bank?', *The Banker*, July 1976, p. 795 suggested that a merchant bank should contain some eleven such organizational characteristics: a high proportion of decision makers as a percentage of total staff, quick decision process, a high density of information, intense contact with the environment, loose organizational structure, concentration of short- and medium-term engagements, emphasis on fee and commission income, innovative instead of repetitive operations, sophisticated services on a national and international level, low rate of profit distribution, and high liquidity ratio.
15 There will of course still be a significant difference in the market status and regulation of these trading bank authorized merchant banks and their non-bank counterparts.

3 MERCHANT BANKING OVERSEAS: A BRIEF HISTORY

1 Anthony Sampson, *The Money Lenders*, London: Hodder and Stoughton, 1981, p. 29.
2 L.H.L. Cohen (ed.), *Clay and Wheble's Modern Merchant Banking: a guide to the workings of the Accepting Houses of the City of London and their service to industry and commerce*, 2nd edn, Cambridge: Woodhead-Faulkner, 1983, p. 5.
3 Sampson, op. cit., p. 30.
4 The Italian, German, and later Austrian firms eventually closed, but the Rothschild family still dominates the British firm and were still in control in France until the Mitterand government's nationalization of most French banks. Sampson, op. cit., p. 33.
5 Under the Louisiana Purchase, the United States paid Napoleon approximately $15 million for France's land holdings in what is

now the United States. The parcel included the Mississippi River basin, stretching from New Orleans and the Gulf of Mexico in the south towards what is now the Canadian border. The purchase doubled the then land size of the United States.

6 Sampson, op. cit., p. 38.

7 For a good overall discussion of the industry's development in London over the 1800s, see Stanley Chapman, *The Rise of Merchant Banking*, London: George Allen & Unwin, 1984.

8 Ibid., p. 180.

9 For a general discussion of merchant banking in Southeast Asia, see Michael T. Skully, *Merchant Banking in ASEAN: a regional examination of its development and operations*, Kuala Lumpur: Oxford University Press, 1983, chs 3 and 4. Alternatively, detailed country-specific coverage is provided in Michael T. Skully, *Merchant Banking in the Far East*, 2nd edn, London: Financial Times Business Publishing, 1980, chs 2, 3, 5, 7, 8, and 10.

10 For specific details, see Michael T. Skully, *Merchant Banking in the Far East*, 2nd edn, London: Financial Times Business Publishing, 1980, chs 5 and 8.

4 MERCHANT BANKING IN AUSTRALIA

1 S.J. Butlin, *Australian Banking and Monetary System, 1817–1945*, Sydney: Reserve Bank of Australia, 1971, p. 2.

2 Prior to most firms gaining Australian foreign exchange licences, this involved arranging letters of credit or bankers' acceptances with overseas banks or through subsidiary companies. Confirming houses are also active in such trade.

3 N.G. Butlin, *Investment in Australian Economic Development 1861–1900*, Cambridge: Cambridge University Press, 1964, p. 148.

4 At least part of the banks' inability to meet this demand was a result of the government's direct control over their operations.

5 It opened for business in October 1949 at 42 Lansell Road, Toorak.

6 The Consolidated Zinc Corporation in 1961 sold its one-third interest to Morgan Guaranty and Lazard Freres, a US commercial bank and investment bank respectively.

7 *The House of Were 1839–1954*, Melbourne: J.B. Were & Son, 1954, p. 437.

8 Though some restrictions were lifted in 1946 it was not until 31 December 1953 that the regulations were fully withdrawn.

9 *Sydney Morning Herald*, 15 September 1949, p. 6.
10 The first Board of Directors consisted of H.T. Armitage, retired Governor of the Commonwealth Bank; Denny Martin, a director of Lazard Brothers and the AFDC's founding father; Francis Rennell, a director of Morgan Grenfell; (now) Sir Douglas Forber, a director of the then National Bank of Australasia; (now) Sir Colin Syme; and Sir Eric Speed as Managing Director. Norman Leggat, an unpublished talk to AUC staff, dated 17 June 1976.
11 R.R. Hirst, 'The development institutions', in R.R. Hirst and R.H. Wallace (eds), *Studies in the Australian Capital Market*, Melbourne: Cheshire, 1964, p. 331.
12 Mainguard (Australia) Limited was acquired by the Hooker group in 1958 and subsequently changed its name to Hooker Projects Pty Ltd. It is no longer active in merchant banking.
13 Hirst, op. cit., p. 331.
14 L. McGregor (Monash University, 1970–71), pp. 64–5.
15 Though often referred to as official dealers, they are more correctly authorized money market dealers.
16 Hirst, op. cit., p. 330.
17 *Australian Financial Review*, 31 March 1960, p. 34.
18 P.J. Rose, *Australian Securities Markets*, Melbourne: Cheshire, 1969, p. 173. This is most likely the first example of a restriction on trading bank shareholdings in merchant banks.
19 H.M. Knight, 'The Merchant Banking Scene, September, 1975', a speech to the Accepting Houses Association of Australia, 11 September 1975, p. 4.
20 Sir Harold Knight, 'An address by the Governor', a speech at the annual dinner of the Australian Merchant Bankers Association, 16 October 1980, Reserve Bank of Australia, *Bulletin*, October 1982, p. 163.
21 C.M. Abbot, 'Merchant Banking in the 1970s', *The Bankers' Magazine of Australasia*, May 1971, p. 347.
22 *Australian Financial Review*, 6–7 August 1970.
23 H.M. Knight, 'Lenders and Borrowers in the 1960's', *1971 G.L. Wood Memorial Lecture*, delivered at the University of Melbourne, 27 September 1971, p. 6.
24 R.T. Kolts, 'Merchant Banking in Australia', *The Bankers' Magazine of Australasia*, May 1974, p. 332.
25 The Federal Treasurer, Mr Frank Crean, the 2nd Reading Speech of the Financial Corporation Bill 1973, a press release dated 11 December 1973. But as the 1971 Sydney telephone directory alone listed eighty-two companies as merchant banks (*Australian*

Financial Review, 15 March 1979) the government estimate was probably much too low.

26 *Australian Financial Review*, 4 January 1973, p. 1.
27 Abbott, op. cit., p. 347.
28 Knight, 'The Merchant Banking Scene', p. 2.
29 Kolts, op. cit., pp. 332–3.
30 Michael T. Skully, 'Australia's Variable Deposit Requirement (VDR) Scheme, 1972–1974', *Economics*, September 1975, provides the specific details of the earlier scheme. The later one operated at the 25 per cent level from 14 January to 6 July 1977.
31 Given the Banking Act, it is doubtful the term 'merchant banks' would have been chosen for the industry's classification.
32 R.H. Dean, First Assistant Secretary, The Treasury, correspondence dated 3 May 1982.

5 MERCHANT BANKS AND AUSTRALIAN FINANCE

1 At one time the break-down of institutional data by the Reserve Bank was much more detailed and hence more useful to researchers. Contrary to the Governor's stated policy of providing more information to the public, the Research Department has been gradually narrowing its institutional flow of funds reporting. The most damaging omission to date was the consolidation of the formerly separate figures of the assets and composition of private and public superannuation/pension funds and the merging of these categories into that of the life offices. Likewise, details formerly provided for the 'other institutions' category elsewhere in the flow of funds supplement have been eliminated. It is to be hoped that the Bank may eventually resume its previous practices.

2 'Australian Ratings' Top One Hundred Financial Institutions', *Australian Business*, 1 May 1985, pp. 72–3. Australian Ratings' views, as published, differ from my own view as to what constitutes a merchant bank in that the AIDC and the authorized money market dealers (AMP Discount, AUC Discount, Capel Court Securities and Trans City Discount) have been classified as merchant banks.

3 Again there is some question as to whether Elders Finance Group should really be classified a merchant bank. Elders Finance & Investments Limited is most certainly a merchant bank, but Elders Finance Group also includes the assets of Elders Lensworth Finance (a finance company) and Elders Rural Finance (again hardly in the merchant banking business). If Elders were reclassified or broken into its component parts, then Partnership

Pacific, presently holding twenty-first place, would be Australia's largest merchant bank.

7 REGULATION AND CONTROL

1 Banking Act 1959–67, Part VII, section 66, p. 23.
2 R.T. Kolts, 'Merchant Banking in Australia with particular reference to small business since 1945', a report submitted for part of an M. Comm. degree, University of New South Wales, 1974, p. 22.
3 Reserve Bank of Australia, *Report and Financial Statement* 1964–65, p. 25.
4 Reserve Bank of Australia, *Report and Financial Statements* 1967, p. 30.
5 *The Vernon Report; Reviews of the Report of the Committee of Economic Enquiry*, Melbourne: Melbourne University Press, 1966, vol. I, p. 261.
6 Treasurer's Press Release, no. 86, 19 June 1984, p. 2.
7 Federal Treasurer, Mr Frank Crean, Second Reading Speech; Press Release, 11 December 1973.
8 The Treasury Press Release, no. 66. 17 October 1975.
9 Australian Merchant Bankers Association, *Australian Financial System Committee of Inquiry: submission by the Australian Merchant Bankers Association*, 1979, p. 30.
10 Bryan Frith, 'Rescued by more growth in project finance', *Far Eastern Economic Review*, 23 September 1977, p. 95.
11 *Australian Financial Review*, 22 May 1981.
12 BA Australia Limited, *Annual Report*, 1981.
13 There are no liquidity requirements in the ACT, the Northern Territory, or Tasmania.
14 *Establishing a Merchant Bank in Australia: a practical guide*, Sydney: Peat Marwick, 1985.
15 Australian Merchant Bankers Association, op. cit.
16 Ibid.
17 'Foreign Investment Policy', Prime Minister's Press Statement, no. 564, 24 September 1975, p. 9.
18 Ibid.
19 In the end, the purchase of its foreign partners' holdings was approved only when Coles was brought in as a 25 per cent owner of the restructured venture.
20 Gregory Hywood, 'Keating's Citicorp Compromise', *Australian Financial Review*, 22 December 1983, pp. 1–2. This promise may not be enforced given the 1985 changes in foreign ownership restrictions.

21 Treasurer's Press Release, no. 141, 10 September 1984.
22 Treasurer's Press Release, no. 136, 29 October 1985, p. 4.
23 Treasurer's Press Release, no. 136, 29 October 1985, p. 5.
24 *Establishing a Merchant Bank in Australia: a practical guide*, Sydney: Peat Marwick, 1985, p. 4.
25 The founders included Australian United Corporation Ltd, Capel Court Corporation Ltd, Darling and Company Ltd, Development Finance Corporation Ltd, and Ord BT Co. Ltd.
26 *Australian Financial Review*, 23 October 1972.
27 As cited in Kolts, op. cit., p. 189.
28 The Association was initially sponsored by Hill Samuel Australia, International Pacific Corporation, MBC International and Partnership Pacific, but also included Australian European Finance Corporation, Australian International Finance Corporation, Australian United Corporation, Capel Court Corporation, CitiNational Securities Corporation, Commercial Continental, Darling and Company, Delfin Industrial Finance Corporation, Euro-Pacific Corporation, Martin Corporation, Ord BT Co., and Westralian International among its founding members. Kolts, op. cit., pp. 190–1.
29 Accepting Houses Association of Australia, Rules No. 4, p. 2.
30 Accepting Houses Association of Australia, Annual Report 1979, p. 7.

8 OVERALL OPERATIONS

1 G. McL. Scott and R.H. Wallace, 'Business Financiers', in M.K. Lewis and R.M. Wallace, *Australia's Financial Institutions and Markets*, Melbourne: Longman, 1985, p. 159.
2 Robyn Goodfellow, 'Forex licence will wrinkle out fuller disclosure in accounts', *Australian Financial Review*, 19 July 1984, p. 49. *Merchant Bank Financial Reporting 1984*, Sydney: Peat Marwick, 1984, examines this divergence problem in some detail.

9 MONEY MARKET ACTIVITIES

1 *Australian Financial Review*, 26 February 1959, p. 7.
2 There is always a temptation to accept smaller deposits and on occasion some firms do. However, any frequent raisings of small deposits could see merchant banks subject to prospectus requirements by the NCSC. As the Campbell Committee recommended: 'In the future, if they solicit small deposits, merchant banks should be subject to the proposed non-bank regulatory framework or issue a prospectus.' However, if 'they deal only in "wholesale"

markets, the Committee sees no need for prudential regulation'. *Australian Financial System: Final Report of the Committee of Inquiry*, Canberra: Australian Government Publishing Service, 1981, p. 328.
3 Reserve Bank of Australia, *Bulletin*, February 1985, pp. 497–8.
4 Investment & Econometrics Research, *Promissory Note Survey*, 27 September 1985, p. 7.

10 DOMESTIC LENDING

1 Barry R. Brownjohn, 'Letter of credit more flexible', and Derek Condell, 'New Developments in A$ financing', *Rydges*, February 1979, pp. 140–2 and pp. 142–4, provide more details on the structuring involved.
2 Letters of awareness or letters of comfort are sometimes also called letters of responsibility. They indicate to the lender that the parent company is aware of the borrowing in question and that it is the company's policy to give its subsidiaries sufficient means to fulfil their obligations and that it will continue to do so over the life of the loan. However, it assumes no legal obligations to do so, nor does it guarantee payment.
3 Representative offices are supposedly prohibited from such activities. M.T. Skully, 'Foreign banks in Australia: a look at some of their experiences', *The Bankers' Magazine of Australasia*, June 1979 and 'The Role of Foreign Banks in Australia', *Australian Financial Review*, 3 November 1980 provide some insights into these limitations. In late 1981 the Reserve Bank was sufficiently concerned to write to local representative offices cautioning them on exceeding their functions. *Australian Business*, 3 December 1981, p. 98.
4 Chase-NBA Group Limited, '*A submission to the Campbell Committee of Inquiry into the Australian Financial System, 1979*', Section 1.
5 Partnership Pacific Limited, *Annual Report*, 1980.
6 BA Australia Limited, *Annual Report*, 1981, p. 9.
7 From the study of merchant bank annual reports in 1979 only a few mention leasing as one of their services and even then leasing was generally conducted through an affiliated specialist company.
8 I.J. Fairbairn, 'A Note on Leasing in the Australian Capital Market', *The Economic Record*, December 1968, p. 512.
9 Partnership Pacific Limited, *Annual Report*, 1981, p. 24.
10 Jennifer Kitchener, 'Leasing Costs to Jump: Survey', *Australian Business*, 21 November 1984, p. 24.

11 Australian Merchant Bankers Association, *Australian Financial System Committee of Inquiry: submission by the Australian Merchant Bankers Association*, 1979, p. 22.

11 OFFSHORE FINANCING

1 BA Australia Limited, *Annual Report*, 1983, p. 7.
2 Correspondence with Hans Hornscheidt, Rural and Industries Bank of Western Australia, dated 4 October 1985.
3 Correspondence with G.A. Kennedy, Australian Industry Development Corporation, dated 27 September 1985.
4 Hamish McDonald, 'Exotic paper chase', *Far Eastern Economic Review*, 15 August 1985, pp. 48–9.
5 Ibid., p. 48.
6 Peter Starr, 'Institutions in borrower orgy', *Australian Financial Review*, 12 July 1985, p. 13.
7 Peter Starr, 'Large Euro raisings help stabilise A$', *Australian Financial Review*, 16 July 1985, p. 45.

12 CORPORATE FINANCE

1 The term underwriting is most commonly associated with the insurance industry. It traces its origins to the early days of maritime insurance whereby merchants agreed to share the risks involved on trading voyages. A main policy would be drawn stating the specifics of the journey and each merchant would then sign it indicating that share of the risk he would assume. As in signing each merchant wrote under the main policy, they became known as the 'underwriters'.
2 Another service, not often discussed in Australia, is that of market support. As security prices can change rapidly and adversely affect the underwriting, an implied function of the underwriter is to support the market price during and immediately following the underwriting. The problem is that such activities can be illegal under the Securities Act.
3 As indicated, Australia has surprisingly few non-listed public equity offerings. Probably the best known unlisted companies are East-West Airlines and the Rothbury Estates but each was a product of special circumstance.
4 Technically, the Commissioner of Corporate Affairs or the appropriate state government minister now has very strong powers to control the exchange as does the National Companies and Securities Commission. In practice, however, these powers are seldom used.

5 Jim Bain of Bain & Co., as cited in *Australian Financial Review*, 5 September 1977.

6 Correspondence with Ralph B. Lee, General Manager, The Stock Exchange of Melbourne Limited, 19 March 1982.

7 J.B. Were & Son, for example, at one time had some eight different investment companies: Were's Investment Trust Ltd (now Australian Foundation Investment Co. Ltd) (December 1928); National Reliance Investment Co. Ltd (1929); Capel Court Investment Trust (Australia) Ltd (1936); Jason Investment Trust (Australia) Ltd (1937); Lombard Investments (Australia) Ltd (1950); Brenton Investments (Australia) Ltd (1950); Clonmore Investments (Australia) Ltd (1956) and Haliburton Investments (Australia) Ltd (1950). It is said that Were intend eventually to have twelve investment companies, each ending its fiscal year in a different month so that, as they pay annual dividends, investors could purchase all twelve and receive a cheque a month.

8 P.J. Rose, *Australian Securities Markets*, Melbourne: Cheshire, 1969, pp. 13–14.

9 Ibid., p. 20.

10 Despite the dangers, there is always the temptation of 'free riding' in the speculative stages of the bull market. Under this process the underwriter intentionally holds back a portion of the issue from the public to create a shortage. The lack of supply coupled with the 'stagging' (an initial rapid increase over the offer price) common at this stage of the market helps push the price up dramatically. The underwriter then carefully sells off its own holding at a substantial profit. The danger is that too much will be held back and the underwriter may be unable to liquidate its investment.

11 *Some General Thoughts on Underwriting*, J.B. Were & Son, February, 1963, p. 5.

12 The sale of newly-created shares by their issuer is referred to as a primary offering while the sale of existing securities by a major shareholder or group of shareholders is a secondary offering. While the former is more common in Australia, the term 'offeror' covers both positions.

13 Australian Merchant Bankers Association, *Australian Financial System: Submission to the Committee of Inquiry*, 1979, p. 20.

14 *Sydney Morning Herald*, 13 June 1981.

15 *Australian Financial Review*, 15 February 1985, p. 74.

16 Lloyds International Limited, *Annual Report*, 1983, p. 12.

17 Anthony Sampson, *The Money Lenders*, London: Hodder and Stoughton, 1981, p. 238.
18 *Australian Financial Review*, 2 July 1985, p. 45.
19 Peter Field, 'The attack on the M & A barons', *Euromoney*, May 1985 p. 89.
20 *Australian Business*, 11 April 1984, p. 141.
21 *Australian Business*, 20 October 1985, p. 8.
22 Interestingly, not everyone believes these independent evaluations are always 'independent'. As the *Australian Financial Review* (26 August 1980, p. 52) commented, 'if a complete snow job is needed, that can be arranged and from organisations with immaculate credentials. At the other end of the scale there are others who will provide scrupulous valuations'.
23 BA Australia Limited, *Annual Report*, 1982, p. 8.
24 The recent introduction of a combined Bachelor of Commerce (Finance) Law degree at the University of New South Wales is another reflection of this trend.
25 *Business Review Weekly*, 3 May 1985, p. 40.
26 'Chanticleer', 'Corporate Advice: room at the top is shrinking', *Australian Financial Review*, 4 April 1985, p. 59.
27 *The Bulletin*, 16 October 1984, p. 111.
28 Capel Court Limited, *Annual Report*, 1978, p. 5.

13 INVESTMENT MANAGEMENT

1 The Development Finance Corporation, for example, set up the Delfin Mutual Fund in 1960; Capel Court together with J.B. Were & Son and the NBA, established a mutual fund similarly in 1960 and five unit trusts in the early 1960s; and Darling & Co. (now Schroder Darling) established the Darling Fund in 1964.
2 Douglas Markell, 'Merchant Banking in Today's Environment', a speech to the Australian Society of Accountants, Chatswood, July 1977, p. 9.
3 *Australian Financial Review*, 20 December 1984, p. 1.
4 R.H. Henderson, 'Notes on the Australian Capital Market, 1946–53', *The Economic Record*, November 1954, p. 180. Interestingly, Australian Fixed Trusts, now part of the ANZ Capital Markets merchant banking group, was responsible for the first unit trusts in Australia.
5 R.R. Hirst, 'Finance for Economic Development', in R.R. Hirst and R.H. Wallace, *The Australian Capital Market*, Melbourne: Cheshire, 1974, p. 502.

6 Graeme Robson, 'The Investment Performance of Unit Trusts and Mutual Funds in Australia from 1969 to 1978', Clayton: Monash University, 1979, provides some analysis of the industry's past performance.

7 UTA estimates of all trusts excluding cash management trusts, Unit Trust Association of Australia, *Annual Report*, 1984, p. 3.

8 Paul Coombes, 'Investors Cash in on High Yield', *Rydges*, September 1981, p. 25.

9 The concern was that the Australian banks would use their investment management or other wholly-owned subsidiaries to offer this service and thereby avoid the then no interest on normal deposits for thirty days or less rule.

10 The management company is expected to pay the costs of issue as well as the actual brokerage commission, typically 0.25 per cent, on those monies placed through stockbrokers.

11 Chris C. Golis, 'Cash Management Trusts—The First Three Years', *JASSA*, December 1983, p. 14.

14 THE FUTURES BUSINESS

1 Since 27 September 1985 the Melbourne Stock Exchange has also operated the Australian Financial Futures Market. As of late 1985, however, it had confined its trading in futures to a limited number of Australian company shares.

2 Treasurer's Press Release, no. 4, 15 January 1979.

3 For more details and examples of contract trading see David Rutledge, 'The Futures Market', in Robert Bruce, Bruce McKern, Ian Pollard and Michael Skully (eds), *Handbook of Australian Corporate Finance*, 2nd edn, Sydney: Butterworths, 1986, pp. 357–77.

4 David Potts, 'Futures Come of Age', *Business Review Weekly*, 19 to 25 September 1981, p. 20.

15 FOREIGN EXCHANGE BUSINESS

1 Reserve Bank of Australia, *Bulletin*, September 1985, p. s46.

2 Elders Finance & Investment Limited, *Annual Report*, 1982, p. 6.

3 Treasurer's Press Release, no. 46, 10 April 1984, p. 1.

4 'BRW foreign exchange poll', *Business Review Weekly*, 24 May 1985, p. 50.

5 Juliet Coops, 'An insight into the financial markets advisory group', *Jobson's Year Book of Public Companies*, 1984/1985, p. 79.

6 Alan Jury, 'Keating's Forex Largesse Takes Market By Surprise', *Asian Finance*, 15 July 1984, p. 39.

7 Edna Carew, 'Forex: A License to Lose Money?', *Euromoney*, August 1984, pp. 121–4.
8 Elders Finance and Investment, *Annual Report*, 1984.
9 'Chanticleer', 'New forex dealers may be forced to gear up', *Australian Financial Review*, 24 July 1984, p. 60.
10 John Hewson, 'On exchange rates you read between the lines', *Business Review Weekly*, 31 May 1985, p. 92.
11 Laura Tingle, 'Disenchantment with forex market development grows', *Australian Financial Review*, 18 September 1984, p. 65.
12 Tony Thomas, 'How the money movers measure up', *Business Review Weekly*, 24 May 1985, p. 39.
13 'The BRW foreign exchange pool', *Business Review Weekly*, 24 May 1985, p. 50.
14 Laura Tingle, 'Australian Dollar Falls. Behind the Boomtime', *Australian Financial Review*, 14 December 1984, p. 13.
15 Lachlan Drummond, 'Foreign Traders Face Hurdle of Buying Expertise, Hardware', *Australian Financial Review*, 7 May 1984, p. 12.
16 Dominic O'Grady, 'From parasites to paragons', *Triple A*, October 1985, p. 38.
17 Angela Mackay, 'BOT Australia retreats from volatile A$ market', *Australian Financial Review*, 14 August 1985, p. 56.
18 Edna Carew, 'Bank issue entry caught in forex market battle', *Australian Financial Review*, 30 March 1984, p. 12.

16 OVERSEAS EXPANSION

1 Euro-Pacific Corporation Ltd, *Annual Report*, 1983.
2 The exploits of this organization make fascinating reading and it is worth scanning at least pp. 383–402 of the Royal Commissioner's *Final Report*.
3 BA Australia Limited, *Annual Report*, 1983, p. 47.
4 *Australian Financial Review*, 21 May 1984, p. 55.
5 Australian European Finance Corporation Ltd, *Annual Report*, 1984, p. 24.
6 Spedley Securities Ltd, *Annual Report*, 1983, p. 1. The acquisition was made by this firm's parent company.
7 For more details of its history, see Michael T. Skully, *Merchant Banking in ASEAN*, Kuala Lumpur: Oxford University Press, 1983, pp. 70–3.
8 It should be noted that PICA was not without its problems and that trouble with its loan portfolio was at least partially a function of the sale. This is particularly evident when one considers that despite some fifteen years of operations, a well-known name,

and well-established branch structure, Elders' purchase price of US$20 million was equal to only 60 per cent of the firm's paid-up capital. In other words, not only was there no goodwill aspect to the purchase price, but these shares were sold at discount from their initial issue price, many purchased some fifteen years ago.

9 For a discussion of the Papua New Guinea merchant banking position and a mention of Fiji's, see Michael T. Skully (ed.), *Financial Institutions and Markets in the Southwest Pacific: A Study of Australia, Fiji, New Zealand, and Papua New Guinea*, London: Macmillan, 1985, pp. 143, 284–6, and Michael T. Skully, *Financial Institutions and Markets in the South Pacific: A study of New Caledonia, Solomon Islands, Tonga, Vanuatu and Western Samoa*, London: Macmillan, 1987 (chapter 4).

17 OTHER ACTIVITIES

1 Tricontinental has since sought to redeem these securities and generally phase out its finance company operations. It found that the previous trust deed on this issue limited its other operations. Maureen Murril, 'State bank buys a PR lemon', *Business Review Weekly*, 12 April 1985, p. 25.

2 Commercial Continental Ltd and Subsidiary Companies, *1981 Annual Report and Notes to the Accounts*, p. 24.

18 STAFFING

1 Paul Ham, 'Henry Morgan (alas not JP) Is Alive and Well Plundering Top People', *Rydges*, July 1984, p. 81.

2 *Australian Business*, 15 February 1984, p. 38.

3 *Australian Business*, 21 November 1984, pp. 125–6.

4 *Australian Business*, 15 February 1984, pp. 36, 38.

5 In early 1984, four BT Australia investment managers left to go to Morgan Grenfell. They reportedly moved not for just more money but rather for a greater challenge. *Rydges*, July 1984, p. 82.

6 Kathryn Bice, 'Expansion opens up in-house training', *Australian Financial Review*, 12 June 1985, p. 31.

7 Robyn Short, 'Finance Sector Staff Faces A Shakeout', *Australian Financial Review*, 7 March 1984, p. 23.

8 Robyn Goodfellow, 'The Mercenaries of Merchant Banking', *Australian Financial Review*, 31 July 1984, p. 13.

19 THE CAMPBELL AND MARTIN REPORTS

1 The Campbell Committee was chaired by the late Sir Keith Campbell who was formerly the Chairman of Citinational, a merchant bank, and the Chairman and Chief General Manager

of Hooker Corporation, a real estate development company. The other five Committee members included R.G. McCrossin, General Manager of the Australian Resources Development Bank; A.W. Coates, General Manager of the AMP Society; K.M. Halkerston, a financial adviser; J.S. Mallyon, Chief Manager of the Reserve Bank of Australia; and F. Argy of the Federal Treasury Department.

2 The Martin Review Group was chaired by Victor E. Martin, the former Chief Executive of the Commercial Banking Company of Sydney and the then Executive Chairman of the Mutual Life and Citizens' Assurance Company. The other three members of the group included R.M. Beetham, First Assistant Secretary of the Treasury's Financial Institutions Division; D.J. Cleary, Deputy Chief Manager of the Reserve Bank's International Department; and Professor K.J. Hancock, Vice-Chancellor of Flinders University.

3 If non-bank is counted as two words the total is then seventy-eight. As the actual recommendation is later repeated again in full on page 786, one could argue a case for an additional forty-one words. Similarly, there are a few mentions of merchant banks on page 449 where the discussion is concerned mainly with local bank ownership of non-bank financial institutions.

4 C.D. Corrigan, 'What happens to merchant banks?', a speech to the Rydges Conference on the Implications of the Campbell Report, 1981.

5 Australian Merchant Bankers Association, *Annual Report*, 1981, p. 5.

6 *The Banker*, September 1982, p. 118.

7 Australian Merchant Bankers Association, op. cit., p. 6.

8 *Australian Financial System: Report of the Review Group*, Canberra: Australian Government Publishing Service, 1984, p. 1.

9 Peter Timmins, as cited in Peter Robinson, 'What the banking changes mean to you and your money', *Sun Herald*, 26 February 1984, p. 41.

10 *Australian Business*, 14 March 1984, p. 117.

11 *Australian Financial System: Report of the Review Group*, op. cit., p. 31.

12 Ibid., pp. 98–9.

13 Ibid., p. 99.

14 Paul Espie, as cited in Malcolm Wilson, 'Merchant banker challenges Martin Report proposals', *Sydney Morning Herald*, 12 March 1984.

15 K. Jarret, 'Elders IXL Limited', a press release dated 24 February 1984.

16 *Australian Business*, 14 March 1984, p. 117.

20 THE FUTURE

1 *Australian Business*, 1 August 1984, p. 14.
2 'Chanticleer', 'The era of Australian merchant banking is just about over', *Australian Financial Review*, 29 December 1983, p. 24.
3 R.R. Hirst, 'Finance for Economic Development', in R.R. Hirst and R.H. Wallace, *The Australian Capital Market*, Melbourne: Cheshire, 1974, pp. 496–7.
4 'Pierpont', 'Trade for the Asking', *Bulletin*, 30 October 1984, p. 128.
5 Hill Samuel Australia was particularly attracted to these factors when deciding to apply for a banking licence in 1982–83. David Clarke, 'Expanded Sector Presents a chance to regain lost grounds', *Australian Financial Review*, 12 November 1984, p. 14.
6 Chris Corrigan, as cited in *Euromoney*, June 1985, p. 214.
7 *Euromoney*, June 1985, p. 214.
8 Partnership Pacific Limited, *Annual Report*, 1984, p. 3.

Bibliography

ABBOTT, C.M., 'Merchant Banking in the 1970s', *The Bankers' Magazine of Australasia*, May 1971, pp. 346–53.

ABGLY, Patricia, 'Fire sale purchase for Elders', *Asian Banking*, July 1984, p. 81.

ACHESON, M.N., 'The Great Banking Invasion', *Australian Financial Review*, 6 and 7 August 1970, pp. 2–3.

ALEXANDER, John, 'High Flyers of Resource Finance', *Australian Business*, 18 March 1982, pp. 42–8.

——, 'Merchant Bank Salary Spiral', *Australian Business*, 17 December 1981, pp. 58–61.

ALLAN, Richard, 'Changes in the Australian Short-Term Money Markets', *JASSA*, June 1978.

ALLAN, R.H., 'The Economics of Intervention in the Short Term Money Market', Ph.D. thesis, Australian National University, 1977.

——, 'Submission to the Australian Financial System Inquiry. The Australian Short-Term Money Markets', Department of Economics, University of Melbourne, 1979.

ARAK, Marcelle & McCURDY, Christopher, J., 'Interest Rate Futures', *Federal Reserve Board of New York Quarterly Review*, Winter 1979–80, pp. 33–46.

ARNDT, H.W., 'Overdrafts and Monetary Policy', in Neil Runcie (ed.), *Australian Monetary and Fixed Policy: selected readings*, London: University of London Press, 1971, pp. 273–304.

AUSTRALIAN BANKERS ASSOCIATION, *Supplementary Submissions to the Australian Financial System*, April 1981.

Australian Financial System: Final Report of the Committee of Inquiry, Canberra: Australian Government Publishing Service, 1981.

Australian Financial System: Interim Report of the Committee of Inquiry, Canberra: Australian Government Publishing Service, 1980.

AUSTRALIAN MERCHANT BANKERS ASSOCIATION, *Annual reports*, various years.

——, *Australian Financial System Inquiry Submission by the Australian Merchant Bankers Association*, 1979.

——, *Submission to the Trade Practices Commission Relating to the Application by the Australian Associated Stock Exchanges for Authorisation of Their New Rules, Regulations, and By-laws*, 25 June 1981.

——, *Third Submission to the Campbell Committee of Inquiry into the Australian Financial System*, March 1981.

Australian Ratings, September 1985.

'Australian Savings Bonds and Special Bonds', *Reserve Bank Statistical Bulletin*, December 1980, pp. 295–8.

BA AUSTRALIA, *Simulated Foreign Currency Loan, Deposit and Promissory Note Facilities*, paper dated July 1982.

BAIN, J.K., 'Problems of the Public Debt Markets', address to the Graduate Management Association, 13 August 1981.

BALL, Brian H., 'The Short Term Money Market in Australia', paper to the Australian Society of Accountants, July 1982.

BALL, R., 'The Australian Stockbroking Cartel', in Albon, R. & Lindsay, G. (eds), *Occupational Regulation and the Public Interest*, St Leonards, NSW: Centre for Independent Studies, 1984.

BALLA, Ignatius, *The Romance of the Rothschilds*, London: G. Bell & Sons Ltd, 1913.

'Banking', *Australian Business*, 14 October 1982, pp. 93–103.

'Banking and Finance', *Australian Financial Review*, 14 May 1985, pp. 39–46.

'Banking and Finance '84', *Australian Financial Review*, 12 November 1984, pp. 1–24.

'Banking Survey', *Australian Business*, 5 May 1983, pp. 60–86.

BARING BROTHERS & CO. LTD, *Merchant Banking Today*, London: Waterlow & Sons, 1970.

BARON. David P., 'Model of the demand for investment bank advising and Australian services for new issues', *Journal of Finance*, September 1982, pp. 955–76.

BAUER, Hans Peter, 'What is a Merchant Bank?', *The Banker*, July 1976.

BEARD, Philip, 'Aussie dollars are Euromarket of the year', *Australian Financial Review*, 4 September 1984, pp. 22–3.

——, 'Australian dollar market expands rapidly', *Australian Financial Review*, 5 September 1985, p. 28.

——, 'Australians plunge into Euromarkets', *Australian Financial Review*, 3 September 1985, p. 13.

——, 'Why Euro A$ bonds are booming', *Euromoney*, August 1985, pp. 95–8.

BEKINGSATE, Christine, 'Merchant Banks given a rap on the level of disclosure, a study by accountants shows inadequacies', *Australian Financial Review*, 25 July 1983, p. 3.

BELCHER, Howard, 'Recent Development in Monetary Control', *The Bankers' Magazine of Australasia*, August 1974, pp. 11–16.

BENNETT, R.L., *The Financial Sector and Economic Development: the Mexican case*, Baltimore: John Hopkins Press, 1965.

BERG, A.R., 'Deregulation of the Australian Capital Markets', Address to the International Corporate Finance Conference, September 1984.

BIVEN, R., 'Cash Flows in the Money Market', *JASSA*, June 1979.

BLAIN, N., 'Accepting houses form their own Association', *Australian Financial Review*, 9 November 1972, p. 20.

——, 'Merchant Banks face a liquidity trap', *Australian Financial Review*, 12 December 1974, p. 10.

——, 'Merchant Banks face a squeeze under new Act', *Australian Financial Review*, 11 December 1974, pp. 2–3.

——, 'Merchant Banks have different lending patterns', *Australian Financial Review*, 13 December 1974, pp. 2–3.

——, 'Merchant Banks move into rural finance', *Australian Financial Review*, 1 January 1974, p. 10.

——, 'No longer free to follow the market place', *Australian Financial Review*, 13 December 1974, pp. 8, 45.

BLANDEN, Michael, 'Why merchant banks are different', *The Banker*, August 1981, pp. 41–6.

BOLTON, Sir George, 'What Future for the Merchant Banks?', *Euromoney*, March 1971.

BOULTON, L.F. & HARPER, I.R., 'The Growth of Money Market Corporations in Australia: Some Preliminary Results', paper prepared for the 12th Conference of Economists, held at the University of Tasmania, 28 August–1 September 1983.

BRAMSEN, Bo & WAIN, Kathleen, *The Hambros 1779–1979*, London: Michael Joseph, 1980.

BRASH, Donald T., 'The role of the merchant banks today', *Accountants Journal*, June 1973.

BRENCHLEY, F. & McGUINESS, P.P. (eds), *The New Money Jigsaw*, Sydney: Magazine Promotions, 1981.

BROADBENT, Jillian, 'The changing money market', *Australian Stock Exchange Journal*, January 1979, p. 22.

BROWNJOHN, B.R., 'Letter of Credit More Flexible', *Rydges*, February 1979, pp. 140–2.

BRUCE, Robert, McKERN, Bruce, POLLARD, Ian, & SKULLY, Michael,

Handbook of Australian Corporate Finance, 2nd edn, Sydney: Butterworths, 1986.

BRYANT, Mark B., 'The audit of a merchant bank', *Chartered Accountant in Australia*, April 1982, pp. 18–20.

BUGG, Ellis J., 'The phenomenon of negative gearing', *Australian Financial Review*, 4 November 1983, pp. 22–3.

BUSHBELL, Noel, 'Competitive environment erodes financial ratings', *Australian Financial Review*, 14 November 1985, p. 39.

BUTLIN, N.G., *Investment in Australian Economic Development 1861–1900*, Cambridge: Cambridge University Press, 1964.

BUTLIN, S.J., *Australian Banking and Monetary System, 1817–1945*, Sydney: Reserve Bank of Australia, 1971.

'Californian Banks Expand in Australia', *The Banker*, November 1970, pp. 1336–7.

CAMERON, R.B., 'The Merchant Banks Arrive', *Investors Chronicle and Stock Exchange Gazette*, 6 October 1972, pp. 37–44.

CAPEL COURT CORPORATION LIMITED, *Quarterly Survey*, various issues.

CAREW, Edna, 'Anything a merchant bank can do, banks can do too', *Far Eastern Economic Review*, 4 April 1980, pp. 97–8.

——, 'Are Merchant Banks here an Endangered Species?', *Far Eastern Economic Review*, 19 September 1980.

——, 'Bank entry issue caught in Forex market battle', *Australian Financial Review*, 30 March 1984, pp. 12–13.

——, 'Bank Relaxes Borrowing Rule', *Australian Financial Review*, 15 February 1982, p. 1.

——, *Fast Money 2: the money market in Australia*, Sydney: George Allen & Unwin, 1985.

——, 'Forex leads the salaries race onwards and upward', *Australian Financial Review*, 26 July 1984, p. 13.

——, 'The immediate problem is drumming up new business', *Far Eastern Economic Review*, 21 September 1979, pp. 91–2.

——, 'Into the arena', *Far Eastern Economic Review*, 2 August 1984, pp. 66–8.

——, 'Loan Council changes cause semi chaos', *Australian Financial Review*, 28 June 1982, pp. 1, 36.

——, 'Merchant Banking Pact to Lift Hedge Market Liquidity', *Australian Financial Review*, 9 May 1983.

——, 'Merchant Banks in Australia', *Jobson's Yearbook of Public Companies 1984/1985*, pp. 46–53.

——, 'Merchant Banks are having an expensive time', *Australian Financial Review*, 7 January 1982, pp. 6–7.

——, 'Merchant banks redefine daily prime rate on bills', *Australian Financial Review*, 14 July 1982, p. 26.

——, 'Paperless settlement—a revolution in the money market', *Australian Financial Review*, 27 August 1982, pp. 12–13.

——, 'Schroder reworks its corporate approach', *Australian Financial Review*, 9 December 1983, pp. 12–13.

——, 'Sydney Exchange to Trade Futures Option First', *Australian Financial Review*, 24 February 1982, p. 39.

——, 'Tonkin Plans Super-Semi Central Borrower', *Australian Financial Review*, 16 June 1982, pp. 1, 53.

——, 'Trusts circle each other in wait for rationalisation', *Australian Financial Review*, 9 September 1983, p. 57.

CAREW, Edna & TINGLE, Laura, 'Behind the Cash Trusts' (three-part series), *Australian Financial Review*, 27, 28, 29 July 1982.

CAROSSO, Vincent P., *More than a Century of Investment Banking: the Kidder, Peabody & Co. Story*, New York: McGraw Hill, 1981.

CARRON, Andrew S., 'The Australian Financial System', in Richard E. Caves & Lawrence B. Krause (eds), *The Australian Economy: A View from the North*, Sydney: George Allen & Unwin, 1984, pp. 195–230.

'Chanticleer', 'Bankers and Brokers in the battle of the bourse', *Australian Financial Review*, 17 January 1980, p. 28.

——, 'Better banks will sort out vanishing merchants', *Australian Financial Review*, 29 December 1983, pp. 23–4.

——, 'Corporate advice: room at the top is shrinking', *Australian Financial Review*, 4 April 1985, p. 40.

——, 'The era of Australian merchant banking is just about over', *Australian Financial Review*, 29 December 1983, p. 24.

——, 'New forex dealers may be forced to gear up', *Australian Financial Review*, 24 July 1984, p. 60.

——, 'The learning curve extracts a heavy toll at Barclays', *Australian Financial Review*, 12 June 1985, pp. 67–8.

CHAPMAN, Stanley, *The Rise of Merchant Banking*, London: George Allen & Unwin, 1984.

Chase–NBA Group Limited, *Submission to the Campbell Committee of Inquiry into the Australian financial system*, 1979.

CHENG, Hang-Sheng, 'Financial Reform in Australia and New Zealand', *Economic Review*, Winter 1983, pp. 9–24.

CLARKE, D.S., 'Macquarie Bank: Adapting to Change', address to the Australian Business Economists, June 1984.

CLAY C.J.J. & WHEBLE, B.S., *Modern Merchant Banking*, London: Woodhead–Faulkner, 1976.

CLEVESON, C.L., 'J.H.D. Marks: millions in a shroud of mystery (Development Finance Corporation)', *Australian Financial Review*, 31 March 1960, pp. 34–5.

Cocks, Graham, 'Hedging Bets on a Foreign Exchange Market in Australia', *Economic Papers*, February 1980, pp. 58–69.

Cohen, A.M., 'Changing Patterns of Cash Flows and Their Implications for Financial Markets', speech to the Council of Authorised Dealers and the Securities Institute of Australia, 8–17 July 1980.

Cohen, L.H.L. (ed.), *Clay and Wheble's Modern Merchant Banking: a guide to the Workings of the Accepting Houses of the City of London and their service to industry and commerce*, 2nd edn, Cambridge: Woodhead–Faulkner, 1983.

Collins, N.G., 'The Role of Merchant Banks in Australia', *The Bankers' Magazine of Australasia*, February 1983, pp. 4–9.

'Commonwealth Government Securities—New Marketing Arrangements', *Reserve Bank Statistical Bulletin*, September 1980, pp. 111–12.

Condel, Derek, 'New Developments in A\$ Financing', *Rydges*, February 1979, pp. 142–4.

Coombe, Brian, 'How the merchant banks rank', *Australian Financial Review*, 26 February 1985, p. 57.

Coombs, H.C., *Conditions of Monetary Policy in Australia*, Sydney: Dept of Economics, Sydney University, 1958.

Corr, John, 'Where the big money is made and lost (Merchant Banks)', *Business Review Weekly*, 15–21 October 1983, pp. 34–6.

Corrigan, C.D., 'Merchant Banking at the Crossroads', *JASSA*, no. 2, June 1982, pp. 19–22.

——, 'What happens to merchant banks', speech to the Rydges Conference on the Implication of the Campbell Report, Sydney, 1981.

Cottrell, Robert, 'On the Defensive', *Far Eastern Economic Review*, 29 August 1985, pp. 46–7.

Crean, F., *The Financial Corporations Act: An Information Document*, Canberra: Australian Government Publishing Service, 1974.

Cripps, M., 'Starting a Merchant Bank', *Money Management*, July/August 1971.

Critchley, Robert, 'Challenging times ahead for Merchant Bank expansion', *Rydges*, February 1980, pp. 122–4.

'Curbs on Merchant Banks Deserves Warning Letter', *Australian Financial Review*, 26 May 1981, pp. 1, 46.

'Currency Futures', *Trends*, September 1981, pp. 5–7.

Curtin, D., 'Too Many Merchant Banks', *Euromoney*, October 1983, pp. 421–31.

DALLEY, Helen, 'Bankers consider their future', *Australian Business*, 14 March 1984, p. 24.

DAS, Satyajit, 'Interest Rate Swaps', *Bulletin of Money, Banking and Finance*, 1983–84, no. 1, pp. 1–40.

DAVIS, A.B., 'Merchant Banking—A Profit Oriented Finance Service', *Rydges*, August 1970.

DAVIS, R.W. & WALLACE, R.H., 'Lessons of the 1960 Bank Credit Squeeze', in Neil Runcie (ed.), *Australian Monetary and Fiscal Policy; selected readings*, London: University of London Press, 1971, pp. 237–61.

DAVIS, Richard, *The English Rothschilds*, Chapel Hill: University of North Carolina Press, 1985.

DAW, E.D., 'Development in the use of commercial bills in Australia', *Currency*, January 1967, pp. 4–6.

DE ROOVER, Raymond, *The Medici Bank*, New York: New York University Press, 1948.

DEWALD, William G., *The Short Term Money Market in Australia*, St Lucia: University of Queensland Press, 1967.

——, 'The Demand for Money in Australia, 1952–1968', Ph.D. thesis, Ohio State University, 1969.

DEWS, Nigel James, 'Australian Money Market Corporation Growth, 1959–1983', B.Econ. (Hons) thesis, James Cook University, 1985.

DEWS, N. & DWYER, J., 'Summary of Implementation of Recommendations of the Committee of Inquiry into the Australian Financial System', *Discussion Papers in Economics*, no. 9, Department of Economics, James Cook University of North Queensland, September 1984.

DIAMOND, W., *Development Finance Companies*, Baltimore: The John Hopkins Press, 1968.

DOMINGUEZ, J.T., 'How will the Semi- and Local Authorities Fund Themselves in the 1980's?', address to the Securities Industry of Australia, Sydney, 8 June 1982.

DONNELLY, P.S., 'The Role of the Merchant Banker', *The Queensland Accounting Bulletin*, vol. 14, no. 15, September 1970.

DRAKE, P.J., 'Stock and Share Markets', in Lewis, M.K. & Wallace, R.H. (eds), *Australia's Financial Institutions and Markets*, Melbourne: Longman Cheshire, 1985, pp. 247–304.

DRANCY, L.R., 'Practical Use of the Bill Market—a market viewpoint', address to the Accepting Houses Association of Australia seminar on bills of exchange, Melbourne, 16 October 1978.

DRUMMOND, Lachlan, 'Foreign traders face hurdle of buying expertise', *Australian Financial Review*, 2 May 1984, p. 12.

ELLIOT, Gregory R., *Australian Banking and Finance in the 1980's and Beyond: report on a forecasting study*, Sydney: State Bank of New South Wales, 1983.

ELLIS, A., *Heir of Adventure*, London: Brown Shipley and Co., 1960.

ELLIS, Noel G., 'How to get International Funds', *The Bulletin*, 29 March 1975, pp. 78–9.

ESPIE, Paul, 'The future of merchant banking', *Chartered Accountant in Australia*, February 1982, pp. 23–4, 26.

Establishing a Merchant Bank in Australia: a Practical Guide, Sydney: Peat Marwick Mitchell & Co., 1985.

'Ethics First for Merchant Banks', *Australian Financial Review*, 25 February 1971, p. 32.

Euro-Australian Dollar Bond Market, London: Orion Royal Bank, 1985.

FAIRBAIRN, I.J., 'The Australian Bills Market', *The Australian Quarterly*, September 1969, p. 50.

——, 'A Note on Leasing in the Australian Capital Market', *The Economic Record*, December 1968, pp. 512–15.

FARMER, James A., 'From the debris of a merchant bank collapse: the spectre of legal challenges to contemporary commercial practices', *Australian Business Law Review*, February 1980, pp. 64–80.

FEHON, C.M., *A critical appraisal of Australia's foreign exchange arrangements 1960–1978*, Melbourne: Committee for Economic Development of Australia, 1980.

——, 'Exchange Risk Management in the Insurance Industry', *The Insurance Record*, June 1982, pp. 226–9.

FERRIS, Paul, *Gentlemen of Fortune: the World's Merchant and Investment Bankers*, London: Weidenfeld and Nicolson, 1984.

FIELD, Peter, 'The attack on the M & A barons', *Euromoney*, May 1985.

Financial Futures in Australia, Sydney: Peat Marwick Mitchell & Co., 1984.

'Financiers Doubts on Merchant Bank Body', *Australian Financial Review*, 23 October 1972, p. 5.

FISHER, Malcolm (ed.), *A New Financial Revolution? An International Review of the Campbell Report*, St Leonards, NSW: Centre for Independent Studies, 1982.

FORD, Thomas C., 'The Financial wholesale function—merchant banking', speech to a Western Australia Institute of Technology seminar, 20 November 1981.

FOTHERINGHAM, K.B., 'The Foreign Currency Hedge Market in

Australia', *The Australian Accountant*, December 1979, pp. 780–5.

FREEMANTLE, James, 'Growth of non-bank financial intermediaries and their impact on trading banks in the Australian money market', M. Admin. thesis, Monash University, 1971.

FRITH, Bryan, 'Financing Queensland's Future Cement Supply', *The Australian Accountant*, May 1979, pp. 212–15.

——, 'Innovators want licence', *Australian Business*, 17 December 1981.

——, 'Merchant Bankers press for easing in investment rules', *The Australian*, 30 May 1984, p. 13.

——, 'Rescued by more growth in project finance', *Far Eastern Economic Review*, 23 September 1977.

FURNESS, B.J., 'Borrowings by Local and Semi-Government Securities', *Reserve Bank Statistical Bulletin*, November 1981, pp. 267–73.

GARDINER, Philip W., 'A quiet revolution in our foreign exchange markets', supplement to *The Australian*, 5 March 1980, p. 2.

GATFIELD, Brian, 'Resource Boom Faces Critical Labor Shortage', *Australian Financial Review*, 23 March 1981, p. 2.

GAY, P.D., 'Interest rate futures—a new option in financial management', *Rydges*, February 1981, pp. 134–8.

GAY, Phil & SCHWARTZ, David, 'How to put interest rate contracts to work', *Australian Financial Review Survey*, 23 November 1981, p. 4.

GEBERT, C.A., 'The Future Role of Non-Banks', *The Bankers' Magazine of Australasia*, June 1968.

GILBERTSON, J.M., 'The Gurley–Shaw Hypothesis', *American Economic Review*, 1958.

GILES, T., 'The major Australian trading banks connected with merchant banks', MBA thesis, University of Sydney, 1977.

'The Global Canvas of Merchant Banks: Who Owns What', *Asian Finance*, 15 January 1983, p. 78.

GOLDSMITH, Raymond W., 'The Development of Financial Institutions During the Post-War Period', *Banca Nazionale del Lavoro Quarterly Review*, no. 97, June 1971.

——, *Financial Intermediaries in the American Economy since 1900*, Princeton: Princeton University Press, 1958.

——, *Financial Structure and Development*, New Haven: Yale University Press, 1969.

GOLIS, Chris C., 'Cash managements trusts—the first three years', *JASSA*, December 1983.

GOODFELLOW, Robyn, 'After setting alight the revolution, it's the chop for merchant banks', *Australian Financial Review*, 1 August 1984, p. 13.

——, 'Forex licence will wrinkle out fuller disclosure in accounts', *Australian Financial Review*, 19 July 1984, p. 49.

——, 'Grey Market goes formal', *Australian Financial Review*, 31 May 1978, pp. 1, 41.

——, 'The mercenaries of merchant banking', *Australian Financial Review*, 31 July 1984, p. 13.

——, 'Merchant banks in top shape as deregulation grows near', *Australian Financial Review*, 18 July 1985, pp. 46–7.

Goss, Richard T., 'The systematic management of foreign exchange risk', *Australian Stock Exchange Journal*, April 1981, pp. 14–15.

Graham, David, 'Merchant banks, the outlook for 1975', *The Bulletin*, 29 March 1975, pp. 80–3.

Guille, C.W., 'Bill Financing by Australian Banks', *Reserve Bank Statistical Bulletin*, September 1981, pp. 134–8.

Gurley, J.G. and Shaw, E., 'Financial Aspects of Economic Development', *American Economic Review*, September 1955.

——, 'Financial Intermediaries and the Savings-Investment Process', *Journal of Finance*, vol. XI, May 1956, pp. 257–77.

——, *Money in a Theory of Finance*, Washington: Brookings Institution, 1960.

Haddock, Richard, 'Letter of credit—a useful financial tool', *Rydges*, February 1978, pp. 104–8.

Ham, Paul, 'The big nine muscle their way into consulting', *Rydges*, December 1983, pp. 74–5.

Hand, Graham D., 'The Euro-Australian dollar bond market', *Commonwealth Bank of Australia Economic Newsletter*, July 1985, pp. 3–6.

Handler, Robert, 'Watershed looming for merchant sector', *The Australian*, 26 August 1983, p. 18.

Harris, I.D., 'Promissory Notes—a new dimension to the Australian money market', *The Chartered Secretary*, April–June 1977, pp. 53–4.

Harris, Robin, 'Investors will soon be wooed by brokers', *Business Review Weekly*, 15–21 August 1981, p. 12.

Haselhurst, David, 'Hill Samuel in the big league', *The Bulletin*, 11 May 1982, pp. 114–16.

Hastings, P., 'Mr J.H.D. Marks, Chairman of Development Finance Corp., behind-the-scenes role for man who guides investment of millions', *Australian Financial Times*, 21 August 1961, p. 27.

Hawthorn, Ian, 'The Coming of Age of the Currency Hedge

Market', *Australian Stock Exchange Journal*, April 1981, pp. 12–13.

HAYES, S.L., 'Investment Banking: Power Structure in Flux', *Harvard Business Review*, March/April 1971.

HENDERSON, R.F., 'Monetary Policy in Australia 1960–61', in Neil Runcie (ed.), *Australian Monetary and Fiscal Policy: selected readings*, London: University of London Press, 1971, pp. 220–36.

——, 'The Scope for Expansion of Banking Lending in Australia', *The Bankers' Magazine of Australasia*, September 1964, pp. 55–70.

HESKETH, Blair, 'Facilities for Syndicated Credit', *The Bulletin*, 29 March 1975, pp. 76–7.

HEWSON, John, 'On exchange rates you read between the lines', *Business Review Weekly*, 31 May 1985, p. 92.

HILL, M.R., 'Bond and Money Markets', in Lewis, M.K. & Wallace, R.H. (eds), *Australia's Financial Institutions and Markets*, Melbourne: Longman Cheshire, 1985, pp. 305–54.

HILLIARD, Brian, 'How the Australian Currency Basket Works', *Euromoney*, June 1981, pp. 144–5.

HIRST, R.R., 'The development institutions', in R.R. Hirst & R.H. Wallace (eds), *Studies in the Australian Capital Market*, Melbourne: Cheshire, 1964.

——, 'Finance for economic development', in R.R. Hirst & R.H. Wallace (eds), *The Australian Capital Market*, Melbourne: Cheshire, 1974, pp. 440–513.

——, 'Postwar Monetary Policy in Australia', in Neil Runcie (ed.), *Australian Monetary and Fiscal Policy: selected readings*, London: University of London Press, 1971, pp. 108–27.

HIRST, R.R. & WALLACE, R.H. (eds), *The Australian Capital Market*, Melbourne: Cheshire, 1974.

——, *Studies in the Australian Capital Market*, Melbourne: Cheshire, 1964.

HOGAN, W.P., 'Monetary Policy and the Financial Intermediaries', in Neil Runcie (ed.), *Australian Monetary and Fiscal Policy: selected readings*, London: University of London Press, 1971, pp. 103–200.

HOLDER, R.F., 'Monetary Policy in Australia', in Neil Runcie (ed.), *Australian Monetary and Fiscal Policy: selected readings*, London: University of London Press, 1971, pp. 162–82.

HORRIGAN, W. & WESTON, C.R., 'Australian Money Markets, the aftermath of Minsec', *The Banker*, January 1977, pp. 43, 45–7.

The House of Were, 1839–1954, Melbourne: J.B. Were & Son, 1954.

HOWARD, John, address to the Australian Merchant Bankers Association Seminar on Financial Institutions in the 1980s, Melbourne, 2 December 1981 (Treasurer's Press Release, no. 216).

Interest Rate Futures, Sydney: Hill Samuel Australia Limited, June 1981.

The Interest Rate Futures Market in Australia, Sydney: Trans City Holdings Ltd, 1983–84.

'International Merchant Banking', *The Banker,* July 1976, pp. 793–832.

'International Merchant Banking', *The Banker,* July 1977, pp. 50–78.

Investment in Australia, Melbourne: The Stock Exchange of Melbourne, 1965.

INVESTMENT & ECONOMETRICS RESEARCH, *Promissory Note Survey,* various issues.

An Investment Guide to the Short Term Money Market: the BA Cash Management Trust, Sydney: BA Australia, 1981.

IRISH, Ron, 'Courting, Resisting and Marriage—the Role of Merchant Banks in Takeovers', *The Chartered Accountant in Australia,* December 1980, pp. 35–40.

JOHNSON, L., 'Origins of Financial Innovation in Australia—A Case Study of the Merchant Bank, Australian United Corporation Limited, 1948 to 1969', B. Comm. (Hons) thesis, University of Melbourne, 1982.

JURY, Alan, 'Interest Rate Futures: holding down the cost of money', *Australian Business,* 3 December 1981, pp. 87–9.

——, 'Make or break time for merchant banks', *Australian Business,* 22 July 1982, pp. 81–6.

JUTTNER, D.J. (ed.), *Interest Rates,* Melbourne: Longman Cheshire, 1982.

KEARNS, A.M., 'The Official Short Term Money Market in Australia, 1959–73', M. Comm. thesis, University of New South Wales, 1975.

KELLETT, R., *The Merchant Banking Arena,* London: Macmillan & Co. Ltd, 1967.

KERR, Ian, 'The neglected blue ribands in Australian bonds', *Asian Banking,* March 1981, pp. 79–81.

KIRKWOOD, J.A., 'Monetary Policy Implementation and the Trading Banks', in Neil Runcie (ed.), *Australian Monetary and Fiscal Policy: selected readings,* London: University of London Press, pp. 91–104.

KITCHENER, Jennifer, 'Merchants tumble on new rating scale', *Australian Business,* 9 January 1985, pp. 23–4.

KNIGHT, Sir Harold, 'An Address by the Governor', speech at the annual dinner of the Australian Merchant Bankers Association, 16 October 1980, *Reserve Bank Statistical Bulletin*, October 1980, pp. 162–5.

KNIGHT, H.M., 'Lenders and Borrowers in the 1960s', the 1971 G.L. Wood Memorial Lecture, Melbourne, 27 September 1971.

——, 'The Merchant Banking Scene—September 1975', paper presented to the Accepting Houses Association, 11 September 1975.

KOLTS, R.T., 'Merchant Banking in Australia', *The Bankers' Magazine of Australasia*, May 1974.

——, 'Merchant Banking in Australia with particular reference to small business since 1945', report submitted for part of an M. Comm. degree, University of New South Wales, 1974.

LAMPE, Anne, 'Merchant Banking '73', *Australian Financial Review*, 8 and 9 May 1973.

'Lawyer Attacks Merchant Banks Role in Takeovers', *Australian Financial Review*, 4 December 1979, p. 51.

LEIGHTON, G.R., 'Exchange Control in Australia—1980', *The Bankers' Magazine of Australasia*, August 1980, pp. 143–9.

LEVIS, Mario, 'The Behaviour of the Australian Forward Exchange Market', *Australian Journal of Management*, June 1982, pp. 61–74.

LEWIS, M.K. & WALLACE, R.H. (eds), *Australia's Financial Institutions and Markets*, Melbourne: Longman Cheshire, 1985.

LINEGAR, Chris, 'The Reserve Bank Makes Some Changes', *Australian Financial Review Survey*, 24 March 1980, p. 10.

LINKLATER, Joan, 'Non-bank currency market emerges', *Rydges*, October 1977, pp. 26–7, 104.

LIVINGSTONE, David, 'The government securities market: unintend(er)ed t(r)aps', address to the Securities Institute of Australia's money market conference, Sydney, 10 June 1982.

LOVE, David, 'Banking in the 1970s', *The Bankers' Magazine of Australasia*, November 1969, December 1969 and January/February 1970.

——, 'Investment Banking Australian Style', *Australian Financial Review*, 11 January 1968, pp. 2–3.

——, 'The Merchant Banks', *Australian Financial Review*, 10 January 1968, pp. 2–3.

LYNCH, Michael, 'Slow Beginning for Futures Contracts', *Australian Financial Review Survey*, 24 March 1980, p. 7.

McCLINTOCK, E.P., 'Evolving relationships between Australian merchant banks and British based companies in Australia',

Australian-British Trade Association Newsletter, no. 64, July 1973, pp. 6–7.

McCRANN, Terry, 'Citinational launches a new era in securities', *The National Times*, 31 January–5 February 1981, p. 49.

——, 'Money Market: why Sydney brokers are opting out', *The National Times*, 24–29 January 1977, p. 49.

McDOUGALL, D.A., 'The Role of Project Financing in Developing Australia's Natural Resources', *The Bankers' Magazine of Australasia*, October 1981, pp. 169–71.

McINTOSH, Ian, 'The Role of Merchant Banks in The Ovens', paper presented at the 1973 AAANZ Conference, Geelong, Victoria.

McKEON, Ashley, 'Fledgling P-note market spreads its wings', *Business Review Weekly*, 31 October–6 November 1981, pp. 43–95.

McKINNON, I., *Money and Capital in Economic Development*, Washington, DC: The Brookings Institution, 1973.

——, *Money and Finance in Economic Growth and Development*, New York: Marcel Dekker Inc., 1976.

MACLEOD, John, 'Australian money markets expand', *The Bankers' Magazine of Australasia*, June 1964, pp. 397–403.

MACLEOD, J.D.S., 'Short Term Money Markets in Australia and New Zealand', *The Bankers' Magazine of Australasia*, June 1961, pp. 465–76.

MAITLAND, Stephen, 'The Challenges ahead for Merchant Banks', *Rydges*, February 1980, pp. 135–8.

MARKELL, Douglas, 'Merchant banking in today's environment', speech to the Australian Society of Accountants, Chatswood, July 1977.

MARKS, Sir John, *Reflections*, Sydney: Estate of John Marks, 1984.

MARSDEN, John, 'Change in the finance industry: its impact on the players', *Chartered Accountant in Australia*, June 1984, pp. 28–30.

MARSHALL, R.H.W., 'Commercial Bill Market', Economic Society of Australia and New Zealand, NSW Branch, *Monograph* no. 264, September 1964.

'MEDICI', 'Hedging your foreign bets', *Australian Business*, 10 June 1982, p. 20.

——, 'D-Day for Merchant Banks', *Australian Business*, 1 August 1984, pp. 14–17.

'Merchant Bank Carpeted Again, Reserve Bank Warning on Credit Crunch', *Australian Financial Review*, 18 December 1981, pp. 1, 16.

Merchant Bank Financial Reporting 1984, Sydney: Peat Marwick, 1984.

'Merchant Bank Ownership About to Revolve', *Australian Financial Review*, 4 June 1981, pp. 10–11.

'Merchant Bank Review', *Marshall's Reports*, July 1985.

'Merchant Bankers Review their Strategies', *Jobson's Investment Digest*, 5 February 1973, pp. 20–2.

'Merchant Bankers Take on TPC', *Australian Financial Review*, 25 June 1981, pp. 1, 4.

'Merchant Banking', *The Australian*, 10 March 1972, pp. 21–4.

'Merchant Banking', *The Australian*, 15 October 1974, pp. 23–5, and 7 October 1975, pp. 15–17.

'Merchant Banking', *Trends*, September 1970, pp. 13–17.

'Merchant Banking—An Identity Crisis', *Australian Stock Exchange Journal*, November 1978, pp. 7, 29.

'Merchant Banking: Another Collapse', *Nation*, November 1981, pp. 7–8.

'Merchant Banking 1973', *Far Eastern Economic Review*, 17 September 1973, p. 64.

'Merchant Banking 1975', *Far Eastern Economic Review*, 26 September 1975, p. 46.

'Merchant Banking 1976', *Far Eastern Economic Review*, 17 September 1976, pp. 35–92.

'Merchant Banking 1977', *Far Eastern Economic Review*, 23 September 1977, pp. 37–108.

'Merchant Banking 1978', *Far Eastern Economic Review*, 22 September 1978, pp. 35–94.

'Merchant Banking 1979', *Far Eastern Economic Review*, 21 September 1979, pp. 43–98.

'Merchant Banking 1980', *Far Eastern Economic Review*, 19 September 1980, pp. 53–104.

'Merchant Banking 1981', *Far Eastern Economic Review*, 18 September 1981, pp. 46–108.

'Merchant Banking 1982', *Far Eastern Economic Review*, 24 September 1982, pp. 51–100.

'Merchant Banking 1983', *Far Eastern Economic Review*, 1 September 1983, pp. 43–86.

'Merchant Banking's More Than Having a Good Chef', *Australian Financial Review*, 22 January 1980, pp. 8–9.

'Merchant Banking Supplement', *Australian Stock Exchange Journal*, November 1977, pp. 10–21.

'Merchant Banks Broaden Role in World Finance', *Australian Financial Review*, 15 November 1967, p. 6.

'Merchant Banks as Corporate Managers', *Money Management*, April 1971.

'Merchant Banks in Developing Countries: The Role of Specialised

Banks in Growing Economies', *National and Grindlays Review*, February 1971, pp. 9–76.

Merchant Banks and Finance Companies in Australia, Sydney: Peat, Marwick Mitchell & Co., 1983.

'The Merchant Banks in the Financial System: the Compartments are Crumbling', *Statetrends*, 1982, pp. 10–12.

'Merchant Banks are Having an Expensive Time', *Australian Financial Review*, 7 January 1982, pp. 6–7.

'Merchant Banks' Performance Best Judged by Pre-Tax Results', *Australian Financial Review*, 21 December 1977.

'Merchant Banks Worry About Campbell', *The Banker*, September 1982, pp. 117–18.

'The Merchant Princes', a five-part series, *Sydney Morning Herald*, 13–19 November 1982.

MERRY, D.H., 'The Changing Role of Trading Banks in the Australian National Economy', *The Economic Record*, April 1959, pp. 78–87.

MINCHIN, Ian H., 'Currency Hedge Market Develops into a Relatively Sophisticated Market', *Australian Financial Review*, 23 March 1981, p. 8.

MISKIN, Philip, 'Bills of exchange will beat liquidity problems', *Rydges*, August 1970.

——, 'How the bill market operates', *Rydges*, May 1969, pp. 40–1.

MITCHELL, Ian G., 'Needless liability created by endorsing bills', *Rydges*, February 1981, pp. 110–13.

'The Money Market', *Australian Financial Review*, 3 April 1984.

'Money Market Supplement 1980', *Australian Financial Review*, 24 March 1980.

'Money Market Supplement 1981', *Australian Financial Review*, 23 March 1981.

'Money Market Survey', *Australian Financial Review*, 26 August 1985, pp. 27–33.

MONTAGUE, David, 'British Merchant Banking in Australia', *The Banker*, December 1969, pp. 1317–21.

MORRIS, Jan, 'The Australian Short Term Money Market', *Chartered Secretary*, May 1971, pp. 139–42.

MORRIS, J. & QUALLS, H., 'The Australian Short Term Money Market', *The Australian Accountant*, May 1972, p. 163.

MOYLE, L.G.C., 'Competition in the Finance Sector', *JASSA*, October 1980.

——, 'New Horizons—The Australian Financial System After Campbell and Martin: Non-Bank Financial Institutions—The Poor Relations?', address to Business Law Education Centre, May 1984.

MULLANE, P.J., 'Merchant Banking Australian Style', *Economics* (Economic Teachers Association of NSW), vol. 8, no. 1, April 1973, pp. 26–9.

MURRAY-PRIOR, Tom, 'Merchant Banks and Bills of Exchange', speech to a Commercial Law Association of Australia seminar, 30 September 1980.

'The New Face of Banks: Banking Survey', *Australian Business*, 1 May 1985, pp. 70–114.

'New Merchant Banks to Try More Selective Approach', *Australian Financial Review*, 1 June 1982, p. 57.

The New Paper Money: Bill Line Facilities and Standby Letters of Credit, Melbourne: Commercial Law Association of Australia, 1980.

NICOL, D.S., 'Raising Equity Capital in the Australian Market', address to the Australian–Canadian Businessmen's Association, 17 March 1982.

NOBLE, B.A., 'Money Market Corporation', *Reserve Bank of Australia, Bulletin*, September 1982.

NORTHCOTT, J.H., 'Official Short-Term Money Market in Australia', *The Australian Accountant*, August 1980, pp. 480–2.

——, 'Recent Developments in the Short Term Money Market', *Economic Monograph*, no. 307, September 1969.

O'GRADY, Dominic, 'From parasites to paragons', *Triple A*, October 1985, p. 38.

OH, John S.A., 'The Long and Short Run Demand for Money in Australia, 1952–1970', Ph.D. thesis, University of Virginia, 1978.

PAGE, Christopher, 'Growth in promissory notes helped by banks', *Australian Financial Review*, 27 June 1985, p. 85.

PARKER, Carol, 'Challenge for The Clearers', *The Banker*, August 1981.

PARKER, M.V., 'Living with the short term money market', *The Bankers' Magazine of Australasia*, November 1968, pp. 141–52.

PARR, Oliver, 'The Growth of Australia's Promissory Note Market', *Euromoney*, June 1981, pp. 147–50.

PATRICK, Hugh T., 'Finance, Capital Markets and Economic Growth in Japan', in Arnold W. Sametz (ed.), *Financial Development and Economic Growth*, New York University, 1972.

——, 'Financial Development and Economic Growth in Under-developed Countries', *Economic Development and Cultural Change*, January 1966.

PERKINS, Ian, 'Merchant Bank Shake-up follows big bank mergers', *Australian*, 31 May 1982.

PERKINS, J.O.N., *The Australian Financial System after the*

Campbell Report, Melbourne: Melbourne University Press, 1982.

——, 'Central Banking in Australia since 1960', in Neil Runcie (ed.), *Australian Monetary and Fiscal Policy: selected readings,* London: University of London Press, 1971, pp. 305–15.

PHILLIPS, J.G., 'Developments in Monetary Theory and Policies', the Fifth R.C. Mills Memorial Lecture, University of Sydney, 29 April 1971.

——, 'Recent Developments in Monetary Policy in Australia', in Neil Runcie (ed.), *Australian Monetary and Fiscal Policy: selected readings,* London: University of London Press, 1971, pp. 69–90.

PHILLIPS, K.M., 'Effects of Recent Changes in the Official Short Term Money Market', *The Bankers' Magazine of Australasia,* July 1969, pp. 407–12.

PHILLIPS, M.J., 'Changing Patterns in Financial Markets', address to the Securities Institute of Australia's money market conference, Sydney, 8 June 1982.

'PIERPONT', 'Trade for the asking', *The Bulletin,* 30 October 1984, p. 128.

POSTAN, M., *Medieval Trade and Finance,* Cambridge: Cambridge University Press, 1973.

POTTS, David, 'Futures Come of Age', *Business Review Weekly,* 19–25 September 1981, p. 20.

A Presentation by the Council of Authorised Short Term Money Market Dealers to the Campbell Committee of Inquiry into the Financial System of Australia, May 1979.

A Proposal to Establish a Currency Futures Market in Australia, Sydney: Sydney Futures Exchange Ltd, February 1977.

RAJANAYAGAM, M.J.L., *The Law Relating to Negotiable Instruments in Australia,* Sydney: Butterworths, 1980.

'Ratings Leave Bankers with Feeling of Inadequacy', *Australian Financial Review,* 29 June 1982, pp. 59–60.

REID, Sir Edward, 'The Role of the Merchant Banks Today', Presidential Address—The Institute of Bankers, London, 15 May 1963.

Report of the Committee Established by the Premier of New South Wales to Report on the Steps Necessary to Establish Offshore Banking Activity in Australia with Particular Reference to Sydney, Sydney: Government Printer, January 1984.

RICHARDS, Gordon, 'Protecting the Corporate Coffers', *Australian Business,* 18 June 1981, pp. 83–4.

RIES, Ivor, 'Merchant banks' future in doubt', *Business Review Weekly,* 13–19 March 1982.

——, 'The Risk in Cash Trusts', *Business Review Weekly*, 3–9 July 1982, pp. 9–11.

RILELY, B.B., *Bills of Exchange in Australia*, Sydney: Lawbook Co., 1976.

ROBINS, Brian, 'Australia: a tougher stance against foreigners in finance', *Far Eastern Economic Review*, 1 September 1983, pp. 83–4.

——, 'Keating turns tough (on Citibank)', *Far Eastern Economic Review*, 15 September 1983, pp. 86–7.

ROSE, P.J., *Australian Securities Markets*, Melbourne: Cheshire, 1969.

——, 'Integration of the Commonwealth Securities and Money Markets in Australia', *Economic Record*, December 1965.

——, 'A Study of the Australian Securities Market', Ph.D. thesis, 1967.

ROSS, H., 'An examination of the short term money market in Australia (with emphasis on the unofficial market)', *Economic Monograph*, no. 321, April 1971.

ROWAN, D.C., 'Monetary Problems of a Dependent Economy: the Australian experience', *Banca Nazionale del Lavoro Quarterly Review*, vol. 7, no. 31, October–December 1954, pp. 204–13.

——, 'Monetary Problems of a Dependent Economy: The Australian experience 1948–52', in Neil Runcie (ed.), *Australian Monetary and Fiscal Policy: selected readings*, London: University of London Press, 1971, pp. 128–51.

——, 'Statutory Reserve Deposits in Australia', in Neil Runcie (ed.), *Australian Monetary and Fiscal Policy: selected readings*, London: University of London Press, 1971, pp. 201–19.

ROWE, Paul, 'One Name Paper Grows in Popularity', *Australian Financial Review Survey*, 24 March 1980, p. 6.

Royal Commission of Inquiry into the Activities of the Nugan Hand Group: *Interim report: Commonwealth terms of reference (e), (f) and (g): October 1983*, Canberra: Australian Government Publishing Service, 1983.

Royal Commission of Inquiry into the Activities of the Nugan Hand Group, *Final Report*, Canberra: Australian Government Publishing Service, 1985.

Royal Commission on the Monetary and Banking System of Australia, *Report*, Canberra, 1937.

RUNCIE, Neil, 'Monetary Policy and Instalment Credit: the central bank's advances policy 1945–63', in Neil Runcie (ed.), *Australian Monetary and Fiscal Policy: selected readings*, London: University of London Press, 1971, pp. 262–72.

RUTLEDGE, David, 'Exchange has an exciting future', *Australian Financial Review Survey*, 23 November 1981, p. 1.

——, 'Futures Market Opportunities for the Fixed Interest Manager', *JASSA*, December 1980, pp. 21–6.

SAMPSON, Anthony, *The Money Lenders*, London: Hodder and Stoughton, 1981.

SANTOW, G.F.K., 'The role of merchant banks in Australia', *Australian Business Law Review*, December 1973.

SCOTT, G. McL. & Wallace, R.H., 'Business Financiers', in Lewis, M.K. & Wallace, R.H. (eds), *Australia's Financial Institutions and Markets*, Melbourne: Longman Cheshire, 1985, pp. 121–86.

SCOTT-KEMMIS, Leigh, 'Love an official dealer', *Australian Stock Exchange Journal*, April 1981, pp. 32–3.

——, 'Promissory Notes—why the market is growing fast', *Rydges*, February 1978, pp. 123–4.

Securities Industry Licensing: an Interim Licensing Information Booklet, Melbourne: National Companies and Securities Commission, December 1981.

SEDGWICK, D. Glenn, *Australian Merchant Banking—Twenty Five Years Young*, Geelong: Deakin University, 1984.

Select Committee on Foreign Ownership and Control, (official Hansard Report), Commonwealth Government Printer, 1972.

SHACK Jonathan, 'Land of sun, surf and merchant banks', *Euromoney*, June 1985, pp. 214–15.

SHARPE, I.G., 'Does Australia need the Financial Corporations Bill?', *Insurance and Banking Record*, April 1974, pp. 197–8.

SHAW, Edward S., *Financial Deepening in Economic Development*, New York: Oxford University Press, 1973.

SHEEHAN, P.J. and DERODY, B., 'The Campbell Report: A Critical Analysis', *The Australian Economic Review*, 1st Quarter 1982, pp. 35–62.

SHELDON, Robert, 'Merchant Banks begin to come of age', *Australia & Financial Times Survey*, 3 September 1968, p. 13.

SIEH, K., 'Merchant banks—auditing under the Securities Industry Code', *Chartered Accountant in Australia*, July 1983, pp. 28–9.

SIMONDS, Peter & TINGLE, Laura, 'Govt. sets low bond tender', *Australian Financial Review*, 30 July 1982, p. 3.

SKULLY, Michael T., 'After the boom, new realism', *Asian Money Manager*, April 1977.

——, *An Australian Bibliography on Merchant Banking*, Accepting Houses Association of Australia, 24 June 1975.

——, 'Australian Financial Institutions and Markets', in Michael T. Skully (ed.), *Financial Institutions and Markets in the Southwest Pacific: a study of Australia, Fiji, New Zealand, and Papua New Guinea*, London: Macmillan, 1985.

——, 'Australian Merchant Banking', *The Banker*, September 1976, pp. 1073–6.

——, 'Australian Merchant Banking, where is it going in the 1980's?', *Australian Stock Exchange Journal*, April 1981, pp. 8–9, 15.

——, 'Australia's Banks Gear up for Growth', *The Banker*, July 1977, pp. 65–9.

——, 'Australia's Variable Deposit Requirement (VDR) Scheme', *Economics*, September 1975.

——, *The Diversification of Australia's Trading Banks*, Lindfield: Centre for Securities Industry Studies, July 1979.

——, 'Growth of Merchant Banks', *Asian Finance*, 15 February 1978, pp. 94–5, 97–8.

——, *Merchant Banking in ASEAN: a regional examination of its development and operations*, Kuala Lumpur: Oxford University Press, 1983, chs 3, 4.

——, *Merchant Banking in Australia: Its Development, Functions and Future*, Accepting Houses Association of Australia, June 1975.

——, *Merchant Banking in the Far East*, London: Financial Times Business Publishing, 1976.

——, *Merchant Banking in the Far East*, 2nd edn, London: Financial Times Business Publishing, 1980.

——, 'Merchant Banking: a problem of definition', *The Bankers' Magazine of Australasia*, June 1977, pp. 107–11.

——, 'Merchant Banks profit from concessions, but will their euphoria endure?', *Asian Finance*, June 1979, pp. 20–1.

——, 'Profits up for Australian Merchant Banks', *Asian Money Manager*, August 1981.

——, 'Tough Competition in Merchant Banking Intensifies', *Rydges*, February 1978, pp. 117–18, 221–2.

——, 'Trading Banks Diversify Outside Banking', *The Banker*, March 1978, pp. 43–7.

SLAYTER, C.W., 'Early birds give interest rate futures market a push as conventionals wait and see', *Australian Financial Review*, 23 March 1981, pp. 6–7.

SPELLMAN, Lewis J., 'Deposit Ceilings and the Efficiency of Financial Intermediation', *Journal of Finance*, vol. XXXV, No. 1, March 1960, pp. 127–36.

STARR, Peter, 'Cowboys find new pastures', *Australian Financial Review*, 8 May 1985, p. 57.

——, 'How the banks rate with their customers', *Australian Financial Review*, 10 September 1985, pp. 1, 54.

——, 'Major trading banks lose in FX rankings', *Australian Financial Review*, 11 September 1985, p. 1.

'Stock Exchange: Futures Market', *National Bank Monthly Summary*, September 1981, pp. 5–7.

STOCKTON, K.J., 'Borrowing Foreign Currency', *The Australian Accountant*, December 1979, pp. 769–73.

——, 'How currency hedging developed', *Rydges*, August 1979, pp. 121–4.

STOKKE, B.R., 'The Merchant Banks', *International Trade Forum*, April–June 1972, pp. 7–11.

STONE, R.C., 'Merchant banking in Australia, 1984–85', *Jobson's Yearbook of Public Companies*, 1984–1985, pp. 54–63.

STROUD, J., 'What is a Merchant Bank?', *Comdec*, Aug./Sept 1982.

SYKES, Trevor, 'Nugan Hand: a sloppy duo's legacy', *The Bulletin*, 20 April 1982, pp. 115–16, 118.

THOM, John, 'Taking care of business finance', an address to the Company Directors Association of Australia's 5th National Biennial Conference, Adelaide, 20 October 1981.

THOMAS, Tony, 'Foreign Exchange: how to navigate the minefield', *Business Review Weekly*, 10–16 July 1982, pp. 41–50.

——, 'Hedge Market's Young Veteran', *Business Review Weekly*, 17–23 July 1982, pp. 26–7.

——, 'How the money movers measure up', *Business Review Weekly*, 24 May 1985, pp. 38–50.

TINGLE, Laura, 'Big Expansion of secondary mortgage market unlikely', *Australian Financial Review*, 28 October 1981, p. 51.

——, 'The decline of the bank bill market', *Australian Financial Review*, 23 April 1985, pp. 1, 61.

——, 'Disenchantment with forex market development grows', *Australian Financial Review*, 18 September 1984, p. 65.

——, 'Learning how to manage the risks', *Business Review Weekly*, 20 September 1985, pp. 121–43.

——, 'The merchant bank rush is just warming up', *Australian Financial Review*, 23 May 1985, p. 53.

——, 'The old hands gain new strength', *Business Review Weekly*, 26 July 1985, pp. 89–93.

TOFT, K.S., 'Training Tomorrow's Merchant Bankers', *The Bankers' Magazine of Australasia*, vol. CCIX, no. 1510.

TOMLINSON, David, 'Merchant princes fight for life in over-banked realm', *The Weekend Australian*, 14–15 September 1985, p. 24.

TOUCHE, A.G., 'Merchant Banks and Company Efficiency', *The Banker*, vol. 120, no. 533, July 1970.

TSUNG, S., 'The Short Term Money Market in Australia', in Skully, Michael T. (ed.), *The Australian Capital Market—some suggestions for improving the operational and allocative efficiency*, Kensington: University of New South Wales, 1978, pp. 206–17.

TSUNG, S. & Ho, H., 'The Unofficial Short Term Money Market in Australia', *The Bankers' Magazine of Australasia*, February 1977, pp. 20–7.

TSUNG, S. & YUILL, R.B., 'The Short Term Money Market in Australia with Particular Reference to the Unofficial Short Term Money Market', paper presented at the 7th Conference of Economists, Macquarie University, Sydney, 28 August–1 September 1978.

——, 'Short-term Money Markets Grow Swiftly', *The Banker*, March 1978, pp. 49–53.

VAGG, Bob, 'Whither the merchant banks?', *Australian Stock Exchange Journal*, vol. 1, September 1972, pp. 39–42.

VALENTINE, Tom, *Finance for Australian Industry*, Sydney: Metal Trades Industry Association, 1984.

——, 'Keeping track of money on the move', *Australian Financial Review*, 15 July 1983, p. 30.

WALKER, G. de Q., 'The Australian revival of the bill of exchange', *Australian Law Journal*, May 1978.

——, 'Bills of Exchange for Mortgage Finance', *Law Society Journal*, April 1979.

WALSH, Maximillian, 'Crean's cash blow', *Australian Financial Review*, 26 October 1973, pp. 1, 22, 58.

WASILIEV, John, 'Taking a look into futures ... the crystal ball shows a tough year ahead', *Australian Financial Review*, 14 July 1982, pp. 12–13.

WATERMAN, M.H., *Investment Banking Functions*, Michigan: University of Michigan, 1958.

WECHSBERG, Joseph, *The Merchant Banker*, London: Weidenfeld & Nicolson, 1966.

WESTFIELD, Mark, 'Keating faces fight on Martin Report', *Australian Business*, 14 March 1985, pp. 23–7.

WESTON, C.R., 'Negotiable C.D.s', *Australian Economic Papers*, December 1971.

'Who wants to be a Merchant Banker? The Field is Becoming Pretty Crowded', *Australian Financial Review*, 7 January 1970, p. 7.

'Why Merchant Banks Chase After Small $', *Australian Financial Review*, 28 July 1982, pp. 1, 12, 13.

WILKINSON, Marian & TOOHEY, Brian, 'Nugan Hand: spies, guns, drugs fall into place', *National Times*, 21–27 February 1982.

WILLMOT, J.P., 'The Pace of Merchant Banks in the Australian Capital Markets', *Australian Stock Exchange Journal*, November 1979, pp. 21–3.

WILSON, Don, 'Evolution of Aust. Merchant Bank Funding', *Australian Financial Review*, 23 March 1981.

WILSON, D.W.A., 'The Australian Intercompany Loan Market', *Economic Monograph*, no. 294, April 1968.

——, 'Merchant Banking in Australia', *Economic Monograph*, no. 310, February 1970.

WILSON, John L., 'The Advisory Role of Merchant Banks in Project Finance', *Australian Stock Exchange Journal*, April 1981, pp. 10–11.

WILSON, J.S.G., 'The Australian Money Market', *Banca Nazionale del Lavoro Quarterly Review*, March 1973, pp. 46–69.

——, *Monetary Policy and the Development of Money Markets*, London: George Allen & Unwin Ltd, 1966.

WILSON, Malcolm, 'How our foreign exchange market is being set up', *National Times*, 1–6 March 1976, p. 48.

——, 'Merchant Banker Challenges Martin Report Proposals', *Sydney Morning Herald*, 12 March 1984.

——, 'Merchants Moving Away From Local Equities', *Age*, 11 November 1982.

WOLF, Harold A. & DOENGES, R. Conrad (eds), *Readings in Money and Banking*, New York: Appleton-Century-Crofts, 1968.

WOLFENSONN, James P., 'How Merchant Banks are meeting the Challenge of size', *Euromoney*, September 1975, pp. 120–1.

WOODROW, G.D., 'Commercial Bills in Australia', *The Australian Accountant*, June 1966.

YOUNG, G., *Merchant Banking: Practice and Prospects*, London: Weidenfeld & Nicolson, 1966.

Index

285